UPSTART CR

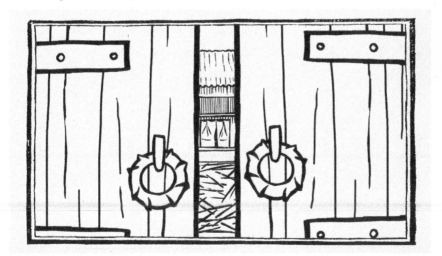

www.penguin.co.uk

Also by Ben Elton

Stark
Gridlock
This Other Eden
Popcorn
Blast from the Past
Inconceivable
Blackadder: The Whole Damn Dynasty
Dead Famous
High Society
Past Mortem
The First Casualty
Chart Throb
Blind Faith
Meltdown
Two Brothers
Time and Time Again

UPSTART CROW

The Scripts

Ben Elton

BANTAM PRESS

LONDON · NEW YORK · TORONTO · SYDNEY · AUCKLAND

TRANSWORLD PUBLISHERS
61–63 Uxbridge Road, London W5 5SA
www.penguin.co.uk

Transworld is part of the Penguin Random House group of companies
whose addresses can be found at global.penguinrandomhouse.com

First published in Great Britain in 2018 by Bantam Press
an imprint of Transworld Publishers

A CIP catalogue record for this book is available from the British Library.

ISBN 9781787630093

Typeset in 11/14 pt Caslon 540 LT Std
India by Integra Software Services Pvt. Ltd, Pondicherry

Printed and bound in Great Britain by Clays Ltd, Elcograf S.p.A.

Penguin Random House is committed to a sustainable
future for our business, our readers and our planet. This book
is made from Forest Stewardship Council® certified paper.

5 7 9 10 8 6 4

CONTENTS

INTRODUCTION

The Crow Folios first emerged in 2015 in the form of a situation comedy broadcast by the BBC and attributed to the pen of comic author Ben Elton. It has since emerged that Elton is not the author and that the Crow Folios are not a sitcom. They are, in fact, the most important discovery in the history of English literature and nothing less than direct verbatim transcripts of episodes from the life of William Shakespeare.

As Jonson had his Boswell, Shakespeare too had a loyal scribe who saw it as his (or her) duty to record the daily doings of the man destined to be recognized as the greatest writer who ever lived. But who was this loyal scribe? The folios offer no clues and so scholars can only guess at the authorship.

The episodes described are confined principally to two locations: Shakespeare's family home in Stratford and his lodgings in London. When the Crow Folios were understood to be a BBC sitcom, this paucity of locations was deemed a simple factor of studio economics. To put it bluntly, the BBC could only afford two decent sets. However, knowing that the Crow Folios are actually sixteenth-century transcripts, we can now draw a very different conclusion. It seems likely that Shakespeare's diligent biographer was a member of either his Stratford or his London household. But which?

Ned Bottom can be dismissed immediately as he could not read or write. This same point almost certainly rules out both Anne and Mary Shakespeare. Few women were properly educated in Elizabethan England and the folios themselves mention Anne and Mary's illiteracy on a number of occasions. The folios do not paint

John Shakespeare in a favourable light and he appears to have been lazy and generally drunk. It therefore seems unlikely he would have had either the energy or the interest to record his son's adventures.

This leaves Kit Marlowe, Susanna Shakespeare and Kate the Landlady's Daughter as viable candidates. Of these, Marlowe seems the least likely. The early papers are packed with evidence that Shakespeare wrote Marlowe's plays, a revelation Elizabethan England's second most famous playwright would not have wanted to make public. What's more, like John Shakespeare, Kit Marlowe was slothful and generally on the piss. Why would he waste time ensuring Shakespeare's legacy when he could be spending it gorging on pie and quaffing ale?

Susanna Shakespeare and Kate the Landlady's Daughter are therefore the only credible candidates. But neither would have had full access to Shakespeare's activities. Perhaps they imagined or used reported speech to chronicle the episodes in Shakespeare's life at which they were not present. Or – as suggested by some scholars – perhaps the two young women collaborated. After all, the folios indicate that after an initial conflict they became friends.

There is, of course, the possibility that Shakespeare himself penned the folios and disguised his authorship by depicting some scenes that do him no credit. The fact that the folios seem most anxious to reflect the Bard's conviction that he was not bald gives some credence to this theory.

Or it could have been a ghost. Or Francis Bacon. Or an ancestor of the actor Mark Rylance.

PRINCIPAL DRAMATIS PERSONAE

WILLIAM SHAKESPEARE – A writer whose plays are generally considered the greatest ever works of English literature. Or a useful sedative which guarantees a restful sleep without recourse to drugs. Opinion remains divided.

ANNE SHAKESPEARE – Will's wife. Previously a milkmaid who only married Will because she was pregnant. Her maiden name was Hathaway and in light of the circumstances of her marriage some scholars have speculated that this was a derivative of 'Have It Away'.

SUSANNA SHAKESPEARE – Will and Anne's teenage daughter. Permanently furious, as indeed you would be if you had a dad who took three or four pages of blank verse to say 'Pass the pie'.

JOHN SHAKESPEARE – Will's dad. A man so dodgy that history records in 1592 he was fined for non-attendance at church, the reason being he owed the entire congregation money.

MARY SHAKESPEARE – Will's mum. A snooty posh bird from the famous Arden family. Now slightly embittered, as indeed you would be if you were married to a grottsome old barfing hog like John Shakespeare.

KIT MARLOWE – Spy. Atheist. Quaffer. Gorger. Shagger of anything on two legs and at a stretch possibly four. He was a seriously naughty boy.

KATE THE LANDLADY'S DAUGHTER – Sweet, fragrant and a raging femmo. A cultured and brilliant young woman prepared to do whatever it took to overcome the appalling misfortune of being born without a cod-dangle. She also really, really wanted to be a star because it was her dream.

NED BOTTOM – Will's servant. Viewed by his master as an amiable dullard without wit or education. Will's low opinion of Bottom may have been because Bottom seems to be one of the few people with the honesty to point out that Shakespeare's plays can be very, very boring. Which is, after all, what everybody secretly thinks.

MISS LUCY – The tavern keeper. Miss Lucy was a real character in Elizabethan London. She was African and possibly an escaped slave and she ran a brothel. The fact that she is depicted in the Crow Folios as having run a pub offers surprising evidence that Elizabethan writers followed modern BBC guidelines and avoided depicting black characters as sex workers.

ROBERT GREENE – Entitled posh boy and snootish pamperloin. Also a writer. His most famous work was *Friar Bacon and Friar Bungay*, a play with the literary distinction of making Shakespeare's works look concise and easy to follow.

EPISODE 1

STAR-CROSSED LOVERS

This fascinating window into Shakespeare's life was the first Upstart Crow folio to be discovered. In it can be found the source of Shakespeare's teen romance *Romeo and Juliet*. History suggests that Shakespeare pinched the plot of *Romeo and Juliet* from Arthur Brooke's 1562 long-form narrative poem *Romeus and Juliet*. But this episode and Shakespeare's great and slightly pervy snogging play (Juliet was thirteen, after all) suggest the similarities are coincidental. A remarkable case of life imitating art.

WILL'S STRATFORD HOME – DAY

Will and his family be all present. His parents, John and Mary Shakespeare, sit in comfort by the fire. His young twins playeth cup and ball. His wife Anne plucketh a goose. His daughter Susanna be upstanding, reading from a manuscript.

SUSANNA: 'Romeo, Romeo! Wherefore art thou Romeo?' Sorry, Dad, how old's this sad weirdo supposed to be?

WILL: The maid be thirteen, my sweet.

SUSANNA: Yeah, cos I'm thirteen.

WILL: Exactly, I . . . I thought it might be fun to hear my Juliet spoke in her true voice, before a middle-aged man with two half coconuts down his bodice gets hold of it.*

SUSANNA: I don't say stuff like this, Dad. I'd sound like a complete turnip!

WILL: Yes, dear, 'tis thy sweet and youthful timbre I would fain hear, not the monosyllabic series of grunts that passes for your conversation.

SUSANNA: Argh! What? Urgh!

WILL: I take the view that having my romantic ingénue say, 'Er, what, shut up, Romeo. You're so weird. Er! Er, shut up! I hate you' would be slightly less effective than mine own timeless poetry.

Susanna sitteth down in high dudgeon.

JOHN: Timeless is the word. As in, feels like goes on for bloody ever.

WILL: You've never given it a chance. You've only seen *Henry the Sixth Part One*.

---

* A fascinating insight into Elizabethan stagecraft. Offering convincing if not conclusive evidence that it might have been a bit crap.

JOHN: Part one? What, you mean there's more? I mean, don't take this the wrong way, son, but God I was bored. I thought I was actually outside my own body watching meself die.[*]

MARY: He sat there cracking his nuts in the quiet bits. I tried to shush him, but he would not be shushed. He's a stubborn man, your father, William. A stubborn common man.

JOHN: Which is why you married me. Posh birds love a bit of rough.[†]

MARY: I married beneath me and now you've done the same, William.

ANNE: And what's that supposed to mean?

MARY: It means that he was seventeen and he got a scheming little twenty-six-year-old tithe-farm milking slap up the duffington, that's what![‡]

ANNE: Ooh, you think you're so posh, Mary Arden. Like you ain't sewn into your winter knickers like everybody else!

Will leaps to his feet in frustration.

WILL: I'm trying to work. I've come from London to hear Sue read my Juliet.

ANNE: Well, I'm not happy, doll. Burbage pays you as an actor, not a writer.[§]

---

[*] Scholars generally believed that the sleep-inducing effect of Shakespeare's plays developed in subsequent centuries, but it is fascinating to note that being suicidally bored was a common reaction even in the Bard's own day.

[†] Mary Shakespeare was indeed a 'posh bird'. She was born into the famous Arden family while John Shakespeare was her father's tenant and a deeply dodgy geezer.

[‡] Anne Hathaway was eight or nine years older than Shakespeare and he barely an adolescent when they conceived Susanna. This has led some scholars to conclude that Shakespeare was a randy little bugger.

[§] Shakespeare started his working life as an actor. It is thought, however, that he continued to give himself occasional parts and scholars believe he cast himself as Hamlet's father's ghost. It therefore seems likely that other actors in the company thought him a self-indulgent arse.

WILL: It's fine. I've sent word to the theatre that the two tunnels which lie beneath the bridge be blocked.

ANNE: Pardon?

WILL: The two tunnels which lie beneath the bridge be blocked. Two tunnels? Beneath a bridge? Anyone?

All do stare at Will most blankly.

WILL: Nose, my loves! Nose! I've told Burbage that my nose be snotted and I would not work this week or next.

ANNE: Well, why didn't you just say 'nose'?

WILL: It's what I do! Now, Susanna, again.

SUSANNA: All right, if I have to.

Susanna commenceth to recite once more.

SUSANNA: 'Romeo, Romeo! Wherefore art thou Romeo?'

She hurleth down the script.

SUSANNA: Dad, nobody talks like this!

WILL: It's poetry. Sometimes I regret teaching you to read.

ANNE: I do think it could be a little less flowery, love. I mean, why doesn't she just say, 'Where are you, Romeo?'?

WILL: Because, my love, it doesn't mean 'Where are you?' It means '*Why* are you Romeo?'

ANNE: That's a bit weird.

SUSANNA: Yeah, Romeo's just his name.

WILL: Exactly. Juliet is saying, 'Why are you a member of a family that I hate?'

ANNE: People will definitely think you mean, 'Romeo, where are you?'

SUSANNA: That's what I thought it meant.

MARY: Yes, I did too.

JOHN: It's bloody obvious.[*]

ANNE: I think to be clear you're gonna have to have Juliet say, 'Romeo, Romeo! Why are you called Romeo?'

SUSANNA: 'A member of a family that I hate.'

ANNE: That'd do it. Although, if I was being really picky, Romeo's just his Christian name, isn't it? And that's not the issue. It's his surname that's the problem.

WILL: Well, yes, actually I was sort of hoping people wouldn't notice that.

ANNE: I think they might.[†]

SUSANNA: Duh!

WILL: So you think she should say, 'Montague, Montague! Wherefore art thou Montague?'?

ANNE: No, cos that'd sound like she's lost her cat.

WILL: Look, it's, it's probably best if you leave this to me, my love. I'm on a bit of a roll. I'm particularly pleased with the comedy scene where a group of rival serving men exchange a series of increasingly obscure insults.[‡]

ANNE: Will, I've told you, don't do comedy. It's not your strong point.

WILL: It is my strong point, wife. It just requires lengthy explanation and copious footnotes. If you do your research, my stuff is actually really funny.[§]

---

[*] Generations have presumed that when Juliet says 'wherefore art thou' she means 'where are you'. Scholars have forgiven Shakespeare this obvious mistake presuming that people would have understood the correct meaning at the time. The folio offers evidence that they didn't.

[†] Anne was wrong. No scholar has ever sought fit to point out this obvious howler.

[‡] This appears to be a reference to the opening scene of *Romeo and Juliet*, which is in fact spectacularly unfunny. A group of serving men bang on about 'Biting their thumbs' at each other in a very boring way. The dullness of the scene is compounded by the fact that the serving men are minor characters typically given to crap actors.

[§] Shakespeare is clearly wrong. Scholars have conducted copious research and written countless footnotes pertaining to Shakespeare's so-called 'comedy' scenes, which have remained definitely not funny.

WILL'S LONDON LODGINGS – DAY

Bottom, a serving man, and Kate, a maid, be going about domestic drudgery.

KATE: So excited to hear about Mr Shakespeare's teen romance. It's such a good idea for a story.

BOTTOM: Yeah, it's all right, I suppose. Better than his usual stuff.

KATE: Has he let slip any hints about the romance plot?

BOTTOM: Er . . . This lad falls in love with this lass and she falls in love with him . . . and they live happily ever after.*

Kate smiles.

BOTTOM: Nice and short, which makes a change from his Henrys.†

KATE: And an amazing part for a girl.

---

* It appears that Shakespeare had not yet finalized the plot. It is tantalizing to speculate how much better the play might have been if he'd resisted the urge to overcomplicate it.

† Will's Henrys are indeed very long, and seem even longer.

BOTTOM: Kate, you've gotta drop that. Just cos your mum rents rooms to my master don't mean he's gonna put you in one of his plays!

KATE: It just seems so unfair that the theatre employs men to perform female roles, when I, a real woman, am ready and eager.

Will entereth, raiment spotted from his journey.

WILL: Ah, Kate! Splendid. Store these new pages in my bureau, would you? (*Handeth Kate some papers and sits down*) And, Bottom, bring ale and pie.

BOTTOM: A 'Good morrow"d be nice.

WILL: Ah, I'm famished. The coach promised a refreshment cart, but oh, not on this particular service, you'll be stunned to hear.

BOTTOM: I hate it when they do that!

WILL: Plus, they were filling ruts twixt Stokenchurch and Chipping Norton and had laid on replacement donkeys. In fact, one donkey for six of us plus bags. Of course, the snortish brute guffed its last after but three furlongs and they had to send for another from Birmingham. We spent two nights in a hedge. And did we see a single rut being filled? Oh no, I was forgetting, this is England. One wouldst more likely see a toothless crone with a tooth than an English rut-filler actually filling a rut. Fortunately I had quill and ink and was able to make passing use of the time.

Kate has been reading the papers.

KATE: My God, Mr Shakespeare, it's brilliant. Timeless, deathless. The most tragical history of Romeo and Julian.

Will stands.

WILL: Oh, er, yes, I . . . That should be Juliet, obviously. 'Romeo and Julian' was but a working title. Early exploratory stuff. It meanteth nothing.[*]

---

[*] It is interesting to speculate that had Shakespeare followed his initial instinct, he would have written the first gay couple in a popular smash, beating the lesbian wedding in *Friends* and Mitchell and Cameron from *Modern Family* by some four hundred years.

BOTTOM: Yeah, right.

WILL: What?

BOTTOM: Well, come on, master. We live in t'same house. I've heard you reading out your sonnets. Especially one to a hundred and twenty-six.

WILL: Those poems are about a platonic hierarchical relationship. God's naughty etchings! Why does everybody presume that just because I write a hundred and twenty-six love poems to an attractive boy, I must be . . . I must be some kind of bechambered hugger-tugger.

KATE: Juliet is an utterly amazing part.

WILL: Yes, I really think I've got her voice.

KATE: You have! You have! She's perfect.

WILL: The real challenge will be to find an actor to do her justice. Master Condell was quite brilliant as Queen Margaret in my Henrys, but I fear he'd be too old to play the ingénue. On the other hand, I don't want a boy. These downy-scrotumed squeakers lack depth.

KATE: Ah-hem!

WILL: Pardon, Kate? Leaping amphibian caught in the ruby pipe, which starts with a swallow but knows naught of birds?

KATE: Pardon?

BOTTOM: I think he means have you got a frog in your throat? But you can never be sure with him.*

A knock be heard.

BOTTOM: I'll get it. As if anyone else was ever going to.

---

* Scholars have long speculated that the dense obscurity of Shakespeare's language would have made him something of a pain in the arse in conversation. This exchange appears to confirm that suspicion.

WILL: Yes, Bottom, or alternatively I could get it and you could write a play and use the money you earn to pay me. Except, hang on, no, that wouldn't work because you can't read or write. So perhaps our current distribution of labour is the sensible and equitable one.

BOTTOM: That's just mean, that is.

Bottom departeth. Kate holdeth the pages most expectantly.

KATE: Ahem.

WILL: What?

KATE: I was hinting that the answer to your Juliet dilemma could be . . .

The maid pointeth at her own visage.

WILL: Oh, Kate, don't go there. Lady acting is illegal. Besides which, girls can't act. Just as they cannot practise law, cure the sick, handle financial matters or stand for any office.

KATE: But no woman has ever been allowed to try any of those things.

WILL: Because they can't do them. God's bodikins, Kate, what's not to get? Now, please, forget this nonsense and let me focus. It's not Juliet I'm worried about, it's Romeo. I can't seem to get a handle on him. His character eludes me.

Kate departeth. Bottom entereth.

BOTTOM: Master Robert Greene is without.

WILL: Rob Greene? Who doth hate my gutlings? What does he want?

Robert Greene strides in full blown with arrogance and pride. He shoveth Bottom in the face as he passes.

ROBERT GREENE: Aaahhh . . . Master Shakey-poet. A word, if you please?

---

* Robert Greene was an English poet and early rival of Shakespeare. He is thought to have died in 1592, but we know that this episode took place in 1596 (when Susanna was thirteen). We can therefore conclude that Greene lived far longer than has previously been supposed.

WILL: Shakespeare, Master Greene. My name is Shakespeare.

ROBERT GREENE: I know your name, sirrah, I was addressing you by trade. Shakey-poet. Just as I would address a house builder as Master Builder or a ship's carpenter as Master Carpenter.

BOTTOM: And what would you call a bear baiter, Mr Greene?

ROBERT GREENE: Master Baiter.

Bottom talks into Will's ear.

BOTTOM: See what I did there?

WILL: Brilliant, loved it.*

ROBERT GREENE: I am come on a mission of great delicacy. My nephew Florian Greene has fallen for a most unsuitable girl, the Lady Rosaline, daughter of a mere country knight. There can, of course, be no question of such a lowly match, so the boy must be kept from her.

WILL: And what part of this unedifying tale of upper-class entitlement is of interest to me?

ROBERT GREENE: Florian travels to Cambridge next week to take his place at the university. You must keep him here till then. You see, this lowly boarding house is far from court and Miss Rosaline will never find him here.

WILL: I am a busy writer, sirrah. Why should I do this?

ROBERT GREENE: Because I am Master of the Queen's Revels and, if you don't, I will deny your plays a licence.†

---

* This is the earliest known example of the familiar 'Master-bater' joke, which has appeared in many different forms over the years.

† To prevent actors and playwrights presenting radical, anti-establishment ideas, no play could be presented without licence from court. Censorship laws continued until the mid-twentieth century before finally being abolished when the authorities realized nobody actually gave a flying toss about actors' and playwrights' radical anti-establishment ideas.

WILL: You mean, you're corruptly using your public position to further your own private interests.

ROBERT GREENE: Ah, duh! I will have the boy sent to you this e'en, bound tight for his blood runs hot. I myself will return in a week for a farewell dinner. A good day.

Greene departeth still full blown with pride.

WILL: Hmm ... I am due at the theatre to discuss my new romance, but now must play nursey nursey, wipey nosey to a rogering, roistering, student clod-hopper. And all because Robert Greene be made Master of Revels. Why be he Master of Revels? What qualifies him to be my judge?

BOTTOM: Well, he's posh and he went to Cambridge.

WILL: Exactly. His very birth did guarantee him advancement, whilst mine precluded it. It is almost as if there be suspended over this sceptred isle a ceiling made of glass against which men of lower birth such as I must always bonk our noggins.[*]

BOTTOM: Do you think that's why you're going a bit bald?

WILL: I am not going bloody bald! I ... I have a very big brain.[†]

---

[*] It appears that Shakespeare coined the phrase 'glass ceiling'. Since he has so often been credited for phrases he did not invent, there is some poetic justice in him being denied credit for one he did.

[†] Historical evidence suggests that Shakespeare was in denial and that he definitely was going bald.

THE RED LION THEATRE – DAY

The actors Richard Burbage, Henry Condell and Will Kempe be all assembled.

CONDELL: Mr Burbage, I am the senior actor of female roles in this company.

BURBAGE: My dear Condell, the ingénue in Master Shakespeare's promised play is a maid of thirteen summers. A young bud scarce yet in bloom.

CONDELL: And your point?

BURBAGE: I think he seeks an actor that doesn't have to shave his ears.

Will doth bustle in.

WILL: Good morrow. Good morrow, all.

CONDELL: 'Don't you good-morrow me, Mr Shakespeare. This new romance you're writing.

WILL: Aye, 'Romeo and Julian'.

BURBAGE: Juliet.

WILL: As I said, 'Romeo and Juliet'.

CONDELL: Burbage says you want me to play some bloody nanny?

WILL: The nurse is a fine comedy role.

KEMPE: Comedy? Oh, don't give it to him, then.

CONDELL: I can do comedy.

KEMPE: Yeah, but only in London, yeah? Not really Florence, is it?

BURBAGE: Yes, we all know you've worked in Italy, Kempe.

KEMPE: Mmm, ooh, did I get an award? Can't remember. Oh, that's right, I did, yeah? A proper one. Not English, Italian, yeah? Commedia dell'Arte. Mmm. Heard of it?*

---

* Commedia dell'Arte was an early form of improvised clowning, which originated in Italy. Like later forms of improvised clowning, it was probably a bit crap.

CONDELL: Since you became big in Italy, Kempe, an unsufferable smuglington hast thou become.

KEMPE: Yeah, but an unsufferable smuglington who's big in Italy.[*]

CONDELL: I am the senior lady actor and I insist on playing Juliet!

WILL: Look, the play isn't even finished. I'm stuck on the character of my Romeo and, what's more, as yet I don't have an ending.

BURBAGE: Surely our young lovers will live happily ever after?

WILL: Mm, well, that's the obvious ending.

BURBAGE: Yes.

WILL: The ending the crowd will want.

BURBAGE: Yes.

WILL: So I thought I'd kill them instead.

BURBAGE: Kill them? Our teenage sweethearts?

WILL: Yes. Theatre should be challenging.

BURBAGE: And entertaining.

WILL: Mainly challenging.[†]

BURBAGE: Oh . . .

WILL: I just need to work out a decent double-death plot.

CONDELL: I can do dying. I'm good at dying.

KEMPE: Yeah, onstage every night. Ah, who said that? Ah, I did so . . .

---

[*] The Italian peninsula was the centre of Western culture between the fourteenth and seventeenth centuries, delivering artistic innovations in painting, literature, philosophy, architecture, mathematics and science. The United States holds a similar position of influence in modern Western culture, having developed reality television.
[†] Here Will Shakespeare establishes a theory of theatre that would eventually result in Harold Pinter.

CONDELL: Mr Shakespeare, I need this role. I can woo Romeo, I know I can. Let me show you. Find a way for me to prove it.

KEMPE: Bit sad though, begging.

WILL'S LONDON LODGINGS – DAY

Will be at his work. Bottom enters dragging a figure who is tied up and concealed within a big bag.

BOTTOM: We've had a delivery.

WILL: Lock up the beef and ale, Bottom. Tell the poor to bar their doors. We unleash the most parasitic creature in Christendom, the English posh boy.*

Bottom is about to open the bag.

WILL: Stay your hand a moment, Bottom. Have you your dagger handy?

BOTTOM: Do you think he's dangerous?

WILL: Possibly. These Oxbridge yobos are extraordinarily strong, having spent their entire lives with literally enough to eat. They join clubs called the Burst Ballsack and the Fisted Peasant, where they gorge and fight and roger and quaff till they coat the walls with gut-porridge.†

BOTTOM: Bit jealous, are we?

WILL: Bloody jealous! Particularly as when they graduate they all get to be bishops and ambassadors and members of the privy council. In England I'm afraid it's not what you know, it's what dead farmyard animals you rogered at university. We can put it off no longer. Unleash the posh boy.‡

---

* This episode suggests that the socially corrosive self-interest of English posh boys goes further back in history than previously assumed.

† The Burst Ballsack and the Fisted Peasant still exist today but have merged and become the Bullingdon Club, of which David Cameron and Boris Johnson were members.

‡ A fascinating historical insight. It had previously been assumed that the practice of rogering dead farmyard animals at Oxbridge parties was instigated by recent members of the Conservative front bench. It seems, however, that the ritual is hundreds of years old.

Bottom doth cut open the bag. The youth Florian, a fey young man, emergeth.

FLORIAN: Rosaline, Rosaline! Wherefore art thou, Rosaline?

Florian doth search the room.

WILL: Goodness, this is, this is spooky. He's asking why his beloved's name is Rosaline.

BOTTOM: Actually, I think he's asking where Rosaline is.

WILL: Probably best to leave the linguistic interpretation to me.

FLORIAN: Where are you, Rosaline? Where are you? I wish I knew where you were!

Bottom turns to Will.

BOTTOM: You gonna admit I was right?

FLORIAN: O brutal love, despised love. Love is the angry thorn upon the false rose and I am a prick.

BOTTOM: Blimey, have we gotta spend a week with this arsemongle?

WILL: Resist your thuggish interjections, Bottom. I see in this lovelorn loon the very model of my Romeo.

FLORIAN: Oh, thou rude and deceiving table. (*Doth thump the table*) Four legs hast thou, yet none are Rosaline's. I would cut off every one and eat upon the floor for but one glance at Rosaline's sweet knees.*

BOTTOM: I'm sorry, but this bloke's a total wankington.

WILL: You must make allowance for his youth and ardour.

FLORIAN: (*Kicketh the floor*) Curse the floor that doth not support Rosaline. (*Picketh up a broom and hitteth the ceiling*) Curse the ceiling

---

* In Shakespeare's *Romeo and Juliet* we first discover Romeo pining over a girl called Rosaline. It seems reasonable to suggest that Shakespeare was influenced by Florian and that Rosaline was a real Elizabethan woman, although whether her knees were indeed sweet will ever remain a matter of speculation.

that doth not shelter Rosaline. (*Slappeth Bottom in the face*) Curse the bondsman that doth not serve Rosaline.

WILL: Well, maybe he is a bit of a wankington.

FLORIAN: Sirrah, who are you?

WILL: My name is Will Shakespeare, Master Florian. And I've been charged with keeping you safe till you go to university.

FLORIAN: Never. I will leave this place at once and search the world until I find my Rosaline.

WILL: I'm afraid that's out of the question.

Florian picketh up a knife.

FLORIAN: Then I will kill myself. Rosaline, Rosaline! Wherefore art thou, Rosaline?

Florian goes to stab himself, then pauses as Kate entereth.

KATE: Mr Shakespeare, I've learned one of Juliet's speeches. And if you'll just let me show you what I've—

WILL: Kate, I'm really, really busy.

Kate poses to perform.

KATE: 'What's in a name? That which we call a rose by any other name would smell as sweet.'*

WILL: Not now, Kate.

KATE: Sorry.

She leaveth.

WILL: Now, Master Florian, don't be foolish. You're going to have to put Rosaline out of your mind.

FLORIAN: Rosaline? Rosaline? Who's this foul trollop, Rosaline?

WILL: Why, your love, I thought.

---

* This is generally considered one of the best bits of *Romeo and Juliet*, although it's even better if you only quote the second half of the sentence starting with 'a rose'.

FLORIAN: Kate. Kate be my love. I will love none but my Kate.

WILL: Kate? You . . . you mean, our Kate?!

FLORIAN: Where she breathes, flowers bloom. Where she sings, pixies dance. Her most billowingly flatulent fartle-barfle be more sweetly scented than all the perfumes of Arabia.*

BOTTOM: Well, you see, you're wrong there. She's not a bad-looking bird, but let me tell you, if she leaves one hanging in a room you're still chewing on it an hour later.

Florian punches Bottom most angrily.

FLORIAN: My Kate doth teach the candles to burn bright. Kate! Kate!

Florian doth hurry from the room in pursuit of Kate. Will taketh up his quill.

WILL: Zounds, I've gotta get some of this stuff down! He's my Romeo all right, and what a bit of luck, him going all diddly doodah over our Kate! We thought to be his jailer, but what better chains to keep him close than those of love?

As Will begins to write, Kate doth enter.

KATE: Mr Shakespeare, something quite interesting has just happened.

WILL: Yes, I know, Kate, Master Florian's taken a shine to you. Just string him along for a week, will you? Let him sing beneath your balcony, write you sonnets, that sort of thing. I'm sure it's nothing serious.

KATE: It is quite serious. He's asked me to marry him.

WILL: Well . . . well, that's very sweet . . . marry?! He can't marry you! Robert Greene thought Rosaline not good enough for his precious

---

* It is reasonable to presume that Florian is employing poetic licence as, considering the Elizabethan diet, neither Kate's breath nor her fartle-barfles would have smelt great. On another note 'all the perfumes of Arabia' is quoted in *Macbeth*. Will probably nicked the phrase from Florian.

Florian and she be the daughter of a knight. Your mum washes my puffling pants.

KATE: Yes, but 'tis not Robert Greene who would marry me, 'tis Florian. And when he does my station will be somewhat elevated – considerably, I might add – above your own.

WILL: But, Kate, if you marry Florian, his uncle will blame me and never license another of my plays!

KATE: Hmm, it's not my problem, though, is it? Particularly since you won't let me play Juliet, even though I'd be brilliant and it's my dream.

WILL: But, Kate, you know very well that it is illegal for girls to do anything interesting!

KATE: Thus, our only recourse is to marry, and if we can marry rich besotted idiots, then all the better.

Kate departeth in high dudgeon.

WILL: Bottom, we have to stop this marriage! We must distract the boy!

BOTTOM: Well, that shouldn't be difficult. The randy little ponce fancies anything in a skirt.

WILL: That's right, yes, of course. So all we need to do is find someone in a skirt whom he definitely can't marry. Oh my God, it's so obvious!

WILL'S LONDON LODGINGS – NIGHT

The table is set for dinner. Florian doth sit while Will and Bottom look on. Master Condell entereth dressed in glamorous female attire.

CONDELL: Yoohoo, masters. See, here I am.

Burbage and Kempe follow on with lute and drum.

CONDELL: I am Mistress Sauce Quickly. A shy but biddable young maid, who's all ripe and hot and drippy. Players!

Burbage and Kempe play most merrily.

CONDELL: (*Singing*) She that craves her true love's joy with a hey ho, the wind and the rain. Who'd do the lot for a handsome boy, for the maid she bonketh every day.*

WILL: Well, Master Florian. (*Both Will and Condell join Florian at the table*) What think you of Mistress Sauce Quickly? Doth she not make your loins tremble and your codpiece cry 'Woof woof'?

FLORIAN: Are you blind? She looks like a man in a dress! Besides, I am spoken for my Kate.

WILL: Ah, but Kate be pure and chaste till wed, while Mistress Sauce Quickly doth promise the lot before dinner.

FLORIAN: Not a bad point, actually.

Kate doth enter, drop-dead gorgeous and like an angel.

KATE: 'Sweet, goodnight! This bud of love, by summer's ripening breath may prove a beauteous flower when next we meet. Goodnight, goodnight, as sweet repose and rest come to thy heart as that within my breast!'†

---

* This song is clearly the source of a very similar verse which appears in Shakespeare's *Twelfth Night*. True to form, when Shakespeare put it in a play he made it four times longer and cut the bit about bonking, which was the only good bit in it.
† This incident – included verbatim in *Romeo and Juliet* – can be established as the first public utterance of this famous passage. It is ironic but also fitting that it was spoken in the context of gender confusion involving a cross-dresser, a subject that held a lifelong fascination for Shakespeare.

Kate doth blow out her candle most saucily with ripe and pouting lips, then departeth.

FLORIAN: Sorry, Mistress Sauce Quickly, that does it. Kate's the one for me. (*Arises*) I shall stand beneath Kate's balcony and strum my lute.

BOTTOM: If that's a figure of speech, don't let the watchman catch you.

FLORIAN: Oh well, in that case perhaps I'll just play her some music.

KATE'S ROOM – NIGHT

Kate all winsome at the window. Will entereth.

WILL: I should be angry with you for pinching my lines like that, but you did do them rather well.

KATE: The verse is so beautiful.

WILL: Look, Kate, crazy as it sounds, perhaps Juliet would be better played by a girl. So, if I were at some point to try – and I only say try – to help you become an actor, would you prefer that to marrying a pervy posh boy?

KATE: Oh, Mr Shakespeare, you know I would, but I am promised now and that is binding in law.

WILL: Well then, we must come up with a plan to get this boy to give you up. And I've got a corker.

KATE: Even better than a middle-aged man in lipstick?

WILL: Yes, even better than that.

AN APOTHECARY – NIGHT

All be dark and sinister. Will doth enter most furtively and greet the old apothecary.

WILL: Good e'en, old apothecary.

APOTHECARY: Good e'en, my master. A dark night for business. Perhaps thy business be dark also?

WILL: Yes, well, I suppose it is a bit. My, erm, friend loves this girl.

APOTHECARY: I see, my master. And this 'friend' has a spotted cod-dangle and a murky discharge.

WILL: Not at all.

APOTHECARY: You take bat spit and goat snot and rub upon your, I mean, your *friend's*, er . . .

WILL: Apothecary, I be not poxed! I just need a simple potion that will render a person seemingly dead, but from which they will fully recover at the appropriate moment.

APOTHECARY: Well, we have Play Dead. Or else you could buy my own brand of the mixture, which is exactly the same but half the price.

WILL: I think I'll stick to the popular brand, thank you. I'm happy to pay a little more for the nebulous sense of comfort that a public brand imbues.

Will hands over the money.

WILL'S LONDON LODGINGS – NIGHT

The youth Florian, all lovelorn, doth strum his lute beneath Kate's window.

BOTTOM: Master Florian, I've come with a message from your true love, Kate.

FLORIAN: Why, sirrah, if you speak Kate's words then you are her mouth.

BOTTOM: Er, not really.

FLORIAN: And so must I kiss thee.

BOTTOM: Er . . . this is not consensual.

Florian doth kiss Bottom most fulsomely upon his lips before recoiling in horror.

FLORIAN: Oh God! Your breath doth stink like you dine on dung! Deliver your message and be gone.

BOTTOM: Mistress Kate has gone to the local chapel. Her countenance was dark and wild. I fear some madness has come upon her. She called for you, master. Hurry, lest you be too late.[*]

Florian departeth in anxious haste.

---

[*] Bottom is clearly acting on Will's instructions, so it seems safe to conclude Will conducted his own life in a manner as chaotic and random as the plots of his plays. With this in mind, it's hard to see how he lived as long as he did.

A CRYPT – NIGHT

Kate sitteth upon a convenient tomb. Bottom and Will stand ready, Will with the potion.

WILL: Right, Kate, you swig the potion, Florian finds you, thinks you dead and breaks off the engagement. I can't see how it can possibly go wrong.

KATE: Well, to play Juliet . . .

Kate drinketh from the bottle and of a sudden faints dead away.* Now the youth Florian approaches.

WILL: And soft, he comes!

Will and Bottom do hide themselves.

FLORIAN: Dark, so dark. I fear my love's not here for surely her bright eyes would be a lantern in the gloom. (*Spies Kate's unconscious form*) What's this? My Kate lies cold. Does she sleep? No, she is dead!

WILL: Now, will he say, 'Oh well, bad luck, I'll just have to forget about her and go to Cambridge'?

FLORIAN: Poisoned! Dead from poison?! Dead!

WILL: 'Oh well, win some, lose some. Plenty more totty in Cambridge'?†

FLORIAN: If Kate be dead then Florian need not live. Perchance, some trace of poison does linger on her lips. A kiss and I will share her fate.

Florian kisses Kate.

---

* Potions like this have been a staple of drama for many centuries. The appropriate character, usually female, simply took a sip and fainted away, then woke up at exactly the right time to further the plot. There appears to have been no scientific basis for these potions but audiences never complained. Possibly because they were asleep.
† Will's naïve expectation that his ridiculous plan will work out mitigates the awfulness of his plots because at least he appears to have believed this shit.

WILL: Blimey. He's taking it a bit harder than I expected.

FLORIAN: And yet no friendly drop remains. Perchance she did brush her teeth and then gargle after drinking it? (*Anguished, he doth draw his blade*) With a dagger I die . . .

And so doth Florian stab himself most horribly in the gutlings. Will and Bottom reveal themselves in all haste.

WILL: No, no! She be not dead, the potion only made her seem dead. She'll wake up any second!

FLORIAN: Bolingbrokes. (*Falls dead*)*

WILL: He dies! Now cracks a noble heart. Goodnight, sweet idiot. Thy heart was big, thy brain tiny.†

Now Kate doth most conveniently awake on cue.

KATE: Soft, I wake. Did the plan work? Did Florian find my still body, think me dead and depart for Cambridge with a shrug?

BOTTOM: Well, two out of three ain't bad.

WILL: Right, good . . . Don't panic, we can deal with this. We just need another brilliant plan.

---

* Florian appears to have died quickly and conveniently although it is in fact almost impossible to stab yourself to instant death. In reality, both Florian and Romeo would have died horribly and agonizingly probably over many bloody hours. It therefore seems likely that the author of this biographical text employed the same theatrical licence as Shakespeare.

† Shakespeare reused this line when writing the death scene in *Hamlet*. Except he used 'Prince' instead of 'idiot' and left out the bit about the tiny brain.

WILL'S LONDON LODGINGS – NIGHT

The assembled company be present, Condell dressed as a woman and Burbage and Kempe holding Florian's dead body upright betwixt them. Bottom completeth laying the table for dinner. Will doth enter with Robert Greene.

WILL: Welcome, Master Greene, to your Florian's farewell feast. Burbage and his company and Mistress Sauce Quickly have joined us to make of it a merry evening.

ROBERT GREENE: Excellent! Excellent! Come, Florian, embrace your uncle. (*Florian, being dead, be most pale, and his tongue doth droop from his mouth*) He looks half dead.

WILL: He is, Master Greene, he is. I did a bit of serious roistering with young Flozza last night. Buckets of oysters, barrels of ale.

ROBERT GREENE: Young sirrah, your hand.

Burbage and Kempe manhandle the corpse of Florian towards Greene and extend its hand. Greene shakes it.

ROBERT GREENE: Good lad. Cold, stiff, unbending. Just as a gentleman should be.

Kate calls out prettily.

KATE: Dinner is served, my masters.

A few moments later all are sat around the table. Florian's corpse is again supported betwixt Kempe and Burbage.

BURBAGE: So I said to Johnny Hemmings – lovely actor, sweet, sweet man – I said, 'Johnny, have you ever played *Gammer Gurton's Needle?*' He said, 'I've played Gammer Gurton, duckie, but the needle came from props.'[*]

---

[*] *Gammer Gurton's Needle* is dense, impenetrable, baffling and spectacularly unfunny. It therefore can be seen as the first play in an English theatrical tradition that was to find its full expression in the plays of Harold Pinter. Unlike a Pinter play, however, *Gammer Gurton's Needle* contains one identifiable gag. The plot concerns a lost needle which is later discovered in the lead character's britches when he sits on it. This is not bad for a five-hundred-year-old joke.

They all laugh, Burbage moving Florian's head.

WILL: Brilliant, Burbage! I always say there's nothing more fascinating than actors talking about themselves. Tell us more!

ROBERT GREENE: What about Florian? Thou hast not touched thy food. Posh boys must quaff and gorge whilst others starve.

Fearful the ruse will be discovered, Will turneth to Kate with utmost urgency.

WILL: Can't keep this up much longer. Let's go for it.

Will addresseth the corpse.

WILL: Tell me, Florian, have you seen anything of the fair Rosaline, whom once you did love so well?

Kate leapeth up in anger.

KATE: Rosaline? Who is Rosaline? You said you loved me, your Kate!

Kate slappeth the corpse's face, whereupon Condell doth leap up, also feigning anger.

CONDELL: Kate?! Young Kate?! Thou said thou didst love me, Mistress Sauce Quickly.

Now Condell smiteth the corpse. Greene doth roar with laughter.

ROBERT GREENE: Bravo, lad! I see you've been roistering as a varsity man should. And er, Master Shakespeare, it seems you have cured my nephew of all silly notions of romance.

WILL: Well, yes, I think you could say we've done that.

ROBERT GREENE: Bravo!

All applaud most merrily. Burbage and Kempe forget that the corpse is in their charge and Florian falleth forward, his face fully in the dinner.

ROBERT GREENE: Well, look now, what's this? Why, he's passed out in his plate! You'd think he was at Cambridge already!

WILL'S STRATFORD HOME – NIGHT

Will and Anne sit before the fire with their pipes, most contented.

WILL: We took him to Cambridge, where not surprisingly they found him cold, uncooperative and expecting advancement without effort or talent. In short, a perfect member of the English establishment. Although he will have decomposed long before he graduates, I imagine he'll get a first.

ANNE: Amazing tale, husband. Particularly the bit about the maid drugging herself in a tomb only for her young lover to think her dead and killing himself before she wakes up.

WILL: Yes. If only I could think of an ending for my play as easily.

EPISODE 2

THE PLAY'S THE THING

This second transcript is a clear source for the
'play within a play' scene from *Hamlet*. However,
no other parts of Shakespeare's famous tragedy are
prefigured in this fascinating episode, so it seems
that Shakespeare had yet to come up with the
brilliant notion that the world was waiting for a play
about a depressed Danish student.

WILL'S STRATFORD HOME – DAY

Will appears to be shouting at Anne in fury. John, Mary, Susanna and the twins sit about the room.

WILL: Ingrate whore! Stinksome strumpet! Foul and false be thy black heart! But blood red will be thy shroud!

ANNE: Argh!

Will appears about to strike his beloved wife but then he pauses.

WILL: Dad, it's your line.

JOHN: Get one of the women to read it.

WILL: Neither of the women can read.[*]

MARY: And I wouldn't if I could. It's a common business.

JOHN: Then, get Susanna to read it. Can't think why else you taught her.

ANNE: There's no point asking Sue for help. She be of teening years and thus a grumpy little bitchington.

Susanna doth growl and sneer most moodily.

JOHN: I dunno why you have to write these new plays anyway. What's wrong with the old plays? The Mumming plays?[†]

WILL: Theatre's moving on, Dad. There's only so many times you can laugh at the Lord of Misrule whacking the naughty Turk with a jingly stick while St George shows the dragon his bottom.[‡]

JOHN: Oh, gets me every time, that one.[§]

---

[*] Scholars have long speculated Anne and Mary could read but pretended they couldn't in order to avoid having to wade through any of Will's plays. Generations of schoolchildren might well have wished they had the same excuse.

[†] Mumming plays were a traditional form of 'entertainment' – essentially a load of shouty old bolingbrokes – that have increasingly been recognized as an excuse for performers and audiences to get completely and utterly pissed.

[‡] Shakespeare was wrong. Research has revealed it wasn't even funny the first time.

[§] Unless you're completely and utterly pissed.

ANNE: Will is trying to do his play, which, believe it or not, I'm actually following. Come on, love, Queen Liz is threatening Queen Mary in the tower.

WILL: Absolutely right, yes. Here we go.

Once more Will commenceth to rehearse.

WILL: 'Blood red will be thy shroud!' And then a nobleman rushes in, 'Majesty, I beseech thee, must not a queen this murder do.'

ANNE: Shouldn't that be, 'A queen must not do this murder'?

WILL: Well, yes, it should, but I always think a sentence sounds better if you mix up the words a bit. It's one of my best tricks.*

SUSANNA: Sounds really try-hard to me.

WILL: Or, put more poetically – 'to me sounds, hard try really'. See? Much better.

JOHN: Queen Elizabeth didn't chop Mary's head off herself, you daft wurzel. She were topped at Fotheringhay.

ANNE: Granddad is right – about the beheading. Queen Liz never done it.

WILL: Yes, my love, I am aware of the facts, but as a dramatist, I take the view that a fat man with an axe saying, 'Close your eyes, love,' *thwack*, isn't quite as compelling theatre as frigid Liz bitch-slapping her cutesome Caledonian cuz Mary in a bit of queen-on-queen action.†

SUSANNA: So creepy, Dad!

ANNE: It does sound a bit creepy. You're better than that, doll.

---

* This offers a fascinating window into Shakespeare's methods and confirms the view held by generations of schoolchildren that much of Shakespeare's writing is in fact completely random and that the Bard himself understood this.
† This is further evidence of Shakespeare's astonishing prescience. These days absolutely everything from pop videos to soaps has to have a bit of lesbian snogging in it.

WILL: Look, I work in showbusiness, girls. Sex sells. We need bums on seats. Or in this case, bum on throne. Because, mark this, Her Majesty has commanded Burbage to produce a play for her feast on the first Sunday after Lamington Eve.[*]

ANNE: The Queen. That is posh.

WILL: Which is why I'm writing my history of Gloriana and her traitorous cuz. It doth flatter Her Majesty most shamelessly. Now, can I please get on? I only came home for some peace and quiet so that I could finish my play. And where is my quill? Or must I pluck another from the chicken's arse?

A chicken runs off.

ANNE: Don't you dare! Poor Mistress Clucky. Whenever you come home with the muse upon you we get no eggs for a week. Her arse be going bald faster than your bonce.

WILL: I am not going bald, I have low eyebrows.[†]

ANNE: Yeah, my dumplings aren't droopy, I've just got a very high belly button.

SUSANNA: Oh shut up, Mum! You're so gross!

ANNE: Here's your quill on the table where you left it.

WILL: Oh, wondrous wife, whene'er I lose a thing you always know its place.

ANNE: Not so much being wondrous, doll, as not being a clueless futtocking arsemongle.

MARY: You're a common woman, Anne Shakespeare. A very common woman!

JOHN: Why do you wanna write about Scots Mary anyway?

---

[*] Lamington Eve is not a thing and never was, which is proof that nobody in England has the faintest idea about any church holidays except Christmas.
[†] Shakespeare was definitely going bald.

SUSANNA: Yeah, Dad, why don't you write a play about normal people?

WILL: Because normal people are boring. The crowd wants plays about posh people. They want gangs of geographically named dukes who wander on at random and say, 'Come, Sussex, Oxford and Northampton, let us to York, there to do battle with Surrey, Cornwall, Solihull and Basingstoke.'*

ANNE: People might enjoy something a bit more realistic. There's plenty of drama in real life. If you want to write tragedy, why not write about the plague?

WILL: The plague? Huh, yes. I can see people just flocking to watch a drama about crowds of the living dead, wandering around with their flesh falling off.†

ANNE: I'd go.

---

* Shakespeare was wrong. Audiences mostly find this sort of scene very boring.
† Evidence that Shakespeare invented the 'zombie' genre, pre-dating *The Walking Dead* by over four hundred years. And imagine how much better *Henry V* would have been if King Harry had found himself battling an army of French zombies at Agincourt.

WILL'S LONDON LODGINGS – DAY

Kate doth practise her acting in front of Bottom.

KATE: 'Caesar, I beg you, go not to the capital today. Woe! Woe! Woe!' Right, what do you think? Come on, I can take it. I welcome criticism.

BOTTOM: It's crap, if I'm honest.

KATE: I know, I know. I need to dig deeper, explore further. Really feel the role.

BOTTOM: Kate, drop it. You can't be an actor.

KATE: Why? Because I'm only the landlady's daughter?

BOTTOM: No, it in't that. You just don't sound like a girl.

KATE: But I am a girl.

BOTTOM: Yeah, but you can't act one, love. We've been through this. It takes a bloke. Women aren't clever enough.

KATE: *Vae mihi quia ego stulta.*

BOTTOM: You what?

KATE: It's Latin for 'Such a shame to be an ignorant woman'.

BOTTOM: Live with it, love.

KATE: Can you at least give me some performance notes?

BOTTOM: All right. Well, your voice for starters, it's too nice. Needs to be all raw and squeaky like this. (*Bottom doth put on a horrid squeaky voice*) 'Caesar, I beg you, go not into the capital today.'

KATE: Well, what about my physicality? Surely at least I move like a girl?

BOTTOM: Well, I suppose. A bit. Although it'd be better with two half coconuts shoved down your bodice. Except they wouldn't fit, would they? No room for falsies cos of your realies.

KATE: Such cruel irony.

Will entereth, his raiment spotted from travel.

WILL: Ah, Kate! Are you here? Splendid. Bottom, ale and pie.

BOTTOM: Good morrow'd be nice.

WILL: Terrible journey! Some pasty-brained arsemongle decided to kill himself on the track.

KATE: Oh, I hate that!

WILL: So selfish! I mean, jump in a lake, eat some hemlock, fall on your sword. Agitate a large bear with a small stick. Just don't throw yourself under the bloody carriage in front of mine!*

Bottom serveth ale and pie.

BOTTOM: Selfish bastable.

KATE: They *didn't* close the road?

WILL: Of course they closed the bloody road! I mean why, for God's sake? Just why? The man is dead. There is a large cart track running from his crotch to his cranium.

BOTTOM: Scrape him up and put him in a bag.

WILL: Just scrape him up and put him in a bag! But oh no, that would mean passing up the opportunity to drive the public insane with frustration. And, let's face it, this is England, so that ain't gonna happen.

KATE: So frustrating.

WILL: And to top it all, our stalled coach had to take on passengers from the one under which the selfish bastable will have hurled himself. Suddenly I find myself squeezed next to

---

* Here, Shakespeare brilliantly reflects the inner workings of the human soul. Modern travellers confronted by a similar situation will profess a grudging sympathy for the victim while secretly harbouring furious resentment that the death of a deeply depressed or mentally ill person has slightly inconvenienced them.

an oafish groundling who spent the entire journey stroking his porker.

BOTTOM: Suppose it passes the time.

WILL: A pig, Bottom, a pig. He did carry home bacon for his daughter's dowry and the beast crawled with vermin. 'Twas not so much a pig that had fleas as fleas that had a pig!

Will hurls down his cloak and stampeth upon it.

KATE: Whenever I crush fleas I always use the time to practise my dancing. (*Kate danceth on Will's cloak whilst playing a flute*) As you know, music and dance are key skills for actors.

WILL: Kate, stop it now. We go through this seventeen times a week. I know I've said I'd help, but you can't be an actor. You're a girl. Where would you put the coconuts?

BOTTOM: That's what I said.

KATE: So unfair!

The dashing blade and naughty rogue Kit Marlowe entereth.[*]

KIT MARLOWE: Morning, all. Let myself in. Kinda go where I please. It's just easier.

Marlowe lounges, putting his boots upon the table most arrogantly.

WILL: Oh, Kit, no, no, always welcome. Always.

KATE: Good morrow, Mr Marlowe.

KIT MARLOWE: Mistress Kate.

WILL: Make yourself at home.

KIT MARLOWE: Yep. Did that.

---

[*] The London theatre scene of Shakespeare's day was small so there can be no doubt that two theatrical titans such as Shakespeare and Marlowe would have known each other. Scholars have speculated that they might even have been friends. The emergence of the Crow Folios confirms that they were, or at least that Shakespeare liked Marlowe and Marlowe liked Shakespeare's ale and pie.

WILL: It's brilliant to see you, Kit. You're so cool and confident. Being your mate always makes me feel a bit more cool and confident.[*]

KIT MARLOWE: Of course it does! So, whisper is you're writing another play? Good work that, man. I can't think how you find the energy.

WILL: Actually I have several on the go at present – alongside my teen romance. Mainly just ideas. 'The Taming of the Vole', which I quite like. 'Seventeen Gentlemen of Verona'. That needs trimming. 'A Midsummer Night's Whimsical Old Tosh'. Still looking for the big idea there.

BOTTOM: I've told ya, just say it's a dream. You can get away with any old dung balls if you say it's a dream.

WILL: Exactly, Bottom, and I hope my quill does wither on Miss Clucky's arse before I resort to such a lazy cop-out.[†]

KIT MARLOWE: It's all a bit so-what so far, Will. You got any more?

WILL: 'The Merchant of Guildford'? Kinda works?

KIT MARLOWE: Kinda doesn't.

WILL: Er, 'A Not Very Funny Story About Errors'.[‡]

KIT MARLOWE: Ouch.

WILL: Well, they all need work, of course, but I have one finished and I'm really pleased with it: 'The Tragical History of Mary Queen of Scots'.

---

[*] Shakespeare clearly had an inferiority complex where Christopher Marlowe was concerned. Scholars find this surprising as Shakespeare was the greater poet. However, Marlowe was single, a hell-raiser, drinker, sexual adventurer, international secret agent and he went to Cambridge. Whereas Shakespeare was a fartsome baldy boots who lived in the Midlands. You do the maths.

[†] Not only was Shakespeare fully aware that *A Midsummer Night's Dream* was a load of old dung balls, but he was also the first writer to use the 'dream' cop-out to explain a crapsome plot.

[‡] Had Shakespeare stuck with this title – rather than the palpably false *A Comedy of Errors* – he would at least have managed expectations.

KIT MARLOWE: Yes! Now we're talking. I'm loving that!

KATE: And such a strong part for a woman.

KIT MARLOWE: Well, you mean for a man playing a woman. Women can't act, obviously.

BOTTOM: That's what I said.

KIT MARLOWE: Where would you put the coconuts?

BOTTOM: No room!

KATE: Please, Mr Shakespeare. I would work so hard. I know I am only an ignorant woman, but I have read *Historia Gentis Scotorum* and so know something of the Stewart Queen's back story.

KIT MARLOWE: Clever girl's an ugly girl, Kate.

WILL: Kate, let it lie. Women are not allowed to act.

KATE: It's so cruel to live in times when women are denied everything! Huh! (*Stormeth out*)

KIT MARLOWE: Birds, eh? So emotional. They're second-class citizens, get over it.

WILL: Anyway, Kit, I was telling you about my new play. It is to be presented to the Master of the Revels, that it may be performed before Her Majesty.

KIT MARLOWE: Oh yes! That'd be great, except probably better if I presented it. Just a thought.

BOTTOM: Here we go, master, be strong.

WILL: Marlowe, I've told you I'm not writing you any more plays.[*]

KIT MARLOWE: Come on, Will. You owe me. It's me that got your work before the public in the first place.

---

[*] This is perhaps the most significant revelation in all of the Crow Folios. Idiotic conspiracy theorists searching to fill their dull pointless lives have long sought to suggest that Marlowe wrote Shakespeare's plays (despite him having died before 90 per cent of them were written). It is indeed ironic to discover that Shakespeare wrote Marlowe's.

WILL: By sticking your name on it.

KIT MARLOWE: It was the only way. What were you? A country bumsnot fresh off the coach. Nobody took you seriously.

WILL: Exactly, I was but a jobbing actor when I gave you *Tamburlaine* and *Doctor Faustus*, but now I want credit for my own work.*

KIT MARLOWE: A bit selfish, Will. Not very attractive.

WILL: Kit, be reasonable. Mine is a unique voice.

KIT MARLOWE: Well, unique-ish. I mean, all you really do is jumble up the words.

WILL: Well, I admit I do do a fair bit of word jumbling – and I'm not apologizing for that. But, but, also I create language. Inventing phrases that I'm sure one day will be in common usage. (*Seizes upon a manuscript*) Look here, Mary Stewart, who is twice damned, being both Scottish and French, she I have dubbed a Frog-Jock.

KIT MARLOWE: Ooh. No, fair play, that is pretty good. I mean, that's just the sort of line I should have written.

WILL: Mm, but you didn't.

KIT MARLOWE: Oh don't quibble, Will, makes you look small. Come on, just give us a play. Because of you everyone thinks I'm this brilliant poet guy, when actually I couldn't be bothered to rhyme dove with ... with ... see? Lost interest already. Verse is just not my gig.

WILL: But why do you care that people think you're a poet? You're a famous roisterer. The most popular man in the city. Your name is like a cold sore.

KIT MARLOWE: Pardon?

WILL: It's on everybody's lips.

---

* *Tamburlaine* and *Doctor Faustus* are of course two towering classics of English literature on which Marlowe's reputation is largely built. The fact that Shakespeare simply gave them to his arch rival is astonishing and has led scholars to suggest that the Crow Folios are an elaborate twenty-first-century fraud.

BOTTOM: Bit rubbish, that one, master.*

WILL: Look, Bottom, improvisation needs a non-critical environment to flourish. You can't do it if you're getting heckled by your servant.

BOTTOM: You need to man up. Comedy's a tough game. It's adversarial.

WILL: I just don't think it needs to be.

KIT MARLOWE: Come on, Will! You totally know why I need this poet thing. It's my cover.

WILL: Oh, yes, of course. I was forgetting, you're a secret agent.

KIT MARLOWE: I'm one of Walsingham's men. Sworn to defend the realm, yet forever in the shadows, and so I play the gadsome poet whilst on my secret work of vital national importance!†

WILL: Hmm ... this work being the entrapping and burning of Catholics.‡

KIT MARLOWE: Absolutely.

WILL: And that's vitally important, is it?

KIT MARLOWE: Well, it seems to be. Walsingham never shuts up about it.

WILL: As a taxpayer, I can't help wondering if the state might not be better employed expending its resources on other important works. Building better roads, for instance, or some rudimentary urban plumbing.

---

* Bottom is, of course, right. The cold-sore gag is a bit rubbish. One can only speculate that Will's plays might have been significantly better if Bottom had pointed out the crap lines more often.

† While there is little doubt that Marlowe did indeed work for famed Elizabethan spymaster Francis Walsingham, the nature of his work is unknown. What can be surmised with relative certainty is that it involved a lot of drinking and shagging.

‡ And, of course, the entrapping and burning of Catholics, which was something of an obsession in Elizabeth's day.

KIT MARLOWE: Well, you'd think, wouldn't you? But, burning Catholics – that's definitely the big thing.

WILL: Just as burning Protestants was the big thing of the last insane bint in a crown who passed England's way.

KIT MARLOWE: Yes, weird, isn't it? But I don't make the rules. I'm just in it for the expense account and the chance to chase foreign girls.

WILL: Well, I'm sorry, Kit, but you're gonna have to have exotic sex at the public's expense without my help. I love you, cuz, but I'm not giving you my frog-jock play and that's final.

KIT MARLOWE: Well, if you won't, you won't, I suppose. Writing plays can't be that hard. Maybe I'll just grab a chicken and write one myself.

WILL: Kit, you be no poet. If you write a play I fear it will be like that which stinks but be not fish. Fertilizes plants but be not compost. And is the last stage of the digestive process but be not a glass of port and a pipe of tobacco.

KIT MARLOWE: Pardon?

BOTTOM: He means crap. You get used to him over time.

KIT MARLOWE: Well, we'll see. No hard feelings. Right, I'm for the tavern. I love you loads.

Marlowe departeth for the pub.

WILL: I hated saying no. He's such a great bloke.

BOTTOM: He uses you.

WILL: He's a mate.

BOTTOM: You're his bitch.

WILL: I am not his bitch!*

---

* This brief exchange establishes yet another astonishing first for William Shakespeare. It has long been thought that the use of the traditionally female insult 'bitch' to demean a man originated with African-American rap poets. It now appears to have been common usage in Elizabethan English.

BOTTOM: You are. You can't see it cos you're too nice. What's more, he gave up too easy. He's up to something. I don't trust him.

WILL: Nonsense, Bottom. Kit's my mate. He would never plot against me.

KATE'S BEDROOM - NIGHT

Marlowe doth machinate against Will and has appeared in Kate's bedchamber.

KIT MARLOWE: It's time you stood up for yourself, Kate.

KATE: Mr Marlowe, Mr Shakespeare is my friend. I can't betray him.

KIT MARLOWE: Would you rather betray your own sex? (*Doth approach the maid with oily, persuasive countenance*) If Will's play were mine, I'd defy the law and let you play the frog-jock queen.

KATE: You'd really make me an actor?

KIT MARLOWE: Absolutely. Imagine it. The curtain calls, the lovely little suppers. The licence to bang on endlessly about poverty and inequality whilst trousering a golden purse.

KATE: And ... even more important than that, the chance to be a strong woman and prove that women are strong.

KIT MARLOWE: Absolutely.

KATE: Particularly women actors, who I imagine will be very, very strong indeed and believe strongly in the fact that women are strong.

KIT MARLOWE: For sure. Totally.

KATE: I'll do it.

KIT MARLOWE: Good girl.

KATE: But where will I put the coconuts?

KIT MARLOWE: One problem at a time.

WILL'S LONDON LODGINGS – DAY

Will doth gorge and quaff with great satisfaction.

WILL: Well, Bottom, today's the day.

BOTTOM: Eh?

WILL: The poet Robert Greene, who is Master of the Queen's Revels, is coming to collect my brilliant play, 'Frog-Jock Mary, Queen of Gingery Savages in Skirts'.[*]

There entereth the odious Robert Greene.

ROBERT GREENE: Ah, Master Shakey-talent. I'm sorry, did I say Shakey-talent? I meant, of course, Shakespeare. Although oft the tongue will tattle what the heart would hide.

WILL: Oft indeed, you preening supercilious plague pustule. Oops! You see, I'm doing it now. (*They laugh*)

ROBERT GREENE: But enough of such merriment. Sirrah, the third Sunday after Lamington Eve approaches. You sent word that you have written a play. Not even a collaboration, but all by yourself.

WILL: You sound surprised, Master Greene.

ROBERT GREENE: Well, 'tis only that all of London's poets are university men – Kyd, Nash, Beaumont, Marlowe, mine own humble self. Whilst you, sir, are a country bumsnot. An oik of Avon. A town-school spotty grotty.[†]

WILL: And so am I like the fulsome cleavage of a buxom saucing wench.

---

[*] It is sad to speculate how much richer historical language would be if Shakespeare's lost two-queen bitch-slap play had survived.

[†] This is true. Shakespeare was the only major poet of the entire English Renaissance who did not attend either Oxford or Cambridge universities. The grip of those two institutions over British arts was as strong then as it is now. To quote Shakespeare himself on the subject, 'The absence of real advances in social mobility in sixteenth-century Britain is absolutely futtocking outrageous.'

ROBERT GREENE: Meaning?

WILL: Much looked down upon.

BOTTOM: I like that one, master. That works.

WILL: Woe to Albion. This sceptred isle doth burst with talent and yet a gaggle of snootish pamperloins from just two universities snaffle all the influence, jobs and cash.

ROBERT GREENE: It is as it should be and as it ever will be, sirrah.

WILL: Ever will be, Greene? I hardly think that centuries hence a tiny clique of Oxbridge posh boys will still be running everything.

ROBERT GREENE: Come now, the appointed day approaches. I would fain have sight of your play to ensure the Queen's person be not offended.

WILL: Offended? My play's a eulogy. Liz will love it.

ROBERT GREENE: *If* she sees it. Christopher Marlowe, a *university* man of proven genius, has also promised a play.

WILL: Kit? He wrote a play after all? Damn, that was quick!

ROBERT GREENE: Come now, I'm a busy man. Give me your play.

WILL: Absolutely. Here it is. (*Doth search his desk drawer in vain*) Erm, I have it but, er, I thought I might, er, drop it off later.

ROBERT GREENE: Later, sirrah? Why later, pray?

WILL: Just want to give it a final polish, you know. Dotting i's, crossing t's.

ROBERT GREENE: At Cambridge we tend to dot our i's and cross our t's as we go along.[*]

WILL: I still have a few days.

ROBERT GREENE: But a few, sir. The Queen has taken to her bed with a chill. She wants this play to cheer her up.

---

[*] When they aren't gorging, quaffing and rogering dead farmyard animals.

WILL: And she shall have it.

ROBERT GREENE: Good day.

Greene doth departeth.

WILL: It's gone! My play, it's gone!

KATE: Oh no! Oh no! Woe!

WILL: We must search every inch of this room!

KATE: Bye.

Kate leaves, clearly with something to hide. Will and Bottom begin to search. Time passes while Bard and servant searcheth.

WILL: It must be here somewhere!

BOTTOM: Well, if it is, we can't find it.

WILL: True, it is beyond our skill. But there is a mystical species that can find anything.

BOTTOM: Wood nymphs!

WILL: Don't be ridiculous.

BOTTOM: Sorry.

WILL: Wood nymphs are treacherous creatures and would find my play only to put it on the fire to warm the toes of their sweethearts, the elves. But there is another enchanted species that will serve.

BOTTOM: Who's that then?

WILL: Why, to find it we have only to take a man and add woe. Know you of what creature I speak?

BOTTOM: Er . . . someone sad? Are sad people good at finding things?

WILL: Why, a man's woe is his wife. And add 'woe' to 'man' and you have . . . woeman.

BOTTOM: Woeman.

WILL: Woman!

BOTTOM: Woman.

WILL: My wife, Bottom! Mistress Anne. She can find anything.

BOTTOM: Honestly, master, it'd be so much easier if you just said Anne.

WILL: It's what I do! Now, hie thee to the coaching house and send word for Stratford.

WILL'S LONDON LODGINGS - DAY

Anne has joined the search.

ANNE: Well, I've found six old quills, three sets of eye glasses and two penneth three farthing down a crack.

BOTTOM: Bit of a relief that. I thought it were piles.

ANNE: But no papist-baiting play.

WILL: But this is terrible! Greene will take Marlowe's play to the Queen in my stead!

ANNE: Marlowe? You mean that bloke you've let take credit for your plays cos he's a posh boy and makes you feel inadequate?

WILL: He does not make me feel inadequate. I just happen to think he's a really great guy.

ANNE: When did you last see the play?

WILL: On the day I returned from Stratford, Marlowe had come over to quaff wine and have a ladsy chat. Kate was here, she will bear witness.

ANNE: Kate, the landlady's daughter? Who's always banging on about being a star? By St Cuthbert's codpiece, husband, do you not know anything about human nature?

WILL: Actually I have a unique and timeless insight into the very heart of what it is to be human. It's absolutely what I do!*

ANNE: Well, you must see that Marlowe's got your play, pinched by false Kate. It's bleedin' obvious.

WILL: Kate and Marlowe? You're saying they've stitched me up like a pair of winter drawers?

BOTTOM: I'd expect it of him, but I'm very disappointed in her.

---

* This exchange appears to confirm what generations of schoolchildren have long suspected – that Shakespeare was not quite as clever as he blooming thought he was.

ANNE: Oh, you're too nice, Will. We all know that. But now it's time to use your unique and timeless insight into conjuring some trick to get the play back.

WILL: I will, wife. I will. In fact, I have!

ANNE: Already?

WILL: Yes. And it's a corker. (*Doth write a note*) Bottom, take this to Burbage at the Red Lion and await me there. If Kate be false, this will sound her out. The play's the crucial factor to catch the conscience of our girly actor.[*]

---

[*] This appears to be an early attempt at what would become a celebrated line in *Hamlet*: 'The play's the thing wherein I'll catch the conscience of the king.' Shakespeare probably rejected the earlier version because it wasn't in iambic pentameter. Every line had to have five beats. Scholars have often asked, 'Why? Just why?' It may have been a form of OCD.

THE RED LION THEATRE – DAY

The players have assembled. Bottom is also present.

BURBAGE: Well, this is most peculiar. All ready were we to begin rehearsal on Marlowe's brilliant 'Mary The Frog-Jock Queen'.

CONDELL: Such a wonderful part for me. The traitor Queen. Half French, half Scottish. A dialect challenge indeed. Bonjour, Jimmy! Comment allez-vous, ya dirty wee bastard?

BURBAGE: Yes. But now Will Shakespeare does insist upon our old friendship that we must post-haste rehearse this fragment of his. You, Mr Condell, will play Katie, a beautiful young lady.

CONDELL: Ah, typecasting, darling.

BURBAGE: And I am Sir Christopher Stooplow, a spy and a charlatan. A comic role, I think.

KEMPE: Uh, comedy? Yeah, that's right, you do a bit of comedy, don't you, Burbage? English comedy. Boring comedy. In Italy, where I'm big, we do proper comedy. Yeah? Ground-breaking. Modern.

BURBAGE: You shut up, Kempe. You play one Shakepike, a genius.

KEMPE: Ah, so no acting required then?

Will arrives.

WILL: Good morrow, sirrahs, I see you have my new pages.

Marlowe arriveth with Kate.

KIT MARLOWE: Will, you sent word you had verse to show us.

WILL: Indeed I do, Kit. Come, friends, be seated and let the play begin.

BURBAGE: Places, everybody, places.

Bottom, Kate and Marlowe do sit and watch as the players take the stage. Will offereth directions.

WILL: Now, remember, speak the speech as I have writ it and don't wave your arms about and try to be funny.*

BURBAGE: I beg your pardon?

WILL: And don't shout. Frankly, if you're going to shout I might as well get Mr Shouty the town shouter to shout my verse.

CONDELL: Cheeky sod!

WILL: And please don't do that actor thing of adding one not very funny grunt and then going around saying you made up the whole thing in rehearsal. And so, let us begin.†

Will takes his seat, the play beginneth.

BURBAGE: The lamentable tragedy of the false maid and the stolen muse!

KATE: Eek!

WILL: Mark Kate, Bottom, see how she doth squeak in fear.

The play continues. Kempe doth enter.

KEMPE: I'm Bill Shakepike. Greatest writer in London and writ have I my finest work, so . . .

Now Condell joins the play.

CONDELL: What ho? Here come I, young Katie, who doth reside with Shakepike.

In the audience Kate is shocked.

KATE: It's me! It's me!

KIT MARLOWE: Stay cool, pretty lady, stay cool!

CONDELL: Hast thou written a brilliant new play, Bill?

---

* This speech from Shakespeare's actual life prefigures the famous advice that Hamlet gives to the players. In the play, Hamlet is gentler, disguising his frustration in flowery language, but here we get the real Will, the true frustrated writer whose every line is at the mercy of some blooming actor.
† Pinching credit for the script is an essential part of an actor's craft, now taught in the first term at RADA.

KEMPE: Have I? Er, yeah, just a bit.

From his seat the Bard doth protest.

WILL: Stick to the bloody script, Kempe!

KEMPE: Just helping you out, mate.

Burbage walks on.

BURBAGE: It is I, Sir Christopher Stooplow. A spy and a false friend. And I will have Shakepike's play for my own!

Marlowe looks most uncomfortable.

BURBAGE: Steal the play, Katie! Steal the play, Katie! Steal the play!

Kate leapeth up in distress.

KATE: I can't bear it! I'm sorry, Mr Shakespeare, but I stole your play and I hate myself. But Mr Marlowe promised me the female lead and I just wanted it so much, because it's my dream!

CONDELL: A girl to play a girl? It's outrageous! Where would you put the coconuts?

KIT MARLOWE: Well, Will, nice trick. You are a clever little bastard, I'll give you that. Here's your play back and no hard feelings, eh?

WILL: Oh, so does this mean we can still be mates, then?

BOTTOM: Bloody hell, master, why don't you just send him flowers?

KIT MARLOWE: Of course we can still be mates. You too, Kate, although you are gonna have to toughen up if you wanna cut it in a man's world. Can't be getting all teary and collapse over a bit of overacting.

BURBAGE: I beg your pardon?

CONDELL: Such an outrage.

KEMPE: Actually, I was brilliant. Fact.

ROBERT GREENE'S OFFICE – DAY

Greene is about to bustle out as Will and Bottom entereth.

WILL: I've got it! I've got my play for the Queen's feast. I only pray I'm not too late.

ROBERT GREENE: Play? Play! You talk of plays? The Queen's chill has grown worse and she is like to die. The kingdom is in crisis. We will have a new monarch by eventide and I must hasten to insert my nose betwixt the next set of royal buttocks before other oily courtiers fill the gap. Be gone, sirrah, with your play.

WILL: But, Master Greene, if you hope to be Master of the new monarch's Revels, surely you'll need a play for the celebration feast.

ROBERT GREENE: Actually, that's true. No other courtier will have a play so soon! Guards, see that Mr Shakespeare doesn't leave!

The guards stand firm as Greene doth bustle out.

BOTTOM: That were quick thinking, master. Your play'll be the first of a new reign. Pretty posh way to kick off your solo career.

WILL: Yes, it really is a brilliant opportunity.

BOTTOM: I wonder who the next king'll be? Unless it's another bird. Oh bloody hell, I hope not! It's just wrong.

WILL: No chance of that. The succession has been settled since the Queen passed child-bearing age. There survives a great-great-grandson of Henry the Seventh, James the Sixth of Scotland. In fact, he'll be James the First of England.

BOTTOM: James of Scotland. Master . . .

WILL: Yes, Bottom?

BOTTOM: I'm just thinking. I may be wrong cos I'm a groundling and it's all crap for us whoever's on the throne – but isn't he a Stewart?

WILL: Yeah, that's right. Son of Mary Stewart.

BOTTOM: Mary Stewart, who your play slags off as a frog-jock queen and traitorous Catholic whoreslap.

WILL: Oh God. I'm on the wrong branch of the family tree!

BOTTOM: A new head on the coins.

WILL: And a new head in the waste-heads basket. I've got to run!

The guards blocketh the way.

WILL: We must burn the play!

BOTTOM: No fire. It's summer.

WILL: Then dissolve it in quick lime.

BOTTOM: Yeah, cos obviously I've got a wheelbarrow full of that in my bag.

They sit.

WILL: Don't suppose you've got any salt and pepper either?

Will and Bottom do eat the manuscript.* Time passes, the play be eaten. Greene returneth.

ROBERT GREENE: Glorious news! The Queen is recovered. The doctors think her like to live another twenty years. And, Master Shakespeare, you have more luck than you deserve. For the first thing the Queen has asked for is a play.

WILL: I had it but it's been stolen by wood nymphs.

ROBERT GREENE: Master Shakespeare, Her Majesty is promised a play and you must provide one. Now!

Bottom has an idea. He pulls a piece of paper from his satchel and giveth it to Will, who in his turn hands it to Greene.

---

* This incident, unknown until the discovery of the Crow Folios, must surely rank as the greatest example of literary self-harm in the history of English theatre. Scholars take comfort in the hope that it was one of the crappier ones, like *The Merry Wives of Windsor* or *Henry VIII*.

ROBERT GREENE: 'The Lamentable Tragedy of the False Maid and the Stolen Muse'. Hmm, interesting title. Where's the play?

WILL: Erm, that's it. It's on the back.[*]

---

[*] This previously unknown play now enters Shakespeare's canon. Being less than a page long, it is likely to prove very popular with schoolchildren.

WILL'S STRATFORD HOME – NIGHT

Will and Anne sit before the fire with their pipes.

WILL: The Queen said my play lacked plot, wit, grace and poetry. There was one thing she liked.

ANNE: Well, that's promising. What?

WILL: That it was only ninety-seven seconds long. I fear I've missed my chance.

ANNE: And eaten a masterpiece. I still can't believe that little minx Kate stole your play.

WILL: I've forgiven her. Kate is a sweet girl really, and Marlowe is so persuasive with the ladies.

ANNE: And the blokes. I hope this little incident has cooled your bromance.[*]

WILL: I like Kit, Anne. He's cool, he's confident, he's everything I'm not.

ANNE: You don't wanna be like that. You're a fartsome baldie-boots, doll. Own it! Kit Marlowe'll probably die in some bleeding tavern fight somewhere. Whereas you will die in your own bed with me, your loving wife.[†]

WILL: You're right, Anne. I'd certainly rather be dull than dead.

ANNE: Hmm . . . Besides, you showed him, eh? Oh, that was such a clever idea. Putting on a play to prick a guilty conscience.

WILL: Yes, it did work rather well.

ANNE: You should put that in a play.

WILL: A play within a play? That's not gonna work.

---

[*] Anne appears to have invented a term that would not be used again until the advent of 'dude' movies in the early twenty-first century. This proves that Will was not the only member of the Shakespeare family to add words to the English language.

[†] An astonishingly astute observation from Anne Shakespeare because on both counts this is in fact exactly what happened. What were the chances?

THE APPAREL OFT PROCLAIMS THE MAN

Malvolio's cross garters in *Twelfth Night* are regarded as the second funniest visual gag in Shakespeare's canon (the first being of course the big donkey-head reveal in *A Midsummer Night's Dream* – see page 68). This episode from the First Folio suggests that it was drawn from real life.

WILL'S LONDON LODGINGS – NIGHT

Will and Marlowe do quaff their ale, which be served by the maid Kate. Bottom sweeps the floor.

WILL: Well, Kit, not so dusty, eh? Things are looking up for me and no mistake. Already I have not one but three plays in Burbage's repertoire, and what's more they're all called Henry the Sixth, which must surely be some sort of record.*

KIT MARLOWE: No doubt about it, Will, you're absolutely ripping London theatre a new arseington. Big respect, cuz.

WILL: Feels good. Can't deny. And there's more. See here? I have an invitation to Lord Southampton's saucy prancings. Think of it, me, a Stratford bumshankle, a-hobbing and a-nobbing with the cock-snobbled folderols.

KIT MARLOWE: Hell of a step up for you. And one in the eye for Robert Greene. Him and his varsity wits think the Southampton prancings their own private literary salon. Huh! He's gonna crap a dead cat when he hears you've been invited! Which is, of course, brilliant. I salute you.

WILL: Thanks, mate.

KIT MARLOWE: Mind you, not sure about this teenage romance thing you've been banging on about. I'm not gonna lie. Sounds lame.†

BOTTOM: Same. I think it's wet.

KATE: I love it.

WILL: Well, as it happens, I've decided to shelve Romeo for now. I need a guaranteed smash to cement my reputation and sadly lovey-dovey smoochie-woochie just ain't gonna cut it.

---

* This record remains so to this day. No writer since has written a series of different plays but given them the same name. The playwright Harold Pinter pulled off the opposite trick by writing basically the same play over and over again but changing the title.

† Clearly *Romeo and Juliet* had a lengthy gestation period.

KIT MARLOWE: Yeah, you've got that right. The plebs want violence and murder.

BOTTOM: Course we do!

WILL: So this morning I knocked out a really satisfying Richard the Third.

BOTTOM: Ugh!

KIT MARLOWE: Bit too much information, Will.

KATE: I mean, why do we need to know?

KIT MARLOWE: Hmm.

WILL: It's a play.*

KIT MARLOWE: Oh, right.

WILL: But even Richard must wait, because the one I'm really pleased with is my big new Jew play.

KIT MARLOWE: Ah, yes! Love a Jew play! No chance you'll give it to me, I suppose?

WILL: No, Kit, I'm afraid not.

KIT MARLOWE: Oh come on! It's just the sort of thing I should be writing.

WILL: Then why don't you?

KIT MARLOWE: You know why.

WILL: Ah, of course, your other job, hunting Catholics for Walsingham's torture chamber.

KIT MARLOWE: Defending the one true, pure and divine faith.

WILL: And this being the one true, pure and divine faith that Henry the Eighth basically invented so that he could dump his Mrs and have it away with bonker Boleyn?

---

* This is the first recorded instance of Cockney rhyming slang, pre-dating the next known occurrence by at least three hundred years.

KIT MARLOWE: Yes, that's the one.

WILL: A romance so spiritually true, pure and divine that it went from rumpy-pumpy lovey-dovey to choppy-whoppy heady-deady in just three years.*

KIT MARLOWE: I don't make the rules, Will!

WILL: Well, I'm sorry, but you can't have my Jew play. I'm on a roll and it's my time to shine.

KIT MARLOWE: Fine, can't really blame you, I suppose. I'm off to the bawdy house for a quaff and a roger.

Marlowe doth rise to leave. He is wearing rakish stripy tights and is clearly most proud of his pretty thighs.

KATE: Pretty hose, Mr Marlowe, very trendy. Très jolie, monsieur.

KIT MARLOWE: Italian, the latest thing.

WILL: Gosh, I envy you, Kit. I could never carry off tights like that. I'm afraid they'd just wear me.

KIT MARLOWE: Oh, don't be ridiculous, you've just gotta strut!

Marlowe doth thrust his codpiece forward. Kate doth squeak and blush most prettily.

KIT MARLOWE: That's all. You're too apologetic. Just get out there and show the world that you don't give a damn. Hey!

Marlowe thrusts once more and Kate doth squeak again.

KIT MARLOWE: I love ya loads.

Marlowe leaves.

WILL: Easy for him to say. The problem is I do give a damn. I crave approval and people sense that in me.

BOTTOM: It's true, you're very needy.

KATE: Not needy. Just nice.

---

* A succinct but telling summation of the English Reformation. One could only wish Shakespeare had employed such admirable brevity in his history plays.

WILL: People don't like nice, they look upon it as weakness. I want to be liked and so for some dark reason located deep in the human soul, people are less inclined to like me. Marlowe, on the other hand, doesn't give a tosslington, so everyone wants to be his mate.*

KATE: I'm just like you, Mr Shakespeare. Girls used to call me a try-hard because I wanted to make friends, but the more I tried the more they'd pull my hair and stab me with their knitting needles. But in the end I made three great pals – Latin, Greek and Mathematics.

WILL: A good lesson for all us fartsome try-hards, Kate. What we lack in easy charm we must make up for with talent and hard work. And mine is finally paying off! I have my big new Jew play ready for Burbage and an invitation to Southampton's prancings in the pocket of my puffling pants. (*Stands most proudly*) Even Robert Greene, who doth hate my gutlings, must now admit I am the coming man!

Will attempts to pose in the strutting manner Marlowe assumed, putting his foot upon the table. He looketh an arsemongle.

---

* Here Shakespeare appears to have identified what modern scholars have come to call the Lennon and McCartney effect. Paul McCartney, being a polite, enthusiastic person who has lived a seemingly blameless personal life, has long been condemned as at best a bit naff and at worst a total wanker. John Lennon, on the other hand, who was mean to just about everybody and in his youth violent to women, is universally eulogized. The difference being McCartney clearly wants to be liked and Lennon appeared not to give a futtock. Marlowe and Shakespeare, friends, contemporaries and sometime collaborators, were the Lennon and McCartney of their time.

ROBERT GREENE'S OFFICE – NIGHT

Robert Greene is in a dark and dangerous mood.

ROBERT GREENE: William Shakespeare – curse him for an oafish country bumsnot. Already are his first three Henrys hits, whilst mine own sublime *Friar Bacon and Friar Bungay* fades in the fickle memory of the mob. (*Takes out a dagger*) Many a time and oft have I thought to dispatch this upstart crow with steel, but such a death would be too quick for one so base. Instead have I employed a crueller weapon. Tomorrow all London will know how Robert Greene doth treat a low pretender to the rank of gentleman. For never more a poet will I be. Instead, I am become a critic. A critic! A critic! Ah ha ha ha ha ha!

Greene laughs manically and stabbeth the air.*

---

* If Shakespeare is indeed the author of the Crow Folios then this depiction of Robert Greene and critics in general is highly subjective. It is, of course, not the case that critics are embittered, jealous, vicious bastables but universally decent, fair-minded, generous, and absolutely and completely objective.

THE RED LION THEATRE – DAY

The players be assembled. Condell holds a paper most gloatingly.

CONDELL: Greene's review is out and it's an absolute stinkington.

BURBAGE: Oh, no! Ouch! 'Upstart crow'. That'll hurt. See, you're right, Condell. He'll hide away for a while after this.

KEMPE: Mm, yeah, nasty. Mind you, might be the wake-up call he needs. So . . .

BURBAGE: I beg your pardon, Kempe?

KEMPE: This is the sixteenth century. He has to move on. Test the boundaries, challenge the form, yeah? Like with his comedy. Comedy isn't jokes, comedy is attitude. It's not what you say, it's what you don't say.

BURBAGE: Do shut up, Kempe.

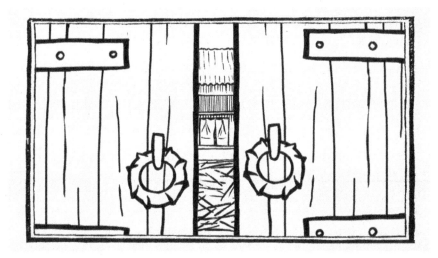

WILL'S LONDON LODGINGS - DAY

The Bard is also reading the review.

WILL: 'Upstart crow'? He calls me 'upstart crow'? I can't believe it. I mean, one welcomes intelligent criticism, but this is just abuse!

BOTTOM: I thought you never read reviews?

WILL: Well, we all say that, Bottom, but it isn't true, obviously. We contrive to bring the good ones to the notice of our friends, while letting the bad ones eat into our souls until the day we die.

BOTTOM: Don't be so soft. It'll be forgot by tomorrow.

WILL: That used to be the case but since printing took off, bad reviews hang around for ever. Woe to Albion that through this new invention any clueless arsemongle may make his puerile twitterings known to the world. As Robert Greene has done with his oh-so-amusing pamphlet, *A Groatsworth of Wit*.

KATE: You have to admit it's a pretty good title.

WILL: Huh! If such little wit be worth a groat, then a king's ransom would not purchase my brilliant gag about waking up in an enchanted forest and falling in love with a donkey.[*]

BOTTOM: Seriously, master, you didn't expect Greene to be nice to you? He's a rival poet. For a genius you don't know much about human nature.

WILL: Actually, understanding human nature is one of my big things.

BOTTOM: Well then, you should be able to see that he's jealous. He's jealous like, erm, like a . . .

---

[*] This appears to be a very early version of Shakespeare's most famous visual gag in which a Fairy Queen falls in love not with an actual donkey but with a man whose head has been transformed into that of a donkey. There is no evidence that Shakespeare had begun working on *A Midsummer Night's Dream* at this point so it appears that Shakespeare dreamed up this visual gag in isolation. This is extremely surprising because it's even less funny out of context.

WILL: The green-eyed monster that doth mock the meat it feeds on?*

BOTTOM: Well, I was gonna say like a talentless turd in tights. Which actually I think is better. The point is, don't let him live in your head rent-free, yeah? Who cares what he thinks?†

WILL: I care! These salty barbs will ruin me! All London will revel in my shame.

BOTTOM: Yeah, cos everyone in London's talking about you, aren't they? Got nothing else to worry about at all, eh? 'Got the plague? Could be worse, I could have been called an uppity crow!' 'Starving to death? Oh, at least you haven't had a bad review!'

WILL: Yes, all right, Bottom.

BOTTOM: Yeah. 'Burned alive for refusing to deny Jesus were made of wine and wafers? Well, that's nothing. Will Shake got called an upstart crow by a posh boy!' 'All your kids dead? Well that's nothing—'

WILL: Yeah, all right, Bottom. I get the gag.

BOTTOM: Yeah. And you know I'm right too.

WILL: I do not know you're right and getting a bad review is much worse than getting the plague because at least with the plague the person that gave it to you dies.

Marlowe enters.

KIT MARLOWE: Good morrow, Will. Mistress Kate. I let myself in. Don't really do manners. Just kinda go where I please.

WILL: Of course, Kit, always welcome. I suppose you've seen Greene's piece in the *Groat*?

---

* This is quoted in *Othello*, which Shakespeare would not write for some years. Scholars agree that, unlike the donkey gag, this one was worth Shakespeare hanging on to.

† The critical consensus is that Bottom is wrong; 'talentless turd' is not better than 'green-eyed monster'.

KIT MARLOWE: Hohoho, absolutely! Oh, you got a serious bitch-slapping! Still, forget about it, eh?

WILL: I can't forget about it, Kit! It, it's eating away at me.

KIT MARLOWE: (*Drawing his sword*) Well, in that case, kill him. Ain't no thing. Challenge him to a duel when you see him at the prancings.

WILL: I can't fight him, Kit, I'm no dashing blade! Where I went to school we did our duelling with conkers and the loser had to give everyone a bite of his carrot. Besides which, I can't go to the prancings now.

KIT MARLOWE: Why not?

WILL: Well, because I'll look a fool. Everyone will have read the *Groat*. I couldn't stand the shame.*

KIT MARLOWE: Oh, Will, please, grow a pair of bolingbrokes! The way to put Greene in his place is to show London you don't care what he thinks.

WILL: But I do care. And all will know it. 'Tis writ upon my face.

BOTTOM: He's transparent.

KIT MARLOWE: Come on, Will! The noble peacock doesn't hang his head. He displays his bumshank with magnificent feathery plumes. Show this churl your feathery bumshank!

WILL: But how?

KIT MARLOWE: Strut, man! Rock some fine thread, put on a show!

KATE: Confidence is attractive.

KIT MARLOWE: Believe me, the only way this review can hurt you is if you let it. Go a-prancing in silken tights of figure-hugging Italian cut and Lord Southampton will see you are a dainty man of taste and breeding and Greene will look a fool that he ever called you upstart!

---

* All artists who have received a bad review believe everyone in the world has seen it and is as obsessed with it as they are.

WILL: Do you know, I think that could really work! If I turn up in form-fitting tights, everyone will see I've got balls! My sweet wife Anne is a pretty seamstress and for a few pence worth of silk will she stitch me hose fit for the thighs of a prince!

KIT MARLOWE: Sounds like a plan!

WILL: Then ho for Stratford. As I always say, the apparel oft proclaims the man.

KATE: I still think that should be clothes maketh the man.

WILL: Well, I imagine that's how it'll end up getting misquoted.[*]

---

[*] Scholars can only marvel at Shakespeare's remarkable prescience. Many of Shakespeare's most popular sayings are actually misquotes, and are often the better for it. For instance, Shakespeare actually said, 'All that glisters isn't gold.' 'Glisters', with an 's'. And he didn't say 'Lead on, Macduff' but 'Lay on, Macduff', which is fine if you're telling him to keep fighting (which is what Macbeth meant) but useless if you're on a country walk and someone insists on hogging the map.

WILL'S STRATFORD HOME – DAY

The family be present. Will doth enter.

WILL: Father is returned. Let joy be unbounded.

The young twins Judith and Hamnet approach Will.

HAMNET: Where's our presents?

WILL: Er, 'Hello, Dad. Nice to see you'?

JUDITH: Did you bring us anything?

WILL: Blimey! Here's your bloody sugar sticks. How did it ever get to be the rule that as soon as a father takes one step outside his front door he's obliged to bring his children presents on his return?* Methinks that in future, less indulgent ages, kids will not be suffered to demand sweets on an almost monthly basis.

ANNE: Well, this is a nice surprise, Will! We weren't expecting you.

The children do crowd their father.

JUDITH: Dad, we've been practising for the May Day stupid dance.†

HAMNET: Mum's making us costumes! Will you watch us?

ANNE: Run along and play, kids. Give your father a minute. (*The children leave*) Good journey, Will?

WILL: Absolutely. Good seat. Clean coach. On time.

ANNE: Well, that makes a nice change!

WILL: Except, hang on, no, that was in my dreams. Unfortunately, I made the mistake of travelling in the real world. So, no, appalling journey.

---

* It appears this outrageous imposition on parents who go away on business is timeless. The modern nightmare of searching the Crap Shop at the airport for a present before settling on a huge sack of chocolate has its archaic equivalence.
† The Elizabethan May Day stupid dance was the same as the modern May Day dance. They were just more honest then.

ANNE: Will you stay long?

WILL: Sadly not, my love. I'm just so busy in London churning out plays, I can only stay a night. I really am becoming quite a success. In fact, I'm invited to saucy prancings at Lord Southampton's.

ANNE: Zounds, that is posh!

WILL: Posh indeed, good wife, and a good show must I make. Which is why I've come home. I need your help. Take this shilling and with it stitch me tights in the Italian style.

ANNE: Italian style, Will? People'll see the contours of your bolingbrokes.

SUSANNA: Oh, Mum!

WILL: That's exactly what I want them to see, Anne. My big bad country boy bolingbrokes!

SUSANNA: I think I am actually going to be sick!

ROBERT GREENE'S OFFICE – DAY

Robert Greene doth fester with jealous rage.

ROBERT GREENE: Again, it seems this upstart crow still flies. Word has reached me that he is seen about the town in fine new tights. 'Tis clear, the rustic fool intends to try to brazen out the shame of my savage review by showing the world the contours of his bolingbrokes. Well, if he be so vain as to think he can come a-prancing amongst educated men, then perchance I can turn that vanity against him.

WILL'S LONDON LODGINGS - DAY

Will doth disport himself most proudly in his new tights.

KATE: Nice bloody tights, Mr Shakespeare!

WILL: Nice indeed, Kate. Strutted have I from Fleet Street to Fenchurch and many a cheeky whistle have I got. I'll wear these to the prancings, brazen out Greene's review and then my big new Jew play will make my reputation as London's best bard.

KATE: Actually, I wanted to mention the big new Jew play, Mr Shakespeare. I read it – I hope that's all right?

WILL: No problem, Kate. Enjoy it? The bit where the wicked Jew poisons an entire convent full of nuns? The end where the Jew gets boiled in a big pot by the righteous Christians?*

KATE: Yes. I was wondering about those bits particularly.

---

* This is pretty tame stuff when it comes to the casual vilification of Jews in this period (and indeed pretty much any period of European history).

WILL: Well, they are good. Nothing like whipping up violent prejudice against small defenceless ethnic groups to get bums on seats.

KATE: Actually, it's that aspect I was wondering about. I just thought, well . . . that you were a bit better than that.

WILL: Oh, here we go. Might-a seen that coming. Lighten up, Kate. Has theatre got so sensitive and correct that a writer can't even start a pogrom without causing offence? Jew-baiting is funny. It's a joke. Get a sense of humour.

KATE: But do you actually feel that, or is it that deep down you know it's mean and cruel and divisive, but you can't resist easy thrills and cheap laughs?

WILL: Look, it's layered. I'm being ironic and post-Renaissance.

KATE: Oh, it's irony, is it?

WILL: Yes, by massaging prejudice I'm actually satirizing it.

KATE: But really though, are you? Honestly?

WILL: It . . . it's a joke!*

There is a knock without. Kate doth spy from the window.

KATE: Goodness, 'tis Robert Greene. Shall I get Bottom to heave a bucket of wee over him?

WILL: Yes!

KATE: Yes!

WILL: No.

KATE: No.

WILL: He must have come about some purpose and I would know it.

---

* Shakespeare for all his genius has no answer, eventually taking recourse in the oldest and weakest excuse for those who thoughtlessly peddle prejudice for their own profit or advancement. 'Just bantz' is the modern equivalent.

KATE: But since he hates you, surely he'll dissemble, concealing his true thoughts and seeking to gull you into further shame.

WILL: You're right, Kate. So what I'll do is I'll hide me behind this chair and bend my little ear to hear the secrets of his heart. For doubtless will he speak his thoughts out loud, as is the custom amongst the dainties.*

KATE: Brilliant idea! You hide, I'll go and let him in.

Kate goes to answer the door. The Bard doth hide behind a chair. Greene doth walk in and seems to find the room empty.

ROBERT GREENE: Good, Master Shakespeare. But soft, the room is bare. That foolish girl mistaken must have been.

Greene spies how the Bard's leg protrudeth from behind the chair. Greene dissembleth, speaking as if to himself.

ROBERT GREENE: 'Tis shame indeed for I am come all contrite to make amends for my foolish slander in the *Groat* and offer a token of my future love.

From his hiding place Will doth muse upon his situation.

WILL: God's conkers, here's a minty fix! He's come to make amends and I am hid. I will reveal myself, but dissemble of the cause.

Will pretends to snore from behind the chair.

ROBERT GREENE: But soft . . . what's this? Why good Master Shakespeare be here after all. Sirrah, are you well?

WILL: Uh, what? What? Oh, yes. (*Emerges*) Er, quite well, sir. Weary was I and so did lay me down to rest behind this . . . chair. Well now, Greene, it seems right strange that one who dubbed me 'crow' comes now a-calling?

ROBERT GREENE: I am come to beg your pardon for the wrong I have done thee.

---

* Here we find the first evidence that the private 'soliloquy', which had been presumed mere theatrical convention, was part of actual Elizabethan life.

WILL: Wow! Really? That's, that's extremely sweet of you. Sweet like the honey'd goat balls that toothless crones do suck on Lammas Eve.*

ROBERT GREENE: Brilliant image from a brilliant poet.

WILL: Thanks! Well, I will grant thee my pardon gladly, cuz.

ROBERT GREENE: And for the new love I bear thee, will I speak further. 'Tis whispered abroad that you would attend the saucy prancings all clad in silken hose.

WILL: Aye, it is true. Spy you these naughty boys?

Will doth strut about in his new tights.

ROBERT GREENE: I beg thee, cuz, to think again. The fashion changeth daily. Silken hose is banished in Florence just now. Instead, purple puffling pants, yellow tights and really silly cross garters are all the rage. Any who come a-prancing dressed not so will make a poor show indeed.

WILL: Really?

ROBERT GREENE: Really.

WILL: Goodness. My heartfelt thanks for telling me this, for I would fain make a good impression.

ROBERT GREENE: Then I will see you at the prancings. Good day!

Greene doth take his leave. Bottom and Kate do enter.

KATE: Well? What did he want?

WILL: He said he was sorry and wanted to make amends.

KATE: Isn't that lovely?

BOTTOM: He's lying. It's bloody obvious.

WILL: It does seem a coddling good turnaround from him that called me 'upstart crow'. 'Tis certain this Greene who was all green like

---

* Interesting note re. Elizabethan sweets: the Honey'd Goat Ball was similar to the modern Ferrero Rocher except instead of hazelnuts they used goats' nuts.

the green-eyed sea monster does not turn joyful pink like the one-eyed trouser monster in so swift a time.*

KATE: Hmm, it is a bit strange when you put it like that.

WILL: He told me my tights weren't fashionable enough and that I should wear purple puffling pants, yellow tights and really silly cross garters to the prancing.

BOTTOM: He's trying to trick you into looking stupid.

WILL: Exactly! So must I go clad in sombre garb like a God-prodding Pure-titty and thus filch him of his gulling.

KATE: Absolutely . . .

WILL: And yet . . . why does this Greene hate me?

BOTTOM: Because he's jealous.

WILL: Exactly, Bottom, because I'm a genius.

BOTTOM: That's not actually what I said.

WILL: And since he knows how clever I am, he must know that if he tells me to wear stupid prancing pants, I will guess his bluffle and come in sombre garb, whilst he besports his dainty leg in finest Italian cross-gartered yellow!

BOTTOM: You're overthinking this, master.

WILL: And so must I practise on him a double-bluffle and go a-prancing in purple pants!

---

* Alongside his many other world literary achievements, it seems that Shakespeare invented the knob gag. This 'one-eyed trouser monster' is a comic epigram of real quality and it is sad that it never appeared in any of Shakespeare's plays.

THE RED LION THEATRE – DAY

The players be assembled.

BURBAGE: Where be Will Shakespeare and his Jew play? This is most frustrating!

KEMPE: Well, bad review, knocks you back. I know the feeling. Except, hang on, I don't, because I've never had one.

CONDELL: Personally I never read reviews.

BURBAGE: Ooh.

CONDELL: Although there was a lovely piece of graffiti about my Fairy Queen scratched on the wall behind the privy at the Red Lion.*

Robert Greene arrives.

ROBERT GREENE: Master Burbage.

BURBAGE: Why, Mr Greene, to what do we owe this honour?

ROBERT GREENE: You know very well. I sent word suggesting a revival of mine own sublime *Friar Bacon and Friar Bungay* for your next production. You have not replied.

BURBAGE: Ah yes, well, lovely idea, *Bungay and Bacon—*

ROBERT GREENE: *Bacon and Bungay.*

BURBAGE: Er, brilliant stuff and all that. It's just that we await a new piece from Mr Shakespeare.

ROBERT GREENE: Really? Shakespeare. Shakespeare. Well, you may yet find you come crawling back to me ere long. This crow you speak of is invited to saucy prancings at Lord Southampton's and methinks he'll put up so poor a show he'll n'er be seen in this town again. (*Laughs*) I'll await your summons. Good day.

---

* The only 'Faerie Queene' in print at this time was Edmund Spenser's epic poem which was not a play and therefore unlikely to have been presented by the Burbage Company. Condell was either referring to a private recital or his 'Fairy Queen' might be a euphemism for something else entirely.

WILL'S STRATFORD HOME - DAY

The family be assembled. Will entereth.

WILL: Unbelievable! It just stopped, stopped dead.

ANNE: Susanna, your father's home, help him with his cloak.

SUSANNA: Oh yeah, that's right, I forgot I'm a slave.

ANNE: What stopped, doll face?

WILL: The coach! We were just pulling into Leamington Spa when it stopped. Barely fifty yards from the post house. No explanation. No apology. He just stood there, for a day. I mean why? Just why?

ANNE: What are you doing home anyway? Did you miss us? I mean, not your mother, obviously. You're not insane!

MARY: I can hear you, Anne Shakespeare! And you're a very common woman!

WILL: To tell the truth, wife, I've had a bad review and must put on a really good show, so—

MARY: Ooh, we might have just the thing, William. Come on, John. Tell him your idea.

WILL: Idea? Dad? What? What idea?

ANNE: Don't listen to him, love, he's a nasty, jealous old arsemongle.

JOHN: It seems to me you've made quite a success of yourself with your ready wit and uncanny command of language, but you're not that bloody clever. I'm as witty as you are, easy!

WILL: Hmm. I'm wondering where we're going with this.

ANNE: He wants to get in on it. Don't you let him!

WILL: You wanna write plays, Dad?

JOHN: No, not plays, I hate your plays. But you're not just a playwright, are ya? You're also a poet, a wit and an all-round smart-arse!

MARY: A raconteur, husband. In Paris they say raconteur, which is French for smart-arse.

JOHN: And I was thinking we could do it together!

WILL: Together?

JOHN: Like a sort of double act. You the famous, witty, successful son, me the grumpy old dad, who's unimpressed by your success and fashionable ways. The only one who can really point out what a knob you actually are.

MARY: Because he's your dad!*

WILL: Maybe? Er, not sure.

JOHN: You're ashamed of me cos I'm a convicted criminal.†

WILL: No, no, I just—

JOHN: Oh, you think you've got above us with your bloody London ways! But I fear you'll never truly be accepted by the cock-snobbled folderols on account of the fact you're a turnip-chomping country bumshankle.

WILL: Not so, father! As you well know I'm invited to Lord Southampton's saucy prancings. And you don't get more cock-snobbled than that! On which subject, wife, I need new tights. It seems, to fit the fashion, I must come all attired in purple puffling pants, yellow tights and really stupid cross garters. You must stitch them for me.

ANNE: And how am I to afford the material?

WILL: Why, from what remains of the shilling I did give thee last time.

ANNE: Well, I've spent it.

WILL: Spent it? On what?

---

* Although clearly Shakespeare rejected this idea, subsequent history has taught us that his father might have been on to something, the entertainment departments of modern television companies having broadcast similar scenarios.
† John Shakespeare was indeed the dodgiest geezer in south Warwickshire.

ANNE: On what? On what, mate? I've got a bloody cottage to run and a family to raise, that's what! I'm having the roof thatched, the chimneys are being swept, I've had the rat catcher round to do the beds. Hamnet's wooden tooth needs re-varnishing and I've bought a ferret for Judith's hair to eat the nits. I've paid off the witch accuser, so he won't accuse me and Susanna of being witches, even though I think she might actually be a witch.

SUSANNA: Oh, God, Mum! Thou art so funny!*

ANNE: And I've bought the twins lovely new outfits for the May Day stupid dance. Beautiful purple doublet and hose for Hamnet and a lovely yellow dress for Judith.

The children descendeth the stairs all dressed in purple and yellow.

HAMNET: Dad, you came back! You're gonna watch our May Day dance!

JUDITH: We love our new clothes, and thanks for this wonderful colourful ribbon.

WILL: Hmm . . . er, look, kids, it's bad news.

HAMNET: You're not gonna watch us.

WILL: Actually, it's a bit worse than that.

---

* Susanna is fortunate that her mother made this joke in the sixteenth century and not a hundred years later. If a passing Puritan had heard such a comment, Susanna would have been barbecued.

WILL'S LONDON LODGINGS – NIGHT

Bottom and Kate be present. Marlowe entereth.

KIT MARLOWE: Just thought I'd drop by to check out Will's tights before the prancings. You know, make sure he's hanging properly. Showing good bolingbroke contours.

KATE: He's already gone, Mr Marlowe.

BOTTOM: Yeah, he were too excited to wait.

KIT MARLOWE: Oh, I bet he was. How'd he look? Pretty cool?

KATE: Hmm . . . not exactly cool.

BOTTOM: He looked like a massive futtocking cod-dangle.

KATE: Robert Greene came round and told him to wear really silly pants, tights and cross garters.*

KIT MARLOWE: Oh, so obviously he realized it was a bluffle to make him look a fool?

BOTTOM: Yeah. But then he decided it was a double-bluffle.

KIT MARLOWE: Hang on, hang on. You're not saying that Will thought that Greene would guess that he would spot his bluff to bluff him into wearing stupid prancing trousers, so thought his actual plan was to twice bluff him into not wearing stupid prancing trousers, so he decided to counter-bluff by wearing stupid prancing trousers?

KATE: Exactly, it's that simple.†

---

* In Robert Greene's plan to make a fool of Shakespeare we see the seeds of Shakespeare's shaming of Malvolio in *Twelfth Night*.

† Kate was used to hearing Shakespeare's plots so found this relatively simple in comparison.

LORD SOUTHAMPTON'S HOUSE – NIGHT

Guests are arriving. Will approaches the footman in his bright yellow tights, foolish cross gartering and purple puffling pants.

WILL: Yes, er, hello, I'm here for my Lord Southampton's saucy prancings.

FOOTMAN: Yes, the artists' entrance at the back door, please, and hurry up, the other clowns have been here half an hour!

Now Marlowe approacheth, all be'cloaked.

KIT MARLOWE: Will! Will! Will! Thank God I've caught you. Greene's been playing you, mate. Trying to make you look a fool.

WILL: No!

KIT MARLOWE: Yes!

Now Greene arriveth full of pomp.

ROBERT GREENE: Well, well, well! Our upstart country bumsnot come a-prancing 'mongst the dainties. Ah no, I see now you are come as a jester to amuse the children. The apparel oft proclaims the man, and you, sirrah, are proclaimed a fool.

WILL: I salute you, Greene. You knew that I would guess that you would guess that I would guess about the stupid pants. And so with fiendish cunning did you triple-gull me.

ROBERT GREENE: No. I just told you to wear stupid pants, and you did! Happy prancing.

Greene entereth the ballroom.

WILL: Well, that's that then. Thank heavens you got here in time to stop me, Kit. If I'd gone in there dressed like this I would have been laughed out of London. As it is, I must skulk away like a lowly oik and miss my chance amongst the folderols.

KIT MARLOWE: Skulk away? Skulk away?! Will, mate, have you learnt nothing from what I've told you? A gentleman doesn't skulk. (*Removes cloak to reveal he be dressed alike in purple and yellow*) He struts!

WILL: Kit! You'd go to the prancings dressed like that? For me?!

KIT MARLOWE: Course I would! You're a mate! Besides, I quite fancied the skit. By the time cool Kit Marlowe's danced a jig or two dressed like this, the whole of London will be wearing purple pants!

WILL: How can I ever thank you?

KIT MARLOWE: I'll leave it with you.

WILL: Right.

The two identically clad friends enter the ball together.

THE RED LION THEATRE - NIGHT

The players be assembled.

BURBAGE: And I hear Shakespeare made a huge success at the prancings after all. Perhaps now he will deign at last to give us his new piece.

Marlowe entereth.

KIT MARLOWE: Actually, Burbage, Will has a bit of writer's block at the moment and he sends his apologies.

BURBAGE: Oh.

KIT MARLOWE: I, however, have been on something of a roll.

BURBAGE: A new play? By you?

KIT MARLOWE: It's just a little thing I dashed off. I think you might like it.

Marlowe produceth a script.

KIT MARLOWE: *The Jew of Malta*. By Christopher Marlowe.[*]

---

[*] *The Jew of Malta* has long been considered one of Marlowe's greatest works, despite the fact it's basically five solid acts of hysterical Jew-baiting. It is interesting to speculate how much Shakespeare's reputation for progressive tolerance and enlightened humanism would have been damaged had Robert Greene not tricked him into wearing cross garters, thus putting him in Marlowe's debt.

WILL'S STRATFORD HOME – NIGHT

Will and Anne with their pipes before the fire.

ANNE: I'm glad you gave that play to Marlowe. Kate was right. There's enough intolerance in the world without clever dicks like you using it to thrill the mob.

WILL: Perhaps you're right.

ANNE: You're bigger than that, doll. You know you are.

WILL: Yes, I think perhaps I am.

ANNE: You should do another big Jew play some time, but give the Jew some sympathetic traits.

WILL: A nice Jew? Bloody hell, pretty radical, Anne.

ANNE: Well, I don't say he has to be nice, just human. I don't know any Jews myself.

WILL: No one does. They were all thrown out of England by Edward the First and none has ever been allowed back in.[*]

ANNE: But I imagine if you prick 'em, they bleed. If you tickle them, they'll laugh just like we do.[†]

WILL: These are bold thoughts, wife, but there may be something in it. I'll let it gestate.

John can now be seen, where he doth sit upon the privy pot before the fire.

JOHN: Gestate? Gestate?! If ya mean 'think about it', then why not just say it?

WILL: I'm not doing a double act with you, Dad. Go to bed!

---

[*] England's historical reputation for tolerance and civilized conduct has partly rested on the fact that we avoided the worst anti-Semitic excesses of the Middle Ages with no mass murders or pogroms. But the only reason for this is that the Jew-baiting bastard Edward the First threw them all out.

[†] Shakespeare was to use this line almost verbatim for his later big Jew play. The man was shameless.

EPISODE 4

LOVE IS NOT LOVE

This episode from the Crow Folios solves one of
the greatest mysteries in all English literature, that
is, the identity of the Fair Youth and the Dark Lady
of the sonnets. Unfortunately it doesn't throw much
light on any other aspect of the sonnets which are,
frankly, pretty comprehensively incomprehensible.
Some literary scholars believe Shakespeare must
have been pisslingtoned when he wrote them.

ROBERT GREENE'S OFFICE - NIGHT

The odious Greene doth sit before his desk.

ROBERT GREENE: Hmm, this upstart crow is ever more advanced in the world, beautifying himself in the feathers of a gentleman.* In vain have I sought to find some chink in the armour of his propriety, some lewd scandal or base crime with which to dispatch him to the dungeon or the gallows. He claims to lead a blameless life. Married, sober, solvent, dull. But all men have their secrets, and when I find Will Shakespeare's I will crush him like a walnut betwixt the iron buttocks of a titan.†

---

* Here Greene quotes a passage from his own description of Shakespeare in his *Groatsworth of Wit*, a book that would have been completely forgotten had it not contained a short paragraph slagging off Shakespeare.

† It is undoubtedly true that Shakespeare's personal life was pretty dull and blameless. Unlike almost all of his contemporary poets, he was not a violent, debauched pisshead. The mundane and parochial nature of Will's character is one of the principal 'proofs' that idiot conspiracy theorists raise as reason to doubt that Shakespeare wrote his plays. Apparently, you're not allowed to be a genius unless you're also a complete futtock-up.

WILL'S LONDON LODGINGS – DAY

Will doth write. Bottom cleaneth. Kate doth flit about most daintily.

WILL: Oh yes! Bloody yes! Nailed it! 'And this by that I prove, love's fire heats water, water cools not love.' Finished! By Jupiter's hairy armpits, bloody finished!

KATE: Finished what, Mr Shakespeare?

WILL: My hundred and fifty-fourth sonnet. The cycle be complete. Result! Oh yeah! Who the bard? Me the bard! Iambic pentameter is my bitch!

KATE: I thought you were working on your wonderful star-crossed lovers play?

WILL: I am, Kate, but a sonnet be like the idle wind. When it bubbleth within, you have to let it out. Besides, these verses be my ticket to immortality. Through them will I live for ever.[*]

KATE: How so, Mr Shakespeare?

WILL: I'm to have them published. Imagine it! A play is but a puff of air, a player's stinking breath doth give it life, but no sooner is it spoke than 'tis lost amid the burps and fartle-barfles of the groundlings. But a published poem lives for ever. People love 'em. Particularly now these short and easily digestible sonnets have made the epic verse cycle look so last century.

KATE: Young people have such short attention spans these days.

WILL: And with publishing, kids have instant entertainment in the pockets of their puffling pants. You see them hanging around together hunched over a book of fourteen-line iambic pentameter thumbing away, transfixed like zombies. Not talking to each other. Not interacting socially. Lost to the world. 'Get off your book

---

[*] Shakespeare was clearly wrong on this point. His sonnets are not the principal source of his eternal fame. In fact, a recent and exhaustive academic study discovered that, with the exception of the one sonnet read at weddings, nobody has read one in its entirety since the nineteenth century.

of sonnets!' cry parents up and down the land. 'You'll develop a hunch.'

KATE: I do worry about how their brains will develop with so little variation of stimulus to challenge their imagination.

WILL: Who cares! The point is sonnets are what the kids are digging and ever shall. Which is why I have for a time abandoned drama and switched to churning out poems. Thought I'd never get them finished. I've been struggling over this last one all morning. Couldn't get the final rhyme.

BOTTOM: So you gave up? Probably best.

WILL: I didn't give up at all. I found my final rhyme, and it's genius. 'And this by that I prove, love's fire heats water, water cools not love.'*

KATE: Except 'prove' doesn't actually rhyme with 'love'.

WILL: Ah yes, but it nearly does, which is even better.

KATE: Hmm, not really.

BOTTOM: Yeah, it's not even close. For 'prove' to rhyme with 'love' you'd have to say 'pruv', which would be just rubbish.

KATE: Or you could say 'loove'. 'And this by that I prove, love's fire heats water, water cools not loove.' I think it could work, at a stretch.

WILL: I don't want it to stretch. A proper rhyme is boring.

KATE: I honestly think people prefer their poems to actually rhyme, Mr Shakespeare.

BOTTOM: Course they do! Like that brilliant one about the cock that couldn't cluck.†

---

* This is indeed the last line of the final sonnet and clear proof that they get worse as they go along.
† The arts establishment deliberately favours the obscure and boring over the robust and popular because they think it makes them look clever. Hence Harold Pinter getting a Nobel Prize for literature. I mean, seriously.

WILL: Have you written any poems lately, Bottom? Can we expect to see a collection of a hundred and fifty-four sonnets attributed to the divine Bottom in the foreseeable future?

BOTTOM: No.

WILL: No? And why would that be?

BOTTOM: Cos I can't write.

WILL: Exactly. Let all stand in wonder at the world's first illiterate literary critic.

BOTTOM: I thought you said all critics were illiterate.

WILL: Don't get clever with me, Bottom.

BOTTOM: Oh, I'm sorry, I thought I was thick. Which one am I – clever or thick? I'm confused.

WILL: Thick, because you can't see how good my rhyme is.

BOTTOM: Cos it doesn't futtocking rhyme!

WILL: Which is the entire futtocking point! Now shut thee that which eateth food but grows not fat, speaketh words but be not wise, and burpeth loud but makes not gas.

BOTTOM: Bloody hell, master, just say 'mouth'. People aren't impressed, you know.

WILL: Sorry, must try harder. My bad!

KATE: Come on, boys, let's not fall out over a rhyme that doesn't rhyme, even though it's a rhyme. Have you really written a hundred and fifty-four sonnets, Mr Shakespeare? That's amazing!

WILL: Well, I find it therapeutic. They help me deal with my moods.

BOTTOM: Like being in love with a bloke.

WILL: I am not in love with a bloke.

BOTTOM: You've written him a lot of poems.

WILL: Not just him, my sonnets are inspired by twin muses. The mysterious fair youth—

BOTTOM: Who you fancy.

WILL: Whom I admire aesthetically. And my other muse, the sultry dark lady.

BOTTOM: Who you absolutely definitely fancy.

WILL: Yeah, I absolutely definitely do. Ever since Kit Marlowe introduced us.[*]

KATE: But, Mr Shakespeare, you are a married man.

WILL: I know that, Kate, which is why I've used my secret passion to create a lengthy series of sonnets, which I will then publish and thus become immortal.

KATE: So much more satisfying to consummate a passion poetically betwixt pure white sheets of paper, rather than physically in the snowy linen sheets of love.

WILL: Hmm. At least, that's what I keep trying to tell myself anyway.

KATE: Me too.

WILL: Well, I must confess I have allowed myself one small romantic indulgence. I have commissioned Burbage and his players to recite my sonnets to my twin muses prior to publication. The first hundred and twenty-six to my Lord Southampton.

KATE: Lord Southampton? Is he the fair youth? Good goss!

WILL: Some might think it be him, but the identity will always remain ambiguous. And the other twenty-eight I will send to Emilia Lanier.

KATE: Emilia Lanier! Daughter of the celebrated Venetian court musician? She's the dark lady?

---

[*] Shakespeare's sonnets have created heated debate regarding the Bard's sexuality. There are many poems eulogizing the beauty of a 'fair youth' which have led many commentators to presume that Shakespeare was either gay or liked it both ways. Other scholars have pointed out that such flowery compliments were fashionable at the time and that Shakespeare may have been writing to order on behalf of another. Modern literary critics tend to say, 'Hey, what does it matter? We're all on the spectrum anyway. Why does everything have to be so binary?'

WILL: Again, I have left the matter open, but between you and me, it's definitely her.[*]

BOTTOM: As if anyone will ever give a tosslington about it either way.

WILL: And now I must journey to Stratford, where I keep the second copies which I intend for publication.

KATE: Goodness, Mr Shakespeare. You keep copies of these passionate poems in Stratford? Aren't you worried that Mrs Shakespeare might read them?

WILL: No chance of that.

KATE: They be too well hid?

WILL: She can't read.

---

[*] This, finally, is the solution to a 450-year mystery. Emilia Lanier did exist and has been put forward as the source of Shakespeare's passion by a number of critics. Another contender was Lucy the African tavern owner, who lived in London at the time and also features in the Crow Folios.

WILL'S STRATFORD HOME – DAY

The family be assembled. Will entereth.

WILL: Home am I. Mother, father, wife, daughter, bring ale and pie. Summon the twins from their dame school, your ever-loving husband, father and son is home. (*The family be grimly silent as Will takes off his cloak*) Yes, well, not a bad journey. Thanks for asking. Only half a day late. Coach crash at the Watford turnpike. Well, it wasn't the crash that delayed us. Amazingly the local watch cleared that up with some efficiency. No, just the fact that all who then passed must slow to a snail's pace to gawp at the wreck. Why do people do that? It occurred to me that there be good and bad in all of us and they be in constant conflict. I've been toying with a soliloquy on the subject. What do you think? 'To gawp or not to gawp . . . that is the question. Whether 'tis nobler to ogle at a coachman squashed under a dead horse . . . or take arms against the urge to perv and by opposing feel a bit better about oneself.' What do you think? Might be useful somewhere. I like the structure.[*] (*The whole family remaineth silent*) Hello? I'm here! Returned with news of ever more success in London. My poetry is much noted.

Now Anne doth turn on Will with thunderly countenance.

ANNE: Oh I know all about your poetry, Will Shakespeare!

SUSANNA: She found the sonnets, Dad. You're so crap, you really are!

WILL: The sonnets? But surely she couldn't read them?

SUSANNA: She made me read them to her.

WILL: Why did I teach that girl to read?! Hoist am I by my own socially enlightened petard.

MARY: I never thought a son of mine could be so base. My own fault for marrying beneath me.

JOHN: The only thing beneath you when you got married was the bloody floor, woman! You didn't have a pot to piss in.

ANNE: Who's this dark lady, Will?

WILL: Dark lady? Is, is there a dark lady?

ANNE: Oh, you know right well there's a dark lady, forsooth.

SUSANNA: Er, nobody says 'forsooth' any more, Mum. It's medieval.

WILL: Oh the, the dark lady in the *sonnets*?!

ANNE: Yes, Will, the lady in the sonnets! The dark-eyed woman with the thick black hair you seem so fascinated with![†]

---

[*] This clearly is an early working of the famed 'To be or not to be' speech from *Hamlet*. This version focuses on an identifiable human foible rather than the vague waffle Shakespeare ended up giving Hamlet, and is far superior.

[†] Shakespeare famously had a forensically astute understanding of the workings of the human soul. But he didn't know that if you don't want your wife to find out you fancy other people, don't write 156 poems about it.

WILL: Well, perchance 'tis thee, Anne, for you have dark eyes and raven hair. In a certain light. Good poetry is never direct or literal. The imagery should be oblique.[*]

ANNE: Read me those bits we marked, Susanna.

Susanna doth read the pages out loud.

SUSANNA: 'Your love is as a fever, frantic mad with ever more unrest.' Yuck, Dad! I mean, seriously, just yuck!

ANNE: Is that about me, Will? Are you frantic mad with restless love for me?

MARY: Is this really a proper conversation for the front parlour?

ANNE: Mary, your husband's taking a dump in the front parlour!

John is revealed to be sat upon the privy pot before the fire.

JOHN: It's raining. An Englishman's home is his privy.[†]

ANNE: Are you having an affair, Will?

WILL: No! No, I ... I ... I ... swear, honestly, truly. You do hurt me with these churlish suspicions and bring to mine eye that which though 'tis water be not drunk, and though 'tis salted be not cod.

SUSANNA: What?

WILL: Tears, girl, tears!

SUSANNA: Yeah, Dad, I know you mean tears. I'm just, like, aghast.

WILL: Look, they can't all be gold, it's work in progress. Now, wife, please. I am a true and faithful husband. No other tufted lady grotto than thine hath given good shelter to the stranger in the

---

[*] It is tantalizing to wonder whether the reason Shakespeare made the sonnets so complex was to disguise their autobiographical nature from his wife.

[†] For the lower orders it was also the cow's privy.

purple helm that doth enter upstanding strong but departs a limp and shrunken weakling.*

SUSANNA: I'm actually going to be sick.

MARY: I shall certainly have to have a lie-down.

WILL: I be married to thee.

ANNE: You're married to me, but you're writing poems about some stinksome whoreslap.

JOHN: And the fair youth. Don't forget the fair youth.

SUSANNA: Yeah, Dad, that is pretty weird.

JOHN: And dangerous. There's laws, son.†

WILL: The fair youth is just a pal. Look, Anne, I . . . I admit that while in London, seen and admired have I many dainties of beauty and experience. And perhaps did idly pen some obscure and somewhat impenetrable verse about them, but I be faithful to thee.

ANNE: Well, maybe you are and maybe you aren't, but I shan't share my bed with someone who's thinking about fair youths and dark ladies. So, until you sort yourself out, you can either sleep in the cowshed with Mrs Moomoo or you can sod off back to London, because I don't like you very much at the moment, Will Shakespeare. I don't like you very much at all.

Anne doth depart most angrily. All do look upon shamefaced Will. John doth speak from his perch upon the privy pot.

JOHN: Do you wanna get in here? Oh no, you're already up to your neck in it.

---

* Shakespeare tended to be a bit coy when it came to describing sex. The raunchiest he got in his plays was describing shagging in *Othello* as making the beast with two backs, which is taken as an image for missionary-style sexual communion. This has led scholars to speculate that Anne never let him do it doggy-style.

† This offers another explanation for the extreme obscurity of the sonnets. Hugger-tuggery was a capital offence in Shakespeare's day and he may have written such wilfully obscure verse in order to disguise his dangerous passion. Lesbianism was simply not acknowledged, although there has always been speculation that Elizabeth the famous Virgin Queen may have preferred making the beast with two tufting muffles.

THE RED LION THEATRE – DAY

The players be rehearsing.

BURBAGE: 'Shall I compare thee to a summer's day?' Oh, I do think that's pretty.

CONDELL: Yes.

BURBAGE: Such a lovely image, one's love like a beauteous August morn.

CONDELL: Fresh, sparkling, sun drenched.

KEMPE: Mm, yeah, unless it's raining. Shall I say you're a bit wet and soggy? Hmm, romantic, don't think so. (*Laughs*)

BURBAGE: Do stop doing that, Kempe.

KEMPE: What? Stop what? Being brilliant? Can't. Why? Cos I am brilliant. (*Laughs*)

BURBAGE: That, that laugh. You keep doing it all the time! Now stop it.

CONDELL: Yes, it doth rattle me to my very teeth.

KEMPE: Oh right, yeah, the laugh. See, the thing is, I see comedy everywhere, yeah? I get stuff you couldn't even begin to get. So . . .

BURBAGE: I understand comedy very well, thank you!

KEMPE: Hm hm! Quite well, Burbage, quite, but if you're a genius like me, there's another level.

CONDELL: Another level, Kempe?

KEMPE: Yeah, I see deep comedy, yeah? Beneath the 'oh it's a bit funny' and beyond to the secret, very funny comedy that only I get. That's why I do my massively annoying laugh. Yeah? To let you in on it. It's a bit of a favour really.

WILL'S LONDON LODGINGS – DAY

Will, Marlowe and Kate be at their leisure.

WILL: Now before I go to Lady Emilia's I wanted your help, Kate. I'm in urgent need of your unique insight into the feminine mind. I'm looking for the understanding that only one woman can bring to the feelings of another.

KATE: Oh . . . my . . . God! Thank you! Thank you! Thank you! Thank you.

Will be most confused at Kate's protestations of gratitude.

KATE: You're finally going to let me be your Juliet.

WILL: Don't be ridiculous, girl! Whatever gave you that idea?

KATE: When you begged use of my unique feminine understanding I . . . naturally presumed—

WILL: Naturally presumed?! God's bodikins, girl, what nonsense! Look, I know we've discussed the idea but the more I think about it, the more I see that what is required to convincingly portray a woman on stage is not feminine understanding or girlish insight. It's a squeaky voice, pouty lips and a couple of half coconuts.

KATE: I just really, really feel that an actual girl would be more convincing. Plus, it's my dream.

WILL: Kate, be realistic. The law states that a woman may not attend university, take a profession, hold public office or own property.

KIT MARLOWE: Men are better than women, by law.

WILL: Exactly. It therefore follows that they must even be better at being women.*

KIT MARLOWE: Well, that's just obvious.

---

* This appears to be a very early example of the phenomenon known as 'mansplaining'. Was there nothing in language which Shakespeare didn't do first?

WILL: Now please, forget these silly notions of becoming an actor and attend to me. I need advice.

KATE: Advice. Be there no men left in Christendom to confide in? Surely even the most ignorant would be a better oracle than I, who, though I read Virgil and Cicero, in Latin, have no cod-dangle, which clearly be the font of all wisdom.

KIT MARLOWE: Kate, do yourself a favour, wind in Mrs Smart-arse. Blokes can't stand clever birds.

WILL: Can we focus? My wife Anne is very angry with me because I've written one hundred and fifty-four love poems to people who are not her.

KIT MARLOWE: Gah, women! I mean, they're so bloody sensitive.

WILL: I know, I know. The point is, Kate, how can I put it right?

KATE: Well . . . I suppose the first question is – do you still love Anne?

WILL: Yes. Definitely. I honestly do, ignorant illiterate milkmaid though she be. It's just that, after thirteen years, I'd really like to lie with someone else.

KIT MARLOWE: Well, duh!

WILL: I'm not going to, I'd just like to. A lot. A really, really lot. Poetry helps me deal with these unworthy urges. I grab my trusty nib, my wrist starts to fly and within a few strokes relief pours out of me.

KATE: Well, I'm sorry, Mr Shakespeare, but if ever things are to be right twixt you and Anne again, you're going to have to stop loving whoever it is you're writing these naughty poems to.

WILL: Uh, if only it were so simple, but the fair youth and the dark lady are my twin muses. 'Tis they who empower my verse. Besides, once the two of them read my sublime and bewitching sonnets, I very much doubt that they'll be able to stop loving me.

EMILIA'S HOUSE – NIGHT

The players do perform the sonnets before Emilia as Will and Marlowe look on.

BURBAGE: '. . . and this by that I prove, love's fire heats water, water cools not lo-ove.'

KEMPE: Doesn't rhyme.[*]

BURBAGE: Your sonnets, my lady.

Burbage doth hand Emilia the sonnets and the players take their leave.

WILL: See how fervently she reads? How grateful she be to be the subject of such divine verse.

EMILIA: Just reading the one about my eyes being nothing like the sun.[†]

WILL: Ah yes, a brilliant opening image, don't you think?

EMILIA: The sun being bright, shining, radiant and above all hot.

WILL: Yes, absolutely.

EMILIA: But you are saying my eyes are not?

KIT MARLOWE: It's a bit of an own goal there, mate.

WILL: Well, not as bright, shining, radiant or hot, obviously. We're talking about the sun, Emilia!

EMILIA: 'If snow be white, why then her breasts are dun.' Dun is an English word for grey-brown, no? As when you say, 'dun cow'.[‡]

---

[*] Scholars often argue that Shakespeare's many crap rhymes are actually the result of changing pronunciation and that in his own time 'prove' did rhyme with 'love'. Yeah, right. And Basingstoke rhymed with elephant.

[†] Emilia is reading Sonnet 130, often referred to by scholars as 'the really, really weird one'.

[‡] Dun Cow was a common name for a tavern in Shakespeare's day, so scholars have speculated that the Bard may have been suggesting that the Dark Lady's breasts were similarly popular.

KIT MARLOWE: Ouch, two–nil.

WILL: Well, yes, but the image is only partially bovine. I'm not suggesting you have but one bosom with four nipples.

KIT MARLOWE: Will, you're really digging a hole for yourself here, mate.

EMILIA: 'The breath of my mistress reeks.' Were you happy with this as well, Mr Shakespeare?*

WILL: I don't know. Should it have been 'stinks'?

EMILIA: So this is supposed to be flattering? Just so I understand.

WILL: I get it. Perhaps I should have explained. This love sonnet is particularly brilliant because besides being a love sonnet, it also satirizes love sonnets. You see? You're getting double bubble.

EMILIA: Ah! This is satirical.

WILL: Yes! Conventionally, love sonnets are ridiculously flattering. They make absurdly overblown claims for the beauty of their subjects.

EMILIA: Well, we wouldn't want that, would we?

WILL: Exactly! The love I show you in my startlingly innovative a hundred and thirtieth sonnet is greater because it recognizes your flaws.†

Emilia slams the pages down upon the table.

EMILIA: Next time bring me sweets.

KIT MARLOWE: Actually, I've written a poem for you as well. 'Emilia, Emilia, by God I'd like to feel ya!'‡

---

* He really did write that. In a love poem. Amazing.
† Shakespeare's explanation is the one scholars have offered over the years to explain a love poem which is actually a series of put-downs.
‡ Due to the extremely homoerotic nature of a great deal of Christopher Marlowe's published work (much of which the Crow Folios suggest was written by Shakespeare anyway), scholars have long presumed that Marlowe was gay. This episode suggests he swung both ways.

EMILIA: Ah! At last! A poem with a proper rhyme. Good day, Mr Shakespeare.

Emilia and Marlowe leave together.

KIT MARLOWE: Perhaps you'll have better luck with your boyfriend?

WILL: Lord Southampton is a *pal*!

LORD SOUTHAMPTON'S HOUSE - DAY

Lord Southampton, a rich and vain young man, lounges with Will as the players read the sonnets.

CONDELL: 'A woman's face with nature's own hand painted hast thou—'

LORD SOUTHAMPTON: Hang on! Stop there. So, you're saying I look like a girl?

WILL: Yes. I don't mean it literally.*

LORD SOUTHAMPTON: Oh, don't you?

Southampton takes the pages from the players.

LORD SOUTHAMPTON: 'For a woman wert thou first created.'

WILL: Now that means—

LORD SOUTHAMPTON: I'm so pretty that when God made me he actually intended to make a girl.

WILL: Yes, but as I quickly add, 'Till nature as she wrought thee fell a-doting . . . by adding one thing.'

LORD SOUTHAMPTON: Which would be a cod-dangle. Hm.

WILL: Well, I don't actually *say* it, but . . .

LORD SOUTHAMPTON: So I'm a Venus with a penis? A strumpet with a trumpet. A Miranda with a stander. A Judy with a protrudy.

WILL: Put very simply.

LORD SOUTHAMPTON: 'And by addition me of thee defeated.' So, to be clear, you think I'm pretty, but because I'm a man you can't have sex with me.†

---

* Shakespeare is clearly lying here, which shows that Shakespeare was no better at complimenting gay men than he was straight women.

† It seems Southampton was a lot better at interpreting Shakespeare than most readers, as this has been the scholarly interpretation for many years.

WILL: I—

LORD SOUTHAMPTON: Get thee hence to your milkmaid wife who is clearly but a beard to your bechambered whoopsidom and returneth not till ye be ready to celebrate God's rich rainbow!

Southampton slaps Will with his own sonnets and retreats. Kempe laughs.

KEMPE: Not laughing at the word whoopsidom, laughing *beyond* the word whoopsidom so actually that's not offensive.[*]

CONDELL: Actually I find it deeply whoopsiphobic.[†]

---

[*] Here is proof that the propensity of comedians to have their cake and eat it when dealing with socially sensitive issues pre-dates the modern age.
[†] Condell's reaction also prefigures modern attitudes. If ever a comedian excuses an offensive line with a cop-out like 'just saying', they will certainly have offended the group who were the subject of the 'gag'.

WILL'S LONDON LODGINGS – NIGHT

Will and Marlowe quaff deeply. Kate doth pour their drinks.

WILL: Blimey, you try and write a nice series of classic love poems and what do you get? The dark lady objects to the tiniest allusion to halitosis and the fair youth seems to have a problem with being told he looks like a girl. I don't know why I bother.

KATE: Twin muses not happy?

WILL: No, Kate, they weren't, which is really weird because all hundred and fifty-four of them are works of genius. And what's more, once they're published, the world will know. Bottom! I want Bottom!

KIT MARLOWE: Yes, I think that's clear from the first hundred and twenty-six sonnets.

Bottom doth enter.

WILL: Bottom, did you deliver my sonnets to Her Majesty's Master of Print that they may be licensed for publication?

BOTTOM: Yeah, I gave them straight over to Robert Greene this morning.

WILL: Greene? Robert Greene?

BOTTOM: Yeah. Looks like he's oiled himself into another top job. He's the new print master.*

WILL: Greene has my sonnets? This is terrible. He'll probably deny me a licence out of spite.

---

* The Crow Folios are the only historical evidence that Robert Greene held any official posts beyond that of debauched poet and embittered critic. However, since he was an Oxbridge man, it is perfectly possible that he was also Lord Chancellor and Archbishop of Canterbury.

Robert Greene enters with guards.

ROBERT GREENE: Oh, I think you'll find it's a little more serious than that, Mr Shakespeare. Guards! Arrest this man for incitement to hugger-tuggery.

Will is taken in irons.

A DUNGEON – NIGHT

Will be chained to the rack. The Lord Inquisitor and Robert Greene attend.

LORD INQUISITOR: Ah, Mr Greene, I am the Lord Inquisitor. Why lies this man upon the rack?

ROBERT GREENE: Sodomy, my lord, sodomy. This inquisition will establish that Mr Shakespeare's vile pornography is nothing more than an incitement to foul hugger-tuggery.

WILL: They're just poems.

ROBERT GREENE: Sodomy is a crime for which circumstantial evidence is always allowable, there being rarely witnesses save the perpetrators, and one of them's looking the wrong way.

Marlowe doth enter in haste with Bottom.

KIT MARLOWE: My lord, I wish to speak in Mr Shakespeare's defence, assisted by my clerk, Ned Bottom. Don't you worry, Will, Bottom and I have been working on a plan!

WILL: Oh God!

LORD INQUISITOR: Proceed.

ROBERT GREENE: Well, I pluck a text at random. 'Wilt thou, whose will is large and spacious.' My lord will, of course, understand in this context 'will' clearly denotes carnal desire.

WILL: The man's very business is literary criticism. He's absolutely right.

ROBERT GREENE: The couplet continues, 'Vouchsafe to hide my will in thine.' This second 'will' being quite obviously a deliberate pun on the word 'willy'.* And, er, uncouth slang for the male sexual organ.

WILL: Damn, he's good.

---

* Further evidence that Shakespeare invented the knob gag. The depths of his originality really did know no bounds.

ROBERT GREENE: I will quote the prisoner's sonnet one hundred and twenty-nine, which addresses this fair youth. 'Th' expense of spirit in a waste of shame.' Clearly in this context 'spirit' is an allusion to seminal fluid.

WILL: He's right. That is how the line is destined to be interpreted.*

ROBERT GREENE: And thus we have an ejaculation in a waste of shame, which can only mean a man. Well, there is no more shameful place in which to expend one's spirit. Apart from perhaps a donkey.

LORD INQUISITOR: Stretch the damned hugger-tugger till he confesses.

KIT MARLOWE: A moment, if you please? Don't you worry, Will, I've got this.

Marlowe accidentally leans on the rack lever, causing it to tighten. Will screams.

WILL: Argh!

KIT MARLOWE: Sorry! Sorry! My Lord Inquisitor.

LORD INQUISITOR: Yes.

KIT MARLOWE: You have the evidence before you, one hundred and fifty-four sonnets, but may I enquire if you've actually read them?

LORD INQUISITOR: I'm not going to lie. Skimmed a bit.

KIT MARLOWE: And do you think that many people are ever gonna read them?

LORD INQUISITOR: Not really, no.

KIT MARLOWE: Of those that do actually read them, how many of those do you think honestly will actually have the faintest idea what it's about?

---

* This is true and the source of much merriment amongst schoolchildren who find the sonnets on their syllabus.

111

LORD INQUISITOR: Well, not very many of them, if I'm honest.[*]

WILL: Well, just a minute—

KIT MARLOWE: And of those who do have a vague idea as to what they're about, how many of those will only have arrived at such an understanding via forced study from joyless schoolmasters?

LORD INQUISITOR: Well, most of them, I imagine. Can't really see them being read for pleasure. Not really a privy book, is it?

WILL: Are you mad? They're brilliant!

KIT MARLOWE: The defence contends that far from being an incitement to sexual depravity, these sonnets are in fact an incitement to a nice long nap.

LORD INQUISITOR: Well, yes, I did nod off once or twice.

KIT MARLOWE: I rest my case.

LORD INQUISITOR: Release Mr Shakespeare.

ROBERT GREENE: I object!

WILL: I bloody object too!

---

[*] Extensive research has revealed that almost nobody who reads a sonnet has the faintest idea what it's about until they look it up on SparkNotes.

WILL'S LONDON LODGINGS – DAY

Will sits with his sonnets. Kate and Bottom attend.

WILL: Well, thanks to you and Kit Marlowe, Bottom, I am acquitted, but only on grounds that my poetry be too wilfully obscure for anyone to bother actually reading.

BOTTOM: Sometimes you've gotta be cruel to be kind.

WILL: I'll no more of sonnets.

KATE: I think you should write one more sonnet, Mr Shakespeare.

WILL: Another one, Kate, why? Who for? None likes them.

KATE: For Anne, your wife. I've been thinking about what you asked me. How to win back her favour. And it seems to me that if 'twere poems to other women which did upset her, then to set it right you must needs pen one to her.

WILL: Of course! Of course! What a subject, a love poem to an illiterate farm wench whom I only married because I'd got her up the duffington. Such a challenge.

Will begins to write.

KATE: Mm, yes.

WILL: The muse be upon me. 'My darling, you are my entire world.'

KATE: Good, nice start.

WILL: 'Though you be old and rather plumpish, sadly . . .'

KATE: Erm . . .

WILL: 'A common, saggy, ignorant old girl . . .'

KATE: Ah . . .

WILL: 'And yet for all that I do love you madly.'

KATE: Erm . . .

WILL: What do you think? Pretty good so far, eh?

KATE: It is good but, as a woman, if I might suggest just one or two tiny cuts.

WILL: But it isn't even finished. That's four lines. I need ten more.[*]

KATE: Honestly, we've got enough.

---

[*] Proper sonnets have fourteen lines. All of which conform to a strict set of rhythmic rules. This was considered VERY IMPORTANT and scholars have devoted much time to study of the form. Curiously, there is no parallel body of research into why anybody GAVE A FUTTOCK.

WILL'S STRATFORD HOME – NIGHT

Will and Anne do sit before the fire. Will reads his new sonnet to Anne.

WILL: 'My darling, you are my entire world. I do love you madly.'

ANNE: Is that it?

WILL: Yes, that's it.

ANNE: Oh, Will, it's lovely.

WILL: Lovely? It doesn't scan and it's missing twelve and a half lines.

ANNE: I don't care. All I ever wanted was my own sonnet. My own sonnet by Will Shakespeare.

WILL: Mm, yes. Although it's not actually a sonnet.

ANNE: I don't care. It says 'I love you', which is all a love poem should do.*

WILL: Mm, a lot of people think that, which personally I find weird. Anyway, I'm done with sonnets. They've brought me nothing but misery and rejection. These a hundred and fifty-four will warm our toes a little and that's all they're good for.

Will goes to throw them in the fire. Anne stops him.

ANNE: Oh, stay thy hand, husband. There's a couple in here might be worth a few groats. There's one about a summer's day that I think could be popular on its first two lines alone. And there's another one about a marriage of two minds that I think might be a big hit at weddings.†

WILL: You think so?

ANNE: Come on, read me mine again.

WILL: Oh God, if I must.

---

* Anne clearly speaks for England here.

† Anne was being remarkably prescient here. Sonnet 116, which begins 'Let me not to the marriage of true minds admit impediments' has indeed been read at millions of weddings over the centuries, even though by the fifth or sixth line most people are completely lost.

EPISODE 5

WHAT BLOODY MAN IS THAT?

In this extraordinary episode from Shakespeare's
life we see quite clearly the genesis of perhaps
his most popular play, the tragedy of *Macbeth*.
Scholars previously thought that Shakespeare drew
inspiration from passages in Holinshed's *Chronicles*,
but this proves otherwise. Amazing to think that
the famous scene in which Lady Macbeth washes
non-existent blood from her hands was inspired by
Anne washing hers after a wee.

A BLASTED HEATH – NIGHT

Owls hoot. Crows cackle. Wild pigs fart. Mist doth envelop all. Will, Marlowe and Kate enter. Bottom follows heavy laden with baggage. Will's temper be sore tried and his puffling pants most spotted with dank dung.

WILL: Once, just once, I'd like to take a coach service that fulfils its obligations to the travelling public according to the promised schedule.

BOTTOM: I don't like this heath. Spooky.

WILL: If they can't manage that, at least be honest about it. Time of departure: when we can be arsed. Time of arrival: some point in the latter part of the sixteenth century.

KIT MARLOWE: Well, in fairness, Will, the coach did throw a wheel.

WILL: Because the lane was rutted and the axle weak, Kit. And why is that? Because the exorbitant fares we pay get to line the puffling pants of bloated shareholders and none be spent on upgrading the rolling stock, mending the tracks or ensuring there be an adequate supply of soft leaves and damp moss in the coach-house privy.

KATE: How far is it, do you think, Mr Shakespeare? I really don't like this heath.

The company do sit upon a rock or tree stump, save for Bottom, who standeth, as befits his lowly place in life.

WILL: Oh, about a dozen furlongs, Kate. Mainly bog with patches of swamp.

KIT MARLOWE: Well, it's better than being in London. You do not wanna be in Southwark with the Black Death in town.

KATE: Such a shame they had to close the theatres.[*]

---

[*] In Shakespeare's day theatres were closed during times of plague. This was because it was wrongly believed that transmission of the Black Death was airborne.

WILL: Hmm, a grim business. We were giving my *Richard* the night it struck. Awful moment. I thought half the audience had nodded off. Big relief to discover they were dead.

BOTTOM: 'Course, some of them had died in their sleep.

WILL: A few, Bottom. Ten at most.

KIT MARLOWE: Well, we'll make a merry crew in Warwickshire and no mistake. You at Stratford and me staying at Sir Thomas Livesey's manor house near by.*

WILL: Particularly with Burbage and his company forced out of London on tour and booked to perform.

KIT MARLOWE: Ah, well, I may skip that. The Livesey children have a French teacher who teases most cheekily whenever I come to visit. Always whispering *l'amour* and then running away. Well, this time I hope to catch her. Prenons un petit seau, avec un chou le-dedans, hein? Which is French. It means 'chase my little cupcake into the larder'.

KATE: Actually, Mr Marlowe, it means 'grab a small bucket with a cabbage in it'.

KIT MARLOWE: Really?

WILL: Gosh, Kit, you're such a cool chap.

KIT MARLOWE: Yes, I am.

KATE: It was kind of you to invite me along as well, Mr Shakespeare. I can't wait to meet your daughter Susanna. I hope we shall be best of friends.

WILL: Mm, well I . . . I'm not sure I'd call her friendly.

KATE: Oh, Mr Shakespeare, I'm sure she's perfect and I shall love her. When I was young I didn't have a lot of friends . . . or any, in fact.

---

* Sir Thomas Livesey was a well-known Warwickshire cock-snobbled folderol. Marlowe clearly chose to stay with him since the quaffing and gorging would have been far superior to that offered at the Shakespeares' house.

119

BOTTOM: Well, that's dead sad, that.

KATE: No, no, Bottom, it was my own fault. I was a bit of a swotty try-hard. Always trying to chat to girls in Latin at slumber parties or discuss the oppression of the female sex. John Knox's book *The First Blast of the Trumpet Against the Monstrous Regiment of Women* had just come out and I was so angry about it.*

An eerie squawking is heard but 'tis only the lonely cry of the crow. Or possibly the belch of a boar.

BOTTOM: God, this heath is really, really spooky.

WILL: Oh, for goodness sake, Bottom, desist. It's the 1590s, not the Dark Ages. A glorious age of reason and logic.

BOTTOM: You still believe in wood nymphs.

WILL: I'm torn. I think the jury's out. After all, if dew be not the tears of scolded fairies, then how do you explain it?

The travellers set off once more upon their weary journey.

KIT MARLOWE: Well, exactly.

WILL: There be no rain in the night yet come morn the ground be soft.

KIT MARLOWE: I mean, how does that work?

Kate doth keep Bottom company as he struggles with his heavy load.

KATE: I did try to make friends. One time I organized a pink-themed girly party with strawberry pudding and raspberry lemonade, but nobody came. Perhaps it was a mistake to write the invitations in Greek.

BOTTOM: You think?

KATE: But this time with Susanna I am determined to make a proper pal.

---

* John Knox was an absolute arsehole and the precursor of similar modern-day arseholes who whine and cry victim when women seek equality and who call themselves things like 'menimists' and troll women on the internet.

Now does appear a most terrifying vision. Three weird sisters do stir at a cauldron.

WITCHES: Double, double toil and trouble; fire burn and cauldron bubble.*

WITCH 1: All hail Will Shakespeare. Owner of your house in Henley Street. Owner of a fine, new, suckling pig. And owner of New Place hereafter.

WITCHES: (*Cackling*) Ha ha ha! Owner of New Place hereafter. Ha ha ha ha ha!

The witches scuttle away, cackling most scarily.

WILL: Well, that was a bit weird.

KATE: Ever so.

WILL: Such strange prophecy. But I am the owner of the house on Henley Street. But I have no new pig and I'm certainly not the owner of New Place.

KIT MARLOWE: New Place?

WILL: The second largest house in Stratford. Own water, extensive family area with room for second cow. Anne and I would kill for that house.

A terrible squealing is heard.

WILL: Angels and ministers of grace, defend us! What be that ghostly shriek?!

Bottom doth enter, carrying a wounded suckling pig.

BOTTOM: Just a bit of roadkill, master. 'Tis a fine suckling pig, still living.

He hitteth the pig most violently.

---

* Shakespeare uses this phrase in his immortal tragedy *Macbeth*. The eerie chant is often misquoted as 'Hubble bubble toil and trouble' which is, in fact, much better.

BOTTOM: Now dead. Good fortune indeed. Mrs Shakespeare'll be thrilled to have a nice pig for supper.

KATE: Well, that's a bit blooming spooky, isn't it?

KIT MARLOWE: What?

KATE: The witches' prophecy. They knew you were owner of the house on Henley Street.

KIT MARLOWE: Which you are.

KATE: They said you'd own a pig.

KIT MARLOWE: Which you now do.

KATE: And then they said you'd be owner of New Place hereafter. Which you just said you'd kill for.

KIT MARLOWE: Kate's right, that is spooky!

BOTTOM: Spooky!

KATE: Spooky!

WILL: Not spooky at all. And yet do I feel my spirits quicken within me. I would love to own New Place. Property is going crazy in Stratford right now.*

Thunder thunders and lightning flashes.

---

* Clearly Shakespeare was to use this encounter from his own life as a plot structure for *Macbeth*, changing the ultimate prize from a nice house in Stratford-upon-Avon to the entire Kingdom of Scotland. It is interesting to note that had Shakespeare been writing in the modern era he might not have made the change, since there have been times when a nice house in Stratford-upon-Avon has been worth more than the entire Kingdom of Scotland. Although with Brexit, who knows?

WILL'S STRATFORD HOME - NIGHT

The entire Shakespeare family be assembled about the room. Will sitteth with Anne. Kate and Bottom are present.

ANNE: Oh God, I'd love that house.

MARY: It's a common little hovel. When I was a girl, I lived in a manor house, but then I was an Arden and of noble birth.

JOHN: Oh, shut up about your noble birth, woman!

Kate hath cornered Susanna in her desire to become pals.

KATE: What music do you like? I'm totally into madrigals.

SUSANNA: They're crap!*

KATE: Yeah, no totally, so lame. Hate them. Shall we make a den and talk about female emancipation?

SUSANNA: Who are you?

KATE: Shall we have a midnight feast?

SUSANNA: Argh!

John Shakespeare doth sit by the fire ever warming his wrinkled and stinking arseington.

JOHN: This New Place looks like a pretty good buy, Will. Put us Shakespeares back on the town map.

MARY: After you comprehensively rubbed us off it.

JOHN: Oh shut up, woman! It was only a bit of fiddling. You used to find it quite titillating till I got nabbed. Anyway, Will, what if those witches' prophecy came true?

KATE: Actually, I don't think witches are witches at all. Just women who don't fit in. Learned, creative, reluctant to accept

---

* Susanna was right. Although highly popular at the time, historical research suggests that madrigals were crap.

the oppressive social and economic restraints forced upon their sex.

SUSANNA: Er, what?

KATE: Men find that threatening and so they burn them as witches. Totally obvious to me.

WILL: Er, Kate, the three learned and creative women we encountered on the heath had huge hooked noses, numerous enormous warts, cackled incessantly and wore pointy hats. Exactly what part of not being a witch are you getting at here?* Anyway, can we please stop talking about New Place. Duncan MacBuff owns it and I'm afraid I could never do business with him.

JOHN: Don't be soft, lad. Why not?

WILL: Because he is Scottish and I am English, so no matter how much I pay or how generous the terms, he will still claim to have been given a raw deal and then bang on about it for ever.†

Duncan MacBuff, a Scotsman, doth enter.

MACBUFF: Ah, Mrs Shakespeare.

ANNE: Speak of the devil.

MACBUFF: I'll trouble you for a jug of milk, unless being English you prefer to deny sustenance to a Scotsman.

WILL: God, MacBuff, again with the victim thing! Let it go! What have you got to feel victimized about?

MACBUFF: King Edward the First invading. His soldiers murdering William Wallace.

---

* Modern feminist readings have supported Kate's view that the hunting of witches was indeed a symptom of a patriarchy seeking to oppress women who refused to conform. Yet Shakespeare is suggesting that perhaps these women really were witches.
† Evidence, here, that the whole Scottish 'victim' thing massively pre-dates the founding of the SNP.

WILL: It happened in 1296! Wallace was topped in 1305! When will you let it drop? God's boobikins, at this rate you'll still be banging on about William bloody Wallace in the next millennium.[*]

MACBUFF: Longshanks did plenty cruel and bloody slaughter to innocent Scots.

WILL: Well, it was your own fault. I'm sorry but painting yourself blue is just not a battle plan.

MACBUFF: It made us look scary.

WILL: It did not make you look scary, it made you look silly.

MACBUFF: We pulverized you at Bannockburn.

WILL: Absolutely, because I am three hundred years old and was there.

MACBUFF: You dishonour a great and noble heritage, sir, but I expect nothing else from an Englishman. The milk, if you please?

ANNE: You're very welcome to go next door to Moll Sluttage, if you wish.

MACBUFF: She is English too and so like you sees it as her birthright to cheat and abuse us Scots, who are, as the world knows, a decent, industrious, fair-minded and egalitarian people, in permanent occupation of the moral high ground. Thank God we're a separate nation!

WILL: Yes, well, I think we can all agree with you on that one, Mr MacBuff. And long may it remain so.

ANNE: There's your milk, Mr MacBuff.

MACBUFF: I shall be back early morning before church for a second jug, unless being English you've murdered me in my bed for being Scottish.

MacBuff departeth with his milk in high moral dudgeon.

---

[*] Shakespeare's plays are often considered prophetic in human insight. It seems that his conversation was likewise.

125

UPSTAIRS – NIGHT

Will and Anne sitteth up in bed.

ANNE: That Duncan MacBuff, he's so bloody self-righteous it drives me potty. It'd serve him right if I did put water in his milk. Or worse.

WILL: Hm? Worse?

ANNE: Oh, it'd be so easy, too. There's a bucket of white lead paint all ready to do the plaster on the half timbering. Do you see what I'm getting at?

WILL: Anne, I've told you, I'll get round to it! Just put it on my dad-job list.*

ANNE: Some blokes'd just take the witches' hint and kill the Caledonian bastable.

WILL: Yes, well, fortunately I'm not some blokes, am I? I'm your husband, whom you do oft call Snugglington or Tiny Knob. And those be no names for a wild and dangerous killer.

ANNE: Yeah, I know. Nice to think about, though. Lovely dream. Night.

Anne doth sleep. Will sleeps also, but wakes. He has a vision, a milk jug floating in the air.

WILL: Is this a milk jug which I see before me? (*Reacheth for the vision*) The handle toward my hand? Come, let me clutch thee. (*The handle moves away. Will follows it*) I have thee not and yet I see thee still.

Will takes a candle and leaves the room.†

---

* Most dads avoid their job list in order to watch football or scratch their balls, but Shakespeare put off painting the woodwork in order to create the greatest body of literature in English history. But it's still sort of the same.

† Years later Will would remember these words, spoken in a dream, almost verbatim, and simply replace the milk jug with a dagger in his dark Scottish masterpiece *Macbeth*.

DOWNSTAIRS – NIGHT

Will arrives in the living room and finds his vision of the glowing jug hovering on the table.

WILL: I see thee yet, in form as palpable as this which now I draw. Thou marshall'st me the way that I was going, and such an instrument I was to use. I see thee still. On thy spout and handle gouts of white paint containing lead, ready to do the outside plaster. (*Takes up the paint pot and approaches the jug*) Which is on my dad-job list that I keep meaning to get round to. (*Pours the paint into the jug*) The bell invites me. Hear it not, Duncan, for it is a knell that summons thee to heaven or to hell.

Lightning flashes, thunder thunders.

UPSTAIRS – DAY

Will awakes with a start. Anne also wakes.

WILL: Wife, a terrible, terrible dream I had. Ah me, my hands be all gooey and covered in pale slop.

His hands are indeed all gooey with pale slop.

ANNE: Yes, well, you've had plenty of those dreams, Will. There's no need to wake me up about it.

WILL: No. I did walk in my sleep. I must put a stop to this before 'tis too late.

Will doth leap from bed and rush from the room.

DOWNSTAIRS – DAY

Bottom sits at the table. Will rushes in.

WILL: Where's the jug?

BOTTOM: What jug?

WILL: The jug of paint— milk!

BOTTOM: The jug for Mr MacBuff? Yeah, he came round really early on his way to church, saw my candle lit and came for his milk.

WILL: Oh no, Bottom! You shouldn't have given it to him.

BOTTOM: What, because he's Scottish? That's just prejudiced.

WILL: No, because I poisoned it.

BOTTOM: Well, that's really prejudiced!

WILL: Could we get off the geopolitical aspect of this for a minute? The crucial point is to stop me from being hung for murder.[*]

---

[*] The correct grammar would, of course, be 'hanged for murder'. Shakespeare deniers will seize upon this slip as proof of their insane conspiracy theories arguing that someone who says 'hung' instead of 'hanged' couldn't possibly have written *Hamlet*.

MACBUFF'S HOUSE – DAY

The Scotsman sits upon a chair. There be white gunk and slop about his mouth and it dribbleth upon his chin. He seems to be dead.

WILL: He's drunk the paint! (*An empty milk jug be lying on its side*) What am I going to do?

BOTTOM: I wouldn't worry. I reckon your plaster's good for at least another year. I don't know what Mrs S is on about.

WILL: I'm not talking about my dad job! I'm talking about MacBuff! He's dead!

BOTTOM: Maybe he's asleep?

WILL: Asleep? Shakespeare doth murder sleep. I've killed him and I'll be found out. Milk will have blood![*]

BOTTOM: God, you're so dramatic, master.

WILL: Mm, yes, funny that. Except, hang on, it's what I do!

Will rushes out.

---

[*] The inspiration, perhaps, for Shakespeare's line 'blood will have blood', which is infinitely better.

WILL'S STRATFORD HOME – DAY

Anne be most prettily dressed in her best attire. Susanna doth fuss about her hem.

ANNE: It's got to be perfect, love. I've never been to a dinner party before.

Kate entereth.

KATE: If you need any alterations, I can do them. I love girly dress-up stuff.

SUSANNA: Yeah, we're OK, thanks! Got this!

Will and Bottom entereth, all agog.

WILL: Anne, I must speak with thee. Susanna, Kate, would you mind?

SUSANNA: Can I stay and she go?

WILL: Please, Sue, I need a moment.

KATE: Come on, I'd love to meet some of your mates.

SUSANNA: That is not going to happen!

Susanna leaveth the scene, followed by Kate.

ANNE: I can't believe I'm going to dinner at Sir Thomas Livesey's. Me, a farmer's daughter, supping with the cock-snobbled folderols!

WILL: Anne, I've killed him.

ANNE: What?

WILL: MacBuff, I've killed him!

ANNE: Don't jape.

WILL: I'm not japing.

BOTTOM: Trust me, you'd know if he was japing, because you wouldn't get it.

WILL: I've murdered MacBuff. In the night I filled the milk jug with lead paint. It was a vision that led me. I thought it was a dream, but it wasn't a dream. I really did it!

ANNE: That's terrible, Will!

WILL: I know! I know!

BOTTOM: Still, it does mean you can buy his house.

ANNE: Actually, that's true, we can buy his house.

WILL: Anne, I don't think you heard me right. I've murdered
MacBuff!

ANNE: Which is terrible, Will, terrible.

*Anne doth smile at Will as if to remind him that it does mean they
can buy MacBuff's house.*

WILL: Wife, how canst thou take this so lightly?

ANNE: Well, I'm not taking it lightly, I'm just trying to see the
upside.

BOTTOM: We live in tough times. Life's cheap. I mean, the average
bloke's dead by the time he's twenty-five.*

WILL: All right. I suppose, put like that, MacBuff should consider
himself lucky.

BOTTOM: Yeah, course he should. Selfish bastable. Well, I mean, how
long did he wanna live for anyway?

ANNE: There's no reason why we should be suspected, not unless
we bring it on ourselves. Tonight we dine at Sir Thomas Livesey's
and we must both appear innocent and carefree. Smiling and
laughing.

WILL: Yes, you're right. Innocent and carefree. Of course, Burbage
and his company are booked for the entertainment, so smiling and
laughing might be harder. I think we should aim for forced grins.

Will and Anne do practise their fake smiles.

---

* People continue to quote this statistic of historical mortality rates as if suggesting
that on average a man was dead by the age of twenty-five. But it's an average figure,
which includes all the infant and childhood deaths. Once a person had survived into
adolescence the odds were that they would survive at least until their forties.

SIR THOMAS LIVESEY'S HOUSE – NIGHT

Servants do prepare the feast. The players await their call to perform.

KEMPE: I'm telling you, it's time to take some risks. Push the boundaries. Mash it up, yeah?

BURBAGE: But, Kempe, we have given *Gammer Gurton's Needle* at every private engagement for over thirty years.

KEMPE: Oh, hello! What are you not getting? *Gammer Gurton's Needle* is old. It is therefore, by definition, crap.

CONDELL: Oh, it's very harsh.

KEMPE: The world's moved on, mate. A little thing called the Renaissance. Heard of it? We've gotta challenge the form, do some proper clowning.

BURBAGE: For God's sake, Kempe, all right, just talk us through it again.

KEMPE: Commedia dell'Arte, mate. Cutting edge. We'll do a lazzi.

CONDELL: Lazzi.

KEMPE: Oh yeah, sorry, forgot, you're English. You don't know about new comedy. It's a pre-agreed scenario around which we'll improvise.

CONDELL: Impro-what?

KEMPE: Improv, mate, yeah? Going with the flow, yeah? Picking up the ball. Free-forming. Finding the comedy, ooh, in the moment.[*]

BURBAGE: But I don't need to 'find' my comedy. I know exactly where it is. I simply take my inflated pig's bladder.

---

[*] The Italian Commedia school of performance was indeed a precursor of the modern phenomenon of 'theatre sports'. Evidence suggests it wasn't any funnier four hundred years ago than it is now.

Condell doth pass a hilarious inflated pig's bladder to Burbage and they perform together.

BURBAGE: I drop it on the floor. I stoop to pick it up. Mr Condell kicks me up the bumshank. I go, 'Oh!' He says . . .

CONDELL: 'Oh, master, now thy arse be as red as thy face!'

BURBAGE: And the whole room explodes in merriment!

Kempe be filled with doubt and contempt.

KEMPE: Yeah. Sorry, mate, but people don't want jokes. They want attitude. We'll do a famous lazzi called 'The Fly'. It's brilliant.

Kempe doth laugh most irritatingly.

CONDELL: I'm only going to do it if you stop laughing that laugh.

KEMPE: Can't, mate. Sometimes it's the only way I have of expressing the breadth and depth of my comic instincts, so live with it, yeah?

SIR THOMAS LIVESEY'S DINING HALL - NIGHT

Sir Thomas, Shakespeare's wife Anne and all the proud company enter the room most merrily.

SIR THOMAS: Well now, Mrs Shakespeare, Lady Livesey and I are most happy to welcome you to our mansion.

ANNE: Oh yes, it is splendid to be dining with the gentry, Sir Thomas. Now that my Will is advancing in the world.

SIR THOMAS: Kit Marlowe, whom you know, of course, will be joining us. He's just finishing a French lesson with our governess.

The sound of sauciness and the cry of 'Ooh la la' be heard.

SIR THOMAS: And we have another guest come in refuge from the plague. Robert Greene.

WILL: Greene?! Here?

SIR THOMAS: He gave you a poor review, did he not?

WILL: Yes, he did. He called me 'upstart' in his *Groatsworth of Wit*.

Robert Greene entereth.

ROBERT GREENE: I am honoured indeed that a great poet like yourself remembers my poor slander. After all, I only studied classics at Cambridge University. Whilst you, great Hermes, did reading and adding up at Stratford Bumbling School.

WILL: I care not for your slanders, Greene. Although methinks a better title than *A Groatsworth of Wit* would be to take 'wit', subtract two Greenes and add a call for silence.

ROBERT GREENE: I do not follow you, sirrah.

WILL: Why, you, sir, are Robert Greene. So two Greenes is 'double you'. Take W from 'wit' and you have but 'it'. A call for silence is a very 'shhh' and add 'shhh' to 'it' and you have a groatsworth of what you write!*

---

* It is interesting to note that Shakespeare's comedy was the same conversationally as it was in writing, in that both require lengthy explanation.

Sir Thomas and the company do laugh most mightily. Now Anne speaketh to Will in a whispered aside, which by strict convention none can overhear.

ANNE: Brilliant, husband! No one would guess you'd murdered a neighbour this morning. (*Turneth to Sir Thomas*) Oh yes, my Will is much raised up in the world. Soon we are to buy ourselves a bigger house here in Stratford.

SIR THOMAS: Ah.

ANNE: New Place, which we have coveted for years. Perhaps you know it?

SIR THOMAS: New Place? Why that belongs to Duncan MacBuff. A fine house for a fine man.

ANNE: Mm. Also dead.

SIR THOMAS: Dead? But I saw him but last week. He was fit and well and, being Scottish, also honest, wise, good-humoured, even-tempered and possessed of a sparkling dry wit. I think it's the accent that I find most attractive. If ever I were to seek counsel from an independent financial advisor, I would want to hear it in a Scottish accent.* Poor MacBuff. We'll miss him.

WILL: It had nothing to do with me. I didn't kill him.

Greene, sat somewhat apart, speaks in the manner of an aside, which by strict convention none can overhear.

ROBERT GREENE: So, this MacBuff dies all of a sudden and the Upstart Crow is all a-tremble at the mention of his name. What is more, the shrewish Mrs Crow would take the dead man's house. 'Tis strange. 'Tis passing strange.

Unaware of Greene's suspicions, the company chatteth most merrily.

SIR THOMAS: I hope young Marlowe hurries himself. We are to have rice pudding and curds and it gets a skin if left to stand.

---

* Fascinating evidence that the Scottish accent was seen as implying comforting fiscal steadiness even before the modern media age. It may be noted that the same air of chirpy sensibleness accounts for the disproportionate number of Scottish weather girls.

A CORRIDOR – NIGHT

Kit Marlowe doth chase the governess. Both cry out in jolly sauciness.

KIT MARLOWE: Ooh oh oh!

GOVERNESS: Ooh la la! *Oo, monsieur.*

KIT MARLOWE: Ah, ha ha ha!

A servant appears carrying a big pot of the aforementioned rice pudding and curds. As Marlowe and the governess pass, the servant loses balance, throweth the pot up in the air and is instantly covered in the slop.

THE DINING HALL - NIGHT

The feast be served and all do quaff and gorge most heartily. Now the gunk-covered servant doth appear in the doorway, his face obscured by gooey pudding. He doth wave his arms about. Will alone sees this vision, for the servant be behind Sir Thomas. Will stands in awe and horror, believing that he has seen the ghost of MacBuff.

WILL: Which of you has done this?! Never shake thy milky chops at me!

ROBERT GREENE: What ails you, sirrah?

WILL: Stay back, vengeful spirit!

SIR THOMAS: He sees some vision. His eye is fixed with terror.

Will tries to point around but as the company turn, the servant has stumbled away.

ROBERT GREENE: Some say it is conscience that maketh men see vengeful vision.[*]

Will sits in fear and shock.

ANNE: No, no, 'tis just a little fit. He has a very active imagination. It's his thing.

Anne whispers most urgently an aside, which by strict convention none can overhear.

ANNE: For lordy's sake! It is just a painting of fear. Like the air-drawn milk jug you saw in your wet dream.

WILL: Look, wife, look!

The slop-covered servant stumbles blindly through the doorway. But before the company can turn to see, Marlowe has appeared and pushed him aside.

---

[*] This exchange is yet another series of almost direct quotes that were later to appear in *Macbeth*, making *Macbeth* arguably the first 'reality play'.

KIT MARLOWE: God save us all. Sorry I'm late. Slight accident. The chef says the curd pud'll be another half an hour. (*Sitteth down beside Will*) You all right, Will? You look like you've seen a ghost. (*Teasing Will most merrily*) Boogedy boogedy!

Once more Greene speaketh in an aside, which by strict convention none can overhear.

ROBERT GREENE: Methinks I see a chance to rid myself of this unctuous oik.

SIR THOMAS: Well, if pudding be delayed, then let us have our show. Bring on the players!

The players enter in the costumes of the Italian Commedia dell'Arte.

KEMPE: Hi, yeah, right, hello, hi. Erm, we're gonna do something a bit different, yeah? It's called a lazzi. It's Commedia dell'Arte. It's cutting-edge comedy from Italy, where I have performed and won several awards. Just saying, so . . . (*Putteth the mask of Punchinello upon his face**) Right, Punchinello, servant to Pantalone. See, my master comes.

Burbage entereth as Pantalone.†

BURBAGE: Well, our servant, I wonder if we shall have any visitors today? (*A knocking at the door*) Oh! Go and see who that is.

Kempe goes off stage whilst Burbage doth gurn most amusingly. Kempe returns.

BURBAGE: Ah, anybody here?

KEMPE: Not a fly, sir. Not a fly.

Kempe drops his mask in order to speak briefly to the audience.

KEMPE: Yeah, loving it, yeah? It's Italian, see. Proper comedy, so . . .

Another knock is heard.

---

* Punchinello with his huge nose and mischievous nature was eventually to enter British culture in the figure of Punch.
† Another well-known Commedia character. Also not funny.

BURBAGE: Ah! Go and see who that is.

Kempe exits and then returns.

BURBAGE: Anyone there?

KEMPE: Again, sir, not a fly, not a fly.

Once more Kempe doth break character in order to address the audience.

KEMPE: Yeah, keeping up so far? Not too challenging or ground-breaking, is it? So yeah, all right.

Once more a knock.

BURBAGE: Ah! This time I shall go myself to . . .

Now Burbage doth exit while again Kempe addresses the audience to be sure they are keeping up.

KEMPE: Yeah, right. Right, this is the funny bit, yeah? This is where it gets really good, right, and if you don't love it, well, it's your problem, so . . .

Offstage there be the sound of fighting. Burbage enters, bloodied and beaten.

BURBAGE: Agh . . . Oh, I have been robbed and beaten! There are hooligans there, you fool!

KEMPE: Yeah, but there wasn't a fly, was there?

This is clearly the big gag but none do laugh and all have straight faces.

KEMPE: Brilliant, yeah? Just a bit.*

Burbage whispers offstage to Condell.

BURBAGE: We're dying on our arseingtons! Condell, quickly!

---

* It is to be noted that this 'lazzo' is in fact a genuine improvisational scenario from the sixteenth-century Italian Commedia, which gives us some indication as to why the art form died out.

Condell doth throw the inflated pig's bladder to Burbage, who catches it.

BURBAGE: What's this here? Oops, my old pig's bladder!

Burbage drops it in an exaggerated comical manner.

BURBAGE: Oops, I dropped it on the floor. I'd better stoop to pick it up!

As Burbage stoops to pick up the bladder, Condell runs on and kicks him in the arseington.

BURBAGE: Ooh!

CONDELL: Oh, master, now thy arse be as red as thy face!

The assembled company doth laugh most heartily while Burbage and Condell do prance and gurn most shamelessly. Kempe doth shake his head in despair.

KEMPE: This is wrong, this is so wrong.

WILL'S STRATFORD HOME – NIGHT

'Tis a dark and sinister night. In the bedchamber Will awakes to spy the ghostly figure of Anne, seeming to wash her hands in mid-air.

WILL: And so, Anne's conscience doth betray her, as mine did me. You do wander in your sleep, Anne. Ever trying to wash away our crime. But all the perfumes of Arabia will not sweeten that little hand.

ANNE: Oh, don't be so soft, I went out for a wee. Don't you wash your hands after visiting the privy?

WILL: I can't go on like this!

Will jumps out of bed and runs out.

THE COWSHED – NIGHT

Bottom doth slumber with Mrs Moomoo, the cow. His master entereth.

WILL: Bottom! Bottom, get up! (*Shakes Bottom awake*) My mind is much troubled. I would seek advice and counsel from the weird sisters.

BOTTOM: You want me to leave this nice warm cow to come with you looking for witches on a blasted heath?

WILL: No, don't be silly, of course not.

BOTTOM: Oh good.

WILL: I'm not going!

Will kicketh Bottom to get him up.

THE BLASTED HEATH – NIGHT

The three weird sisters do stand about the cauldron muttering.

WITCHES: Double, double toil and trouble; fire burn and cauldron bubble!

Bottom enters nervously.

BOTTOM: Er, hello? Er, ladies, sorry to bother you while you're cooking, but my master's all of a doodah. He thinks Robert Greene suspects him of murdering MacBuff.

The witches look up.

WITCH 1: Tell Will Shakespeare to fear not. No man born of woman shall accuse him of this crime.

WITCHES: Ha ha! Ha ha!

BOTTOM: Oh, well, that sounds all right. What's in't pot?

WITCH 1: Eye of newt and toe of frog.

WITCH 2: Wool of bat . . .

WITCH 3: And tongue of dog.

BOTTOM: Can I have a bit?

WILL'S STRATFORD HOME – NIGHT

Bottom has returned and addresseth Anne and Will.

BOTTOM: So they said that no man born of woman could e'er accuse you.

WILL: But this is brilliant news! Greene, like all men, was born of woman!

ANNE: We're off the hook!

WILL: Absolutely! We have it on the authority of three homeless derelicts with clear mental-health issues. And quite frankly, the way I'm feeling that's good enough for me. As long as Greene was born of a woman, I'm in the clear!

Greene doth enter most unexpectedly.

ROBERT GREENE: In that case, sirrah, you will hang! For untimely was I ripped from my mother's womb, born by the Caesar method!

WILL: No, the prophecy!

ANNE: Hang on, what difference does that make? You're still born from a woman. I mean, tummy or front bottom, it's still a birth, isn't it?*

ROBERT GREENE: Shakespeare, you murdered MacBuff and I will see you hang!

MacBuff doth enter most dramatically. All recoil in horror.

ANNE: Argh!

WILL: See! See! He returns! The vision has come again!

ROBERT GREENE: I see him too! Argh!

In terror Greene doth flee, departing the scene.

MACBUFF: I'll trouble you for a jug of milk, Mrs Shakespeare.

Will, Anne and Bottom look shocked.

WILL: Mr MacBuff, you're – you're alive!

MACBUFF: Of course I'm alive! I'm Scottish. We're more than alive! We are vibrant, creative, uniquely generous, strong, fair-minded, even-handed, good-humoured.

WILL: Look, I . . . I saw you out cold in your parlour yesterday morning. I, I thought you were dead.

MACBUFF: I was just having my morning nap after church. A big jug of milk always makes me sleepy and I get it all slopped over me.

WILL: But the milk . . . I . . . I, I poured it from the . . .

Will looks to where he thought the paint bucket was kept.

ANNE: The milk bucket! That be Mrs Moomoo's milk bucket, husband. And if you're looking for the paint to do the plaster, it's over here beside the wash tub.

Anne picks up the paint bucket, which be brimming with paint.

MACBUFF: Such milk, Mrs Shakespeare – full, creamy – I came to thank you. And as a neighbourly token, here is a gift of sweetmeats for the children.

---

* Anne highlights that the whole 'man born of woman' plot twist was absolute illogical crapplington but, inexplicably, Shakespeare chose to use it unchanged in *Macbeth*.

ANNE: Oh lovely!

MACBUFF: Yeah, taken have I a solid base of nougatine, spread upon it burned caramel and enfolded all in a sweetened cocoa paste.[*]

ANNE: Oh, that sounds utterly delicious.

MACBUFF: Then dipped it in batter and deep-fried it.[†]

ANNE: You see, now you've gone too far.

MACBUFF: Ah, I bid you goodnight.

MacBuff leaves.

BOTTOM: No need to kill him for his house. Simply sit back and wait for him to die of a heart attack!

ANNE: And be owners of New Place hereafter![‡]

There is a terrible scream. Susanna entereth covered in red.

SUSANNA: I can't stand her any longer! She's driven me mad! Mad, I tell you!

WILL: Susanna, where is Kate?! Susanna, your hands be blood red! You've murdered Kate! Kate! Kate!

Kate appears with a plate of strawberry pudding and a glass of red berry juice.

KATE: Yes, Mr Shakespeare?

Susanna takes up a knife most dramatically and doth grab Kate by the throat.

SUSANNA: If you don't get her away from me, I will murder her!

KATE: We were just having a girly slumber party with strawberry pudding and raspberry lemonade, Mr Shakespeare, but I think Susanna might have had enough now.

---

[*] This seems to be extraordinary evidence that the Mars bar was invented three hundred years earlier than previously thought.

[†] As was the deep-fried version.

[‡] Shakespeare later bought the Stratford property known as New Place, thus fulfilling the weird sisters' prophecy. No mention of Duncan MacBuff is made in the surviving records of this transaction.

WILL'S STRATFORD HOME – NIGHT

Will and Anne are sitting by the fire, smoking their pipes.

ANNE: You know, it seems to me, husband, all these doings'd make a really good play.

WILL: Yes, you're right. Of course! A light and breezy comedy about a laughable misunderstanding over some milk.

ANNE: Well, actually, I was thinking more of the weird sisters, the ghost at the feast, the conscience-struck wife endlessly washing her hands in the night. You know, a proper blood-and-guts thriller.

WILL: No, no, I think comedy's the way to go. 'Two Milky Jugs' by William Shakespeare.*

---

* If Shakespeare did write this play it is lost in the mists of time. Which is a great shame.

EPISODE 6

THE QUALITY OF MERCY

There is no mention of Shakespeare's *Merchant of Venice* in this episode from the First Folio, but it is clear that its most famous scene was inspired by the events depicted here. The pound-of-flesh argument was not Will's idea at all but Kate's, and it seems it took place in a real courtroom. Frankly, this doesn't make it remotely more plausible.

MISS LUCY'S TAVERN – NIGHT

The place be full and rollicking with blades and wenches. Will doth quaff with Marlowe.

KIT MARLOWE: A toast, Will, a toast. To the age of exploration, and for once I'm paying. Every ship returning from the New World brings riches to Albion's shore. Everyone's coining it in!

Lucy the tavern owner approacheth.

LUCY: You've got that right, Kit. I'm making plenty gold myself. You should get a piece of it, Will. Timid bull don't pleasure no cow.

WILL: No thank you, Lucy, I'm aware that the city sharp boys in their Italian-designed tights are coining it big on the New World commodity market. Also that the occasional bonus even trickles down to smaller investors like yourselves. But I'm a conservative sort of bloke. I prefer to keep my money in my puffling pants.

KIT MARLOWE: Rubbish! You told me you were investing in Burbage's new theatre.

WILL: Bricks and mortar, Kit. Very different. Solid. Respectable. Why invest in malodorous leaves and tuberous root vegetables from a mosquito swamp in north Virginia, when you can build here in London? Using bricks made of solid dung and straw.

KIT MARLOWE: Well, it's your loss, mate. Robert Greene is setting up a syndicate to buy the cargo off the next ship that docks. He needs investors and this fella's in.

LUCY: Me too. I'm saving up to buy a warship so I can cruise the Ivory Coast freeing slaves.

WILL: I've often wondered how you won your own freedom, Lucy. Perchance I'll immortalize the story in a play.

LUCY: I bribed my way out with a diamond ring, which I cut from the man who first stole me from my home.

WILL: Goodness, you cut off his finger?!

LUCY: It wasn't on his finger.*

Lucy doth clear the empties and depart.

WILL: Thoroughly invigorating woman. I'd miss her if she did go off and be a lady pirate.

The odious Robert Greene who hateth Will's gutlings approaches.

ROBERT GREENE: Ah ... *quid agis*, Marlowe?†

KIT MARLOWE: *Omne bene, gratias*, Greene.‡

ROBERT GREENE: *Ni illud velum sic habis bonum mane*, Shakespeare.§

WILL: Er ... er ... er ... Wait, I know this ... um ...

ROBERT GREENE: Ah, yes. I was forgetting, you speak but little Latin. Sad. Come now, Marlowe, have you money for your investment? I would fain not stay a moment longer in these immoral surroundings than I must.

LUCY: Hey, Mr Greene. Here again so soon?

Greene be covered in blushes and confusion.

LUCY: You are a naughty boy.

ROBERT GREENE: I know not what you mean. I am here to speak to Mr Marlowe. 'Tis true I occasionally visit this establishment, but only in order to raise up fallen women with Bible reading.

LUCY: It is unlike you to take the missionary position.

Lucy doth depart.

ROBERT GREENE: The money, Marlowe. *Da mihi pecunia.*¶

---

* Here is very interesting evidence that the fashion for 'cock rings' pre-dates the 1980s London club scene.
† The Latin translates to: 'Good day to you, Mr Marlowe'.
‡ The Latin translates to: 'Good day to you, Mr Greene'.
§ The Latin translates to: 'And greetings also to you, Mr Shakespeare'.
¶ The Latin translates to: 'Please give me the sum you wish to invest'.

KIT MARLOWE: *Hic pecunia mea.** Bung that on whatever's in the next ship.

ROBERT GREENE: Mr Shakespeare, *vis ad obsedendam in unico tempores opportunitate?*[†]

WILL: Erm, *vis* . . . that's 'would' . . .

KIT MARLOWE: He's asking if you wanna invest.

WILL: Oh er, right, well, er, *non ego non . . . non . . . quid . . . tibby . . . keepus cashus . . .*

ROBERT GREENE: No matter. Most of the cargo is already sold. The sacks of potatoes are spoken for, likewise the bags of tobacco. Before long the only thing left on that boat will be a couple of cases of *syphilis sive morbus gallicus.*[‡]

Greene and Marlowe do laugh most merrily.

KIT MARLOWE: Oh, sorry, Will. You wouldn't get it, Latin joke. Need to have gone to Cambridge.[§]

---

* The Latin translates to: 'Here's my investment.'
† The Latin translates to: 'Would you like to take up this marvellous investment opportunity?'
‡ The Latin translates to: 'Syphilis (or French disease).'
§ Shakespeare's lack of a classical education made him the butt of snobbish jibes all his life. And beyond it. Ben Jonson famously sneered that Shakespeare knew 'little Latin and no Greek', proving that Jonson was a pompous, patronizing twat.

WILL'S LONDON LODGINGS – DAY

Will sits.

WILL: Deum, daem, dadum, dadum, da-bloody-dum! It's no good, Kate. It won't stay in that which supports a hat but be not a hook, has a crown but be not a king and is fringed with hair but be not my bolingbrokes.

KATE: Pardon?

BOTTOM: He means his head, love.

KATE: You will, Mr Shakespeare. You will! You already have your schoolboy Latin to build on. I taught myself from scratch.

WILL: Mm, yes, but I think it's easier for girls. Their heads being otherwise so empty that there's more room to learn things.

KATE: Yes, because that's really logical.*

BOTTOM: I dunno why you care anyway. I mean, how many dead Romans are you gonna be chatting with?

WILL: Apart from the obvious social advantages of knowing Latin, all legal documents are writ in the language of the Caesars. If I'm to be a theatre owner, I must be able to read the contracts.

KATE: Theatre owner? Such an exciting idea, Mr Shakespeare!

WILL: Isn't it? Yes. Burbage must move his productions to south of the river to escape the wrath of the God-prodding Pure-titties who run the city.†

---

* We might expect that Kate – with all her spirit and intelligence – would come up with a better comeback to Will's outrageous male entitlement. Perhaps she told him to futtock off and die but Shakespeare's mysterious chronicler, to spare his blushes, failed to report it.

† In Shakespeare's day many considered theatres nothing more than debauched centres of drunkenness and lechery. That would certainly make the National a bit less futtocking dull.

KATE: Oh, I hate those God-prodding Pure-titties. They're so grim. There's no singing, no dancing—

WILL: Yes and, most crucially, no point. I search the Bible in vain for the passage that tells us that putting horseshoe nails on the inside of your codpiece will give you a front-row cloud in heaven. Still, the Pure-titties' righteous fury could be the making of me, for Burbage has asked me to come in with him as investor and producer.

KATE: Such a joyful happenstance.

WILL: And, what's more, he has hinted that if I can but finish my great teen romance in time, it will open the new house.

BOTTOM: But why don't you just tell him it's finished?

WILL: Because it isn't.

BOTTOM: Well, it is if you want it to be. Liberate yourself, just stop writing. Put a big full stop and you're done.

WILL: But nothing will be concluded of plot or character.

BOTTOM: Trust me, no one'll notice. They're not really following anyway.* Your plays are too long. I mean *Richard the Third* was nearly four hours! That's just wrong.†

WILL: People cheered.

BOTTOM: Yeah, they were glad it was over! Didn't you get that?

WILL: Bottom, your barbs do bite most bitterly.

BOTTOM: Well, no one else'll tell you except me. You give 'em too much.

---

* It would indeed be an interesting experiment, even in our modern age, if the Royal Shakespeare Company did just half a play, or maybe the first and last acts. Would anyone notice? Really? And we'd all be out in time for the pub.

† Bottom is right. The Ancient Greeks laid down many rules of theatre which are considered useful even to this day. If only they'd been clear that four-hour history plays are TOO FUTTOCKING LONG.

WILL: Kate, you don't agree with this, do you?

KATE: Well, they are quite long, Mr Shakespeare. I mean it's all great, it's just sometimes less is more.

BOTTOM: Short play's a good play. You don't want Juliet's balls dropping halfway through the balcony scene.

WILL: Well, that's true, and 'tis ever a danger with these beardless youths that we must employ to play the ladies.[*]

KATE: Of course, if an actual girl were playing the role . . .

BOTTOM: Oh God, here we go! Would you let it drop, woman?! Girls can't act.

WILL: No, no, Bottom. I confess, I'm beginning to come round to Kate's way of thinking. I would love to hear my Juliet in the true voice of a maid. Sadly, we're constrained by law.

KATE: So frustrating! A woman may not disport herself onstage for fear she be thought a trollop.

WILL: It does seem silly, but there it is. If ever I'm to hope to sneak you into Burbage's company, it must be in disguise. You must make him believe that you be that which though it have teats have no breasts, and though it have balls be not a game of tennis.

KATE: You mean a man, right?

WILL: Yes, I mean a man.

BOTTOM: A bit tortured that one if I'm honest, master.

WILL: You have to let 'em roll and then edit later.[†] Now, I must be on my way. I am to meet Burbage to discuss our great venture.

KATE: Let me come.

---

[*] Adolescent boys were indeed employed to play all female parts in Shakespeare's day. With a play as long as *Hamlet*, Gertrude might have gone onstage a boy soprano and taken her bow as a beefy baritone with a bum-fluff moustache.

[†] This is a fair point from Shakespeare. Unfortunately, he never edited later.

WILL: You, Kate? How so?

KATE: I speak Latin, I understand compound interest. I can be your secretary.

WILL: But you're a girl. Girls can't be secretaries, it's unheard of.

KATE: Exactly! And so I shall come disguised as a man. And if I can do that without discovery, then surely I can audition as a boy to play Juliet?

WILL: Well, I suppose I could do with a Latin speaker on my team.

BOTTOM: Oh no! I don't like this at all. This is just rubbish, this is.

WILL: You have an objection, Bottom?

BOTTOM: Yes, I have got a flippin' objection! I can't read, I can't write, I own nothing and I'm sewn into my underwear, but at least I've got more rights and status than any bloomin' bird. You start edging women into the workplace, then where's that gonna leave all of us pig-ignorant blokes?*

---

* It would take several centuries for history to provide an answer to Bottom's question and when it came it was brutal.

THE RED LION THEATRE - DAY

Will and Kate do enter most furtively, Kate dressed in the clothing of a boy.

WILL: Now, Kate, be ever vigilant. The tiniest mistake can see you unmasked as a weak and timorous girlie.

KATE: What sort of mistake? Any hints?

WILL: Well, do not under any circumstances discuss your feelings.

KATE: Not discuss feelings? What do men talk about?

WILL: Sex, beer and sport. On the subject of feelings – if a rehearsal begins, do not cry at the sad bits. And if blood sports be suggested and a pack of dogs be set upon a tethered goat for fun, you must cry, 'Kill, kill!' not, 'But he looks so sweet. Why do we have to hurt him?'

KATE: And of course there's the most important factor of all in pretending to be a man.

WILL: What's that?

KATE: I must ne'er be seen to perform a multitude of tasks all at the same moment. For 'tis a fact well known that men cannot perform a multitude of tasks all at the same moment.

WILL: Actually, that's a fundamental misunderstanding on the part of you girls. In fact, men can perform a multitude of tasks all at the same moment. We just prefer to sit around drinking beer.[*]

Burbage, Condell and Kempe enter, full strutting and proud.

BURBAGE: So, Master Shakespeare, we come as promised to discuss plans for our new theatre. And who's this?

WILL: Cuthbert, my secretary. A young fellow who would make a life in the theatre.

---

[*] A truly astonishing revelation that the clichéd business of women claiming men can't multitask pre-dates female newspaper columnists.

KATE: Oh, you bunch of hugger-tuggers, anyone get any minge last night? Wahey, I love minge!*

BURBAGE: Seems a very pleasant fellow, Will. Come and sit down, Cuthbert. I tell you what, perhaps later on we'll go bearbaiting, eh?

KATE: Brilliant! And I certainly won't cry!

BURBAGE: So, Will, as you know the God-prodding Pure-titties in the city have forced our company beyond London's walls. So we plan to build south of the river in Southwark.

WILL: Yes, England's first purpose-built theatre. Think of it, Burbage, we're actually inventing the form.

BURBAGE: Absolutely. It falls upon us to lay the very foundation stone of theatre architecture. So, a playhouse. What is it?

CONDELL: A big space for people to stand in.

BURBAGE: Yes, that's a good beginning. (*Doth make the mark of an 'O' upon the paper in front of him*) Yes, what else? What else?

KEMPE: Stage at one end, probably.

BURBAGE: A stage for certain, a stage. (*Doth mark a stage within the 'O'*)

WILL: This is so exciting. And since our building will be only for the production of plays and not also for boozing and bearbaiting as has been the custom to date, there's no limit to the effects we can install. Traps, drapes, screens. With such devices great battles and mighty tempests can be presented.†

KEMPE: Yeah, but really? Not sure.

BURBAGE: You have an observation to make, Kempe?

---

* Either Kate had a time capsule and had seen an episode of *The Inbetweeners* or men have always been a bunch of utter wankingtons.
† Will was expecting a lot from a sheet of a twine and a bit of old curtain, but then drama types always have been wont to over-enthuse.

KEMPE: Just sayin', but battles? Tempests? A bit dated? Wrong thing to say? Brr, don't care, said it now, so . . .

CONDELL: Dated, Kempe?

KEMPE: Not gonna lie. All that shouting. All that, 'Oh I'm a king and my army's all dead.' That's not relatable. That's not interesting.

WILL: Then what do you suggest?

KEMPE: Well, instead of setting the big scene in a battle, why not set it in . . . a king's counting house?

WILL: In an office?

KEMPE: (*Nods*) Observational, see? Minimal is the new epic, yeah? Instead of having heroic characters struggling with war and murder, they could all be really ordinary and worried about really tiny things, like, 'Oh, did you use my quill?' 'Ah, was that your quill?' 'Well, yeah, that was my quill. It's got my name on it.' 'Oh, sorry.' 'Well, you can borrow it, if you ask, maybe. Please respect my stuff.' That sort of thing. It'd be brilliant.

BURBAGE: Do shut up, Kempe.

CONDELL: We must consider the auditorium too. We'll need a toilet, methinks. Will's plays be very long.

BURBAGE: Very, very long.

KEMPE: Incredibly long, like mad long.

WILL: They're not long!*

BURBAGE: A bit long, Will. (*Once more doth make his mark upon the plan*) Yes, we'll definitely need a big trench out the back to piss in.

KATE: And numerous closeted stalls for the ladies. Twenty or thirty, I'd say, otherwise there'll be a queue.

BURBAGE: The ladies? You think we should cover for them?

KATE: Well, of course. While there be no ladies onstage, many do attend the play.

---

* Here is evidence that despite his literary prowess, Will suffered from massive self-delusion. His plays are definitely mad long.

BURBAGE: Yes, well, I suppose we could knock up a little shed and put a bucket in it. (*Doth mark the plan with a crude depiction of a bucket in a shed*) So . . . the conveniences – a twenty-yard pissoir for the men and a single bucket in a cupboard for the ladies.

KATE: But, Mr Burbage, a single stall? Surely you can see that in times of greatest traffic, such as the interval, a large queue will form of angry ladies with their legs crossed. Remember, sirrah, that what we design here today will set the pattern for theatres across future centuries.*

BURBAGE: So, as I say, a twenty-yard pissoir for the men and a single bucket in a cupboard for the ladies.

WILL: (*Whispers*) Have a care, young Kate, for your outrageous special pleading for your own sex will unmask you!

KATE: It's just so unfair!

BURBAGE: Right, lunch. I have a meat pie.

Burbage takes from his satchel a fine meat pie.

KEMPE: Meat pie.

CONDELL: Meat pasty.

WILL: Meat pie.

All do produce their meaty repasts. Kate, however, produces naught but vegetables, green leaves and bright petals.

KATE: And I've made a lovely little salad, which you're all welcome to pick at. Just some fresh leaves and carrot goujons. Also some rose petals just for scent and colour, but you can eat them.†

Condell doth throw down his pie in fury.

CONDELL: You're a bloody girl, aren't you? An ambitious little bitchington trying to steal my job!

---

* If only Kate designed our modern theatres.
† Kate's choice of lunch suggests that the fashion for slightly ridiculous and arbitrary salad ingredients pre-dates the invention of Marks and Spencer.

KATE: No! Minge! Flange! Anal!

Kate doth shock even herself with this last laddish allusion.

BURBAGE: We get one like you every fortnight. Silly little girls pretending to be boys, in the pathetic hope that they'll be as good at being girls as boys are.

CONDELL: Be gone, you foul sluttage, and find yourself a husband!

Defeated, Kate retreateth.

BURBAGE: So . . . theatre design complete. Now, if you want to be in on this venture, Will, you've got to invest. Four quid minimum shares. Are you in or out?

WILL: In, Burbage. I journey to Stratford this very e'en to get the cash. For there is a tide in the affairs of men, which taken at the flood leads on to fortune.[*]

All are most bemused at the Bard's verbosity.

BURBAGE: Meaning?

WILL: Well . . . I'm j-just reiterating really that I'm going to Stratford to get the cash.

All return to their repast embarrassed.

KEMPE: His stuff's too long.

CONDELL: Very long.

BURBAGE: Very, very long.

---

[*] Shakespeare tries out a line that would later appear, unimproved, in *Julius Caesar*.

WILL'S STRATFORD HOME - NIGHT

All the family are gathered. Will doth enter.

WILL: God, what a journey! Lost a whole half day stuck behind a seriously unhelpful shepherd, who simply refused to pull his sheep over to the side of the lane. Let me tell you, when we finally did edge alongside, we all made some seriously rude gestures out of the carriage window. Which was satisfying, but considering it took three hours to pass him, rather tiring on the arm.

ANNE: Well, I'm glad you're back, love. Your dad-job list is getting longer than a Pure-titty's sermon.*

WILL: Aye, mistress, such was the longing I felt for thee, so fervently did tug the bonds of love, that I must needs forswear all other thoughts and hasten to thy side.

ANNE: What do you want?

WILL: The family savings.

ANNE: Our savings?

WILL: Yep. All of them. The whole four quid.

ANNE: But what about our plans to buy New Place? And Susanna's dowry? She be thirteen and thus fast approaching marrying age. And she's such a gobby little bitchington I really don't think we're gonna offload her for less than ten bob.

SUSANNA: Shut up! God, you're so weird! Everything I do is wrong! Shut up!

ANNE: And I've told you ten times to move your cup and plate and tidy away your clothes.

---

* It is a little-known historical fact that the length of sermons delivered by the puritanical God-prodding Pure-titties was a major cause of seventeenth-century Catholic revivals, some worshippers preferring to risk being burned at the stake rather than sit through any more of them.

SUSANNA: I'm busy! Why is it always me? Ask the twins. Shut up!

WILL: 'Tis true, wife. Unless we can happen upon a youth who finds selfish lethargy and impenetrable self-righteousness attractive, we may be stuck with her for quite a while.

SUSANNA: I did not ask to be brought forth into the world!*

ANNE: What do you mean, you want our savings?

WILL: I want them in order to double them. Treble them! Burbage and I intend to build a theatre on the South Bank.

Will taketh the family money box and looketh within.

WILL: Wife ... nearly all the money's gone!

ANNE: Our savings ... stolen?!

WILL: Yes! We, we had four pounds and now there's only one!

John sits shamefaced by the fire.

MARY: Oh, the shame of it. Your own son!

WILL: Mum?

MARY: He took it, your father. To think, me, an Arden married to a thief.

JOHN: Oh yeah, cos it's all about you, isn't it?

MARY: He's been fined again. Illegal wool trading. He bought and sold sheepskin without paying the excise. Oh, the shame of it. The very shame!†

WILL: Dad, be this true? Are you become a criminal?

JOHN: Criminal? Oh well, depends how you define 'criminal'.

---

* Historians often speak of the 'teenager' as a modern phenomenon, beginning in the 1950s. This record of Susanna Shakespeare suggests that the essential teenage characteristics of furious entitlement and aggrieved self-pity have been a part of family life for much longer than previously supposed.

† It is true that John Shakespeare was arraigned before the courts on just these charges. The Bard's dad was a seriously dodgy geezer.

WILL: Somebody who has broken the law.

JOHN: But which law? Real law or natural law?

WILL: Real law.

JOHN: What about all the bankers and traders who've tempted thousands to lose everything in a fruitless search for mythical El Dorados? They're the real criminals.

WILL: Yes, if by 'the real' you mean 'also'. None of this makes it all right for you to steal my life savings!

JOHN: Look, I was desperate. When you turned down my idea for a dad–son double act, it was the last straw.

WILL: This is my fault?

MARY: Well, I do think you might have considered the idea, William.

JOHN: I still think we can make it work.

WILL: I have to find three pounds in the next week, and shameless, self-indulgent, cross-generational fame-whoring ain't gonna do the job!

ROBERT GREENE'S OFFICE – DAY

Will sits before Robert Greene.

ROBERT GREENE: So, Mr Shakespeare, you wish to invest, after all?

WILL: Yes, I . . . I have a pound and would hope for a great return, as you promised.

ROBERT GREENE: I also said you should hurry, sir. All the investments are made – the potatoes, the tobacco, the spices.

WILL: But what about those cases of syphilis whatnot you mentioned? You said there might be some of those left?

Greene turneth away and speaketh to himself in the manner of an aside, which by strict convention none can overhear.

ROBERT GREENE: And so does this upstart crow's lack of education condemn him. I have him in my clutches. (*Turns back to Will*) Hmm . . . well now, let me see. (*Produceth a ledger and studieth it*) Yes, it seems in fact there are a number of cases of syphilis reported on a ship just docked.

WILL: Then I would beg you, let me invest in one.

ROBERT GREENE: By all means. Although, *caveat emptor*, for the purposes of my duty of care, you are aware of the nature of that in which you would invest?

WILL: Who cares? It's been imported from America. We in England will instantly adopt anything from America. What is a potato but a starchy tuber? What is tobacco but a dried weed? What is a corn cob but a big yellow bobbly dildo? I would invest in the very next case of syphilis that be brought ashore.* I have a pound.

ROBERT GREENE: I fear the minimum stake would be two.

WILL: I have but one.

---

* It is not surprising that Will had not heard of syphilis. The dreaded disease was a recent phenomenon in the West at this point and its name only recently fixed.

Greene turneth away and speaketh to himself in the manner of an aside, which by strict convention none can overhear.

ROBERT GREENE: The trap shuts. (*Turns back to Will*) Why, sir, let me lend you another.

WILL: Really? You . . . you'd do that for me?

ROBERT GREENE: And for surety on the capital?

WILL: Name it, my house, my wife . . .

ROBERT GREENE: No, sir, nothing so onerous. Let us just say that for my one pound, I would want merely one pound back.

WILL: Well, that seems very reasonable.

ROBERT GREENE: Of your flesh.

WILL'S LONDON LODGINGS - DAY

Will prepares to depart for the theatre. Kate and Bottom be at hand.

WILL: So, the investment's sorted, I'm off to the Red Lion. Burbage is conducting preliminary auditions for my Juliet and if I'm not careful he'll choose the wrong boy.

Kate puts down her needlework.

KATE: Oh, Mr Shakespeare, let me try again. Please!

WILL: Kate, I've told you. In order to be a girl you must first be a boy.

KATE: Give me another go. Give me some hints. I . . . I just need to get deeper into character.

WILL: Well . . . all right. Supposing we go to the tavern where the new American potato tuber be served – diced into batons and fried.*

BOTTOM: Oh God, I love them!

WILL: Aye, all men do. Women also. And here, Kate, lies the rub, for without care you will be exposed.

KATE: How so, Mr Shakespeare?

WILL: When the diced potato tuber be offered, do not refuse to order your own, only then to steal it from another's plate.

KATE: Oh my God, I so do that.

WILL: For then will all at table know you are a girl.

KATE: I'll be *so* careful. Will you also lend me another suit of clothes so they don't recognize me from last time?

WILL: All right. But we have to hurry!

Will, Kate and Bottom do depart for Will's chamber most urgently.

---

* This is the very first allusion to chips in all English literature.

WILL'S LONDON LODGINGS - DAY

Will, Kate and Bottom be in the bedchamber. There be a pile of garments hurled upon the bed. Bottom holds up further raiment. Will sitteth in frustration and despair. Kate be in an agony of indecision.

WILL: Kate, you must decide!

KATE: I can't! I can't!

WILL: Every garment from the wardrobe hath been hurled upon the bed and yet you still claim that you have not a single thing with which to robe yourself!

KATE: Full, round and plumpish all do make me look.

WILL: But, Kate, can't you see, this is a case in point. As with the diced fried tuber batons, girls can't stop being girly. 'Tis at the very core of their nature. A man would simply grab the first pair of puffling pants to hand, give them the sniff test and if they be not actually rotted with his dung, shove 'em on!

BOTTOM: I've only ever owned a single pair. I've had these on for fifteen years.

WILL: You must decide.

KATE: All right. Which do you think? These or these?

WILL: Er, those.

KATE: So you hate these? You think I look full round and plumpish in these?

WILL: No, you asked me, by Jehovah's nostrils! You, you forced a choice upon me and then you turned that choice into a slight! Was ever there a thing so girly? This is impossible!*

KATE: All right! (*Indicates the puffling pants she has on*) I'll go with these.

WILL: Finally! And actually, for what it's worth, I think you look very nice in those puffling pants.

KATE: Yeah, right, as if. I do not. You're obviously lying.

WILL: Oh God, look, Kate, I'm sorry but I'm not doing this. It's quite clear that you can never convince as a man. And therefore there is no possibility of your ever earning the opportunity to convince as a woman. Now I have far more pressing concerns.

KATE: You wait, Mr Shakespeare. I will find a way to prove my worth.

WILL: Kate, gentle Kate, thou provest thy worth every day with thy joyous smile, thy girlish laugh and the soft tender grace that all Eve's daughters bring to the rough world of men.

KATE: Oh, Mr Shakespeare, you are like he who gives support. Like that which sweetens all that it covers. You are a great poet and are like the heavens.

WILL: Kate, your words move me, but I would fain know their meaning.

KATE: Why, he who gives support is a patron. That which sweetens all that it covers be but icing. A great poet is a bard.

---

* Some critics argue that Shakespeare is indulging in gender stereotypes here.

And the heavens of course be starred. Put them together and you get . . .

WILL: Patron-icing bard-starred.*

KATE: I'll leave it with you.

Kate does ever depart with her head held high.

BOTTOM: God! Her and her women's emancipation stuff.

WILL: Mm, yeah. Talk about having a diced fried tuber baton on her shoulder.†

---

* Kate scores a historical first here. This is the first recorded instance of a woman calling a man a patronizing bastard.

† Etymologists have always believed that the expression 'to have a chip on one's shoulder' derives from English naval shipyards and refers specifically to wood chips. It is extraordinary to discover that the term refers to potato chips and was, like so much else in the English language, invented by Shakespeare.

THE RED LION THEATRE – DAY

It be the auditions for a boy player to perform the role of Juliet. Will, with Burgage, Condell and Kempe, doth sit in judgement.

BOY ACTOR: I think I'm outward-going and with a great personality. It's my dream to play Juliet and I really, really want it.

BURBAGE: Thank you. Next.

BOY ACTOR: But you haven't heard my back story. My mum's just got the plague! I was bullied at dame school! I'm bringing up my sister's son!

BURBAGE: I said next!

BOY ACTOR: You'll see. I'll be a futtocking star and then you'll look like dicks!*

Boy actor departeth in high dudgeon.

BURBAGE: Crappage! Crappage! They all be crappage! (*Casteth aside his audition call sheet in high fury*) At this rate our theatre will be built before we find our Juliet.

Condell can contain his resentment no longer.

CONDELL: But you've got your bloody Juliet. Me! Except, oh, that's right, once an actor who plays women reaches a certain age, the roles dry up.

WILL: My dear Condell, Juliet be but a maid of thirteen.

CONDELL: And Romeo be fourteen, yet no doubt Burbage here will be playing him. Oh yes, it's all right for actors who play men. They can be geriatric and still get romantic leads. We actors who play women are tossed away in favour of younger actors who play women.

BURBAGE: Enough of this carping. We've a play to cast and a theatre to build. Speaking of which, Will, have you your four pounds' investment?

---

* It is surprising to discover that the X-Factor-style deluded sense of entitlement is a much more venerable aspect of English theatrical tradition than previously thought.

WILL: At any moment, Burbage. I expect news of my investment on the hour.

The servant Bottom arriveth.

BOTTOM: Mr Shakespeare, we've just got a note from the Board of Trade.

WILL: Ah, brilliant! (*Taketh the note and openeth it*) Not brilliant. I'm ruined. My investment was in twice-poxed sailors.

Robert Greene enters in triumph, accompanied by armed men.

ROBERT GREENE: Your ignorance condemns you, sirrah. *Syphilis sive morbi gallici* is but the recently coined term for the 'French disease', but since the name be conjured by the poet and astronomer Hieronymus Fracastorius in his Latin lyrical verse cycle, an oikish country bumsnot like you knows not of it.*

WILL: I'm sorry, Burbage. I'm broke and cannot invest in your theatre.

ROBERT GREENE: Oh, I think your problems are a little more urgent than that, sirrah. I would have my pound back and if it be not in monies then let it be in flesh!

WILL: But I have no monies.

ROBERT GREENE: Then these officers of the law will keep you safe until a court of law orders that my debt be paid.

BURBAGE: But, Greene, a pound of flesh cut from a man means certain death.

ROBERT GREENE: Hmm. Yes.

WILL: I'll get a lawyer. I'll fight this case.

ROBERT GREENE: Your case is hopeless, sirrah. I have my signed bond. There is not a man in London who will represent you. Take him away.

---

* *Syphilis, sive morbi gallici* is the title of the 1530 poem by Girolamo Fracastoro and the origin of the word syphilis.

A COURTROOM – DAY

A full public court is in session. The clerk calls order.

CLERK: All rise for his honour Sir Robert Roberts, judge presiding.

All stand as the judge entereth.

JUDGE: Be seated.

All sit, save Will, who be the accused.

JUDGE: Who will speak for the prosecution?

ROBERT GREENE: I, my lord, will prosecute. Being a Cambridge graduate, I am of course a qualified lawyer.*

JUDGE: And who will speak for the defence?

ROBERT GREENE: I fear none, my lord, for this case is so hopeless that there be not a single man in London who will speak for this wretch.

Kate steppeth forwards, disguised as a male lawyer.

KATE: Not so, sir. I am a man and a lawyer. And I will defend this wronged man.

JUDGE: You, sirrah, who are you?

KATE: I am Cuthbert Capulet, your honour.

JUDGE: Do you wish to argue that Master Greene should not take his bond?

Will recovers from his surprise at seeing Kate so attired and does speak to her in the manner of an aside, which by strict convention none can overhear.

---

* In Shakespeare's day, an Oxbridge degree clearly entitled a man to practise law. In our own age, of course, it also allows a man to become Prime Minister and run the National Theatre.

WILL: Go for it, good Kate. Nail him with some brilliant Latin stuff.*

KATE: On the contrary, my lord. If Mr Greene wishes to cut a pound of flesh from my client then he must, for it is his legal right.

WILL: What?!

JUDGE: Master Greene, you may extract your bond.

ROBERT GREENE: Oh, how sweet will be this unkindest cut of all.

Greene doth produce a terrifying knife and approach Will most sinisterly.

WILL: Please, Master Greene, the quality of mercy is not strained. It droppeth as the gentle rain from heaven upon the earth beneath.†

ROBERT GREENE: Not even iambic pentameter can save you now!

KATE: Tarry a little. There is something else.

Greene's knife is at Will's throat.

KATE: This bond doth give thee here no jot of blood.

ROBERT GREENE: (*Removeth the knife*) I beg your pardon?

KATE: Take then thy bond. Take thou thy pound of flesh, but in the cutting it, if thou doth shed one drop of Christian blood—

ROBERT GREENE: No blood? How can I avoid it?

KATE: Exactly, sirrah. If you must take your flesh, you must needs also steal blood, and thus would my client die.

JUDGE: Well, I must say, this does alter things a bit. Will you still take your bond, Master Greene? I shall be happy enough to try you straight away after for murder.

---

* Shakespeare drew on this as inspiration for the final scene in his *Merchant of Venice* in which Portia, disguised as a man, argues on behalf of Antonio, and which was of course a lot longer.

† Shakespeare reproduced this verbatim in *Merchant of Venice* despite the fact that it's really not a very good line. What, for instance, does 'not strained' mean? There is no record of anybody ever saying that mercy *was* strained so it seems odd that Shakespeare should deny it.

ROBERT GREENE: But, my lord, this Capulet's argument is utterly spurious. Why, flesh contains blood. Flesh be not flesh without it. You do not visit the butcher and say, 'A pound of beef and don't forget to leave the blood in,' do you?

JUDGE: Actually, that's very true. Master Greene is entirely and absolutely right. Your whole pound-of-flesh argument is in fact wafer-thin rubbish. I'm sorry, Mr Shakespeare. You're gonna have to let him carve a steak off.*

WILL: But I'll die.

JUDGE: Mm, sorry. Right, lunch recess.

Will doth quake with terror as Greene approacheth with his knife. Meanwhile the judge produces a lunch box in which is contained ... a salad. Kate does spy this abnormality.

KATE: A ... a moment, Mr Greene!

Greene pauseth, his knife at Will's throat.

KATE: Your honour, may I approach the bench?

JUDGE: Come.

KATE: Just wanted to say, nice gown. Really loving it.

JUDGE: Thanks so much. I thought it might make me look a bit full, round and plumpish.

KATE: So, a salad-eater who thinks a perfectly nice gown makes him look fat. Or should I say, makes *her* look fat. You're a girl.

JUDGE: It's true!

Judge Roberts takes off her beard to reveal the smooth round face of a gorgeous girly.

---

* Quite apart from Greene's point that flesh contains blood, Will is required to deliver the debt, not Greene to take it. Greene had only to demand that Will pay up his dues, blood or not. The whole thing is just futtocking ridiculous and yet Will saw fit to use it as the killer scene in *Merchant of Venice*. The man certainly had some bolingbrokes.

JUDGE: Ever since I first came to London as a young girl, I've known that it's a man's world. And to prosper I must needs become one. Please, do not expose me!

KATE: Don't worry, I get it, I really do. Just let my client walk and your secret's safe.

The judge puts her beard back on and bangeth her gavel.

JUDGE: Case dismissed!

ROBERT GREENE: What?!

JUDGE: Costs awarded against the plaintiff. Set at . . .

WILL: I need four quid.

JUDGE: Four pounds! (*Now turning to Kate once more*) I love your shoes.

KATE: Thanks, Judge Robert.

JUDGE: Please, call me Bob.[*]

---

[*] Scholars have speculated that evidence of this very 'Bob' can be found in another historical source, the venerable *Blackadder Chronicles*, an ancient but fragmented family history which came to light in the 1980s. Whether this Judge Bob is indeed the same person who was briefly in a cross-dressing, trans-inquisitive relationship with Edmund Blackadder during the mid-sixteenth century will always remain a point of speculation.

WILL'S STRATFORD HOME - NIGHT

Will and Anne sit in comfort before the fire with their pipes.

WILL: Kate saved my sweet, white, country arseington and no mistake. If the judge hadn't turned out to be another woman I'd be a couple of giblets short of a playwright.

ANNE: Yeah, well, it's lucky you didn't have to rely on her stupid pound-of-flesh argument. It's bloody obvious flesh contains blood! If the end of one of your plays hinged on such a half-baked notion all would boo and jeer and call thee a total wankington.

WILL: Mm, yes. Absolutely. Although it might work, you know, if I buried it in a lot of iambic pentameter.

ANNE: Well, it's your call, love. You're the genius.

WILL: Yes, wife, I absolutely am.[*]

---

[*] Audiences do not usually boo and jeer and call Shakespeare a total wankington but most critics agree it's only because they are fearful of looking stupid.

EPISODE 1

THE GREEN-EYED MONSTER

This episode in Shakespeare's life was undoubtedly
the inspiration for the Bard's immortal *Othello*,
which is generally considered to be one of his
better efforts. These days thankfully the leading
role is always played by actors of colour. If this long-
overdue social advance had occurred fifty years
earlier, Sir Laurence Olivier might have avoided
making an absolute twatlington of himself with
his exaggerated deep voice, made-up accent and
weird walk, which he claimed was 'how black
people walk'.

WILL'S STRATFORD HOME - DAY

Will be staying home with his family. He taketh up his quill.

WILL: So, here we go again. Application to the ancient College of Heralds for a Shakespeare coat of arms.

MARY: I don't know why you're bothering. We tried this years ago and got nowhere then.*

JOHN: Ah, but I was broke then and I'm not any more. Well, Will ain't. Money talks and it's gonna say – John Shakespeare, gentleman.

WILL: Glaring contradiction in terms though that may be.

MARY: If you really want to be a gentleman, you could start by not constantly fossicking about with your dangling tackle.

SUSANNA: He hangs on to it while he's talking to people. I'm like, please, just die!

JOHN: Only having a bit of a fossick. It's not a crime!

WILL: One of the few things you do which isn't.†

ANNE: Why waste our money on trying to make that dirty old goat posh?

Will doth ever confront his father.

WILL: Because his shame reflects on me, wife. I am the most divinely gifted poet in Christendom and yet, because I'm also the son of the dodgiest geezer in south Warwickshire, all the other snootish poets do laugh at me and call me the oik of Avon.

JOHN: Ha ha ha, brilliant!

---

* Mary and John Shakespeare did indeed apply for such an honour, even before their son's success. The cock-snobbled folderols at the College of Heralds suggested that they futtock offeth.

† Shakespeare is exaggerating. John Shakespeare was only dragged before the Stratford courts twice. Although he may not have been caught on the other occasions.

Will turneth away in great disgust.

WILL: But this is England and so spurious, unearned social status
will polish even the most stinksome turdington. By which of
course I mean you, Dad. (*Sits down*) Thus must I bribe the odious
Robert Greene that the Shakespeares may be gentlemen – or in
Dad's case, genitalman.

ROBERT GREENE'S OFFICE – NIGHT

Will doth visit the loathsome Robert Greene, who doth hate his gutlings.

ROBERT GREENE: Give it up, Mr Shakespeare. You will never win a coat of arms. Your family be turnip-chewing country bumshankles without influence or connection. I doubt if you have so much as dined with a single person of rank or education in your entire life.

WILL: It is true, Master Greene. Never did I dine with folderols nor ever sup with pamperloins, but I do have five pounds.

Will placeth monies on the table.

ROBERT GREENE: Mr Shakespeare, attempting to bribe an official of the crown is a criminal offence.

WILL: Bribe, sirrah? 'Tis but a gift. A token of my esteem. A very generous token of my esteem.

And so the Bard doth push the money closer to Greene.

ROBERT GREENE: In which case, I accept it with thanks.

Greene puts the money in his desk.

ROBERT GREENE: Application denied. The door is behind you. Good day.

Second Folio: Episode 1

WILL'S LONDON LODGINGS - DAY

Will enters in high fury.

WILL: Unbelievable! The lickspittle nincombunion kept my money and gave me nothing.

BOTTOM: And him a gentleman. Who'd have thought it?

WILL: Such corruption. To cheat a man offering an honest bribe.[*] But I can scarce credit it. Can you credit it, Kate?

Kate be buried in a book.

KATE: What? Sorry, wasn't listening. Caught up in my new book. Sir Walter Raleigh's latest biggie, 'The Discovery of the Large, Rich and Beautiful Empire of Guyana, With the Relation of the Great and Golden City of Minoa, brackets, Which the Spaniards Call El Dorado, closed brackets'.

BOTTOM: Catchy title.[†]

KATE: Isn't it?! I just can't get enough of these thrilling accounts of adventure and discovery. Queued all night for this one. Got it signed, too. Which, incidentally, Sir Walter charged for, which I thought was a bit off considering without us he'd be nothing.

WILL: S . . . sorry, without who, Kate?

KATE: Us. His fanaticals. We made him.

WILL: This would be a man who, among other things, established the first English colony in North America, named Virginia for the Queen and brought potatoes to these shores?

---

[*] It seems that the Bard cannot speak without unveiling a human truth. Here he recognizes that people only despise financial skulduggery when perpetrated by someone richer than them. They see their own small infringements as nothing more than natural justice. For instance, a person may despise the multimillionaire tax-avoiding lord while excusing their own slightly inflated holiday insurance claim because the bastards can bloody afford it.

[†] Unbelievably, this really was the title of Raleigh's book. Fortunately for him he never had to plug it on a chat show.

KATE: Yes, that's right.

WILL: And you made him?

KATE: Absolutely.

WILL: Kate, it be a man's achievements that raise him up. Fame itself is ephemeral. It be like the tasty snack that a fond mother packs for the eager schoolboy against the hunger of the long afternoon.

KATE: What?

WILL: Gone by lunchtime.*

BOTTOM: But you wanna be famous, don't ya?

WILL: As a poet, Bottom. If fame itself be more important than the means by which it be got, then will there dawn a day in Albion where we simply watch a gaggle of inadequates sitting about in a house and call *them* famous?

KATE: I think that could actually be quite an interesting social experiment.

WILL: It might start out that way, Kate, but it would soon degenerate into a fatuous game of who bonketh whom.†

BOTTOM: Basically what he's saying is if anyone ever wants his signature he's gonna charge them for it.

WILL: Yes, I am! And in fact I'm already laying the groundwork, signing my name only occasionally and spelling it differently each time to increase the rarity value.‡

Marlowe enters full merry.

---

* Not one of Shakespeare's better lines. It is fortunate for Ben Elton that he is no longer credited with writing the folios or he'd have to take responsibility for this disappointingly lacklustre image.

† This is uncanny. Shakespeare not only predicted *Big Brother* but actually understood that it would be riveting for a couple of series before degenerating into repetitive disappointment.

‡ Finally an explanation is found for the perplexing lack of written evidence of Shakespeare's existence.

KIT MARLOWE: Morning all! I ascendeth the stairs, so best thee get this party starteth.[*]

They laugh.

WILL: Kit, splendid! Bottom, bring ale and pie!

BOTTOM: Funny, after all your vast and innovative vocabulary, you still haven't heard the word 'please'. Manners maketh man, you know.

WILL: Very clever, Bottom. Shaming me with my own phrase.

KATE: 'Manners maketh man' is not your phrase, Mr Shakespeare.

WILL: Isn't it? I think it is.

KATE: No, it isn't. It was first quoted by William Horman in his Latin textbook *Vulgaria*, published in 1519, forty-five years before you were born.

WILL: Well, perchance some naughty sprite didst pluck it from my brain, dance back through time to 1519 and whisper it in William Horman's ear at the very moment he was writing his *Vulgaria*.

Kate and Bottom look incredulous.

WILL: Could happen.

Bottom bringeth ale and pie.

KIT MARLOWE: Actually I won't bother with the ale and pie, Botsky.

WILL: No quaffing or gorging? How so? Feel you like that which though it be not brandy doth burn the throat, though it be not stew doth contain bits of carrot, and though it be not a costermonger's cap doth get thrown up in the street at New Year.

KIT MARLOWE: Pardon?

WILL: Sick, Kit. Are you feeling sick?[†]

---

[*] It is unlikely but not impossible that Pink was acquainted with the Crow Folios when she wrote her first hit.

[†] This one's not exactly a zinger either. Perhaps the Bard was feeling poorly himself that morn.

KIT MARLOWE: Oh right! No, no, not a bit of it. No, I've been quaffing and gorging all night. Out with my new best mate.

Marlowe doth place his boots upon the table most arrogantly.

WILL: New best mate? Surely I be not usurped?

KIT MARLOWE: Oh, don't be ridiculous, Will.

WILL: Phew!

KIT MARLOWE: You're not my best mate. I mean, you're a mate, definitely. You know, good mate, not my best mate.

WILL: Right, yeah, k-kind of how I like to play it too. (*Attempteth the same casual pose as Marlowe but his legs be too squat and ungainly to do so with convincing swagger*) Don't wanna get in too deep. But tell us about this new friend of yours. Perhaps I might meet him and then we could be best mates together.

KIT MARLOWE: Well, I don't know, Will, I mean, the guy is pretty cool. Real player. You know, soldier, statesman, bona fide Moorish prince.

WILL: No? Really? Actual African royalty?

KATE: How fascinating! I am obsessed with stories of travel and adventure.

KIT MARLOWE: Ah, well, this guy's got loads of them. Name's General Otello. Docked yesterday and me being the coolest doodle in town he sought me out.

WILL: Oh, how I envy thee, Kit. You have all of London at your feet and I cantst not even style myself a gentleman.

KIT MARLOWE: I thought you were gonna buy your family a coat of arms?

WILL: Yes, but Robert Greene be Chief Herald and says my lack of connection amongst the dainties doth preclude all advancement.

KIT MARLOWE: Gah, damnable snob. How about this – a snootish pamperloin like Greene be dying to meet the Moorish prince.

Why not host a dinner, hm? I can bring Otello, you can invite Greene.*

WILL: What a brilliant notion, Kit. If I host a dinner for foreign royalty, Greene could ne'er deny my status.

Kate be most excited.

KATE: Oh my God! An African prince? Coming here? Oh, please let me attend, Mr Shakespeare, please.

WILL: Kate, sorry but no. This is a party to impress Robert Greene and you be but a landlady's daughter. Although that is a point, Kit – what of girls? No dainty dinner be fit without the gentle sex and I know no posh birds at all.

KATE: Oh, I think you do.

WILL: No, don't think so.

Kate takes up a blanket and wraps it round her shoulders.

KATE: (*Putting on a posh voice*) Why, sirrah, do you deny the Duchess of Northington? Then I think foul scorn upon thee. For though I have the body of a weak and timorous girly, I have the heart and stomach of a proper posh bird.†

WILL: Gosh, Kate, that is so good. You really do sound to the manner born.‡ What a brilliant performance.

---

* Then, as now, the English lost all sense of proportion at the prospect of minor royalty. In fairness, the phenomenon is not confined to England (witness Sarah Ferguson's continued employment on American daytime TV).

† This appears to be a deliberate reworking of Queen Elizabeth's famous speech at the time of the Spanish Armada. She spoke of having 'the heart and stomach of a king', which is a powerful image unless you think about the stomach of her own father, Henry VIII, which was like a pasty sixteenth-century Space Hopper.

‡ This phrase appears to have meant 'posh' and Shakespeare would go on to use it in *Hamlet*. The Bard might have been a bit pissed off had he known that four hundred years later the phrase, with a punning change of spelling, would be far better known as the title of a Penelope Keith sitcom. Mind you, he nicked plenty of stuff himself.

KATE: (*Quickly*) Well, as you know, performance is my passion because I really, really want to be an actress and it's my dream.

WILL: Stop it, Kate. Lady acting is illegal, but for one night only you will play the duchess.

Bottom doth attempt to act as if to the manner born.

BOTTOM: And I can act like a lord. What what what!

WILL: Mm, except we'll also need someone to wait at table, so perhaps you could break the habit of a lifetime and act like a servant?

WILL'S LONDON LODGINGS – NIGHT

Dinner is laid. Kate doth enter resplendent in a beautiful gown.

KATE: How do I look in my gown?

WILL: Wonderful, Kate. The very image of an alluring young posh bird. Better even than when Mr Condell wore it as Margaret in my Henrys.

KATE: Which is amazing really. What with him being a middle-aged man and me being only a real girl, you'd think he'd have the edge.

WILL: I can't change the law, Kate.

KATE: But thou darest not even try, despite all of the false promises you have made to me. 'Tis certain you will never play a female role yourself.

WILL: Well, I dunno. I have been deemed a goodly actor in my day.

KATE: Ah, but the law states that to play a girl one must have bolingbrokes and you have yet to grow a pair.

WILL: I will not quarrel on this special e'en, Kate. Soon we are to meet Prince Otello. I've been thinking I might use him in a play. I feel sure I could build a most wonderful drama around such a wild and passionate figure.*

KATE: Why do you presume Prince Otello will be wild and passionate?

WILL: Because he is African, obviously! Thus will he be primal, organic ... I mean, lovely, of course. Just more ...

KATE: Organic?

---

* This can of course only refer to Shakespeare's cross-racial masterpiece *Othello*. *Othello* would, for the next three and a half centuries, provide white male actors (who already believed they were better at playing women than women) an opportunity to claim they were better at playing black people than black people.

WILL: Exactly. In England we trace our culture back to the classical models of Greece and Rome, but the Moor is untouched by the example of ancient civilizations. Like the Scots.[*]

KATE: Well, if we're talking ancient civilizations there's Carthage, obviously.

WILL: What?

KATE: Carthage, where the Carthaginians came from.

WILL: Yes, Kate, I imagined that Carthaginians came from Carthage. They're not gonna hail from Stockton-on-Tees, are they? But . . . what about them?

KATE: Well, they were an ancient African civilization who led the world in dyes and textiles and their general Hannibal terrorized Rome.

WILL: Oh right, *those* Carthaginians? Well, obviously there are exceptions.

KATE: Or the Numidians. Carthage's greatest rival, who sided with the Roman republic in the second Punic war. They were Africans too.

WILL: Really? Numidians, you say?

KATE: And then of course there's the Egyptians.

WILL: Well yes, but the ancient Egyptians weren't Africans, obviously.

KATE: You are aware that Egypt is in Africa, Mr Shakespeare? I mean, I only ask since I happen to know you think Verona is a port and Bohemia has a coast.[†]

---

[*] It is true that the land now known as Scotland was never conquered by the Romans. Let's face it, the Scots were just too futtocking hard. Well, in a country where the thistles are waist high and the men wear skirts, you're going to toughen up a bit.

[†] These two famous mistakes appear in Shakespeare's plays, something which has caused much amusement amongst cock-snobbled folderols.

WILL: Ah no, methinks you overstate your case. Egypt may be in Africa, but the ancient Egyptians weren't African.

KATE: You mean, they were white?

WILL: Well . . . perhaps lightly tanned.

KATE: But when their civilization stopped being so glorious they suddenly started getting darker?

WILL: Kate, the ancient world played by different rules. Christ himself hailed from Judea and yet, as everybody knows, he was blond with blue eyes.

KATE: The only blond and blue-eyed man in the whole of the Middle East?

WILL: Don't be ridiculous! Of course not. His disciples were blond and blue-eyed too. Except Judas who was dark and swarthy. Look at any painting.*

BOTTOM: The Virgin Mary in our church is a ginge.

The odious Robert Greene doth enter, all strutting pride.

ROBERT GREENE: I am come as bidden, Mr Shakespeare. Full surprised though I be for we are not friends.

WILL: Come now, Greene, I know we have fought in the past, but like the sweet-nosed maid who doth follow the fully loaded turding cart, I would put all that behind me.

Greene spies Kate in her expensive gown.

ROBERT GREENE: And who, pray, is this?

WILL: Why, the noble Duchess of Northington, Mr Greene.

ROBERT GREENE: Charmed, I'm sure. (*Now speaketh in the manner of an aside*) Step aside will I a moment and speak my innermost thoughts, which by strict convention cannot be heard. Does the

---

* And indeed every Hollywood movie or God-bothering TV Bible story since. The myth that Jesus would have looked like a middle-class California hippy circa 1968 dies hard.

crow think me a fool? Why this duchess is none but the landlady's daughter, no doubt so attired as to make a show for the Moor. I'll not expose the sluttage yet. Knowledge is power! (*Turneth once more to the maid Kate*) Do you know Prince Otello, your grace?

KATE: I have not had the pleasure but do long to. What proper posh bird does not go diddly doodah over the prospect of a prince?

ROBERT GREENE: Yes, of course. (*Once more speaketh in the manner of an aside*) So this unworthy girl would set her cap towards the Moor. Well, she is passing pretty and he just returned from war and longing no doubt for honeyed words and soft caresses. 'Tis clear, 'tis certain, a soldier's blood will run hot in sight of this ripe peach, and where there is passion there is always jealousy.

Marlowe entereth, followed by Otello the Moorish prince.

KIT MARLOWE: Pray, bid welcome to General Otello, Prince of Morocco.

OTELLO: Greetings! Men who share the blood of beasts are brothers. My assegai will kill your enemies. (*Waveth his spear*) My shield will protect your women. My wildebeest will give you milk and fertilize your herb gardens.

WILL: Wow! Thanks!

Will and Kate engage in conversation in the manner of an aside, which by strict convention none can overhear.

WILL: So not wild and passionate at all then?

KATE: Oh goodness, Mr Shakespeare! Otello? More like *Hot*ello! He really is orgasmic!

WILL: You mean organic?

KATE: I kinda think I know what I mean.

Will turns once more to Otello.

WILL: General, allow me to introduce you to Mr Greene, a great and renowned poet, whose sublime play *Friar Bacon and Friar Bungay* is, I imagine, in constant repertory at the Marrakesh Grand.

OTELLO: A poet. I am honoured. Rude am I in my speech and little blessed with the soft phrase of peace.

KIT MARLOWE: Ha, don't believe a word of it! This bloke's got more gob than a Cheapside renting knave.

ROBERT GREENE: Well then, perhaps the prince would regale us with a tale or two. (*Once more speaketh in the manner of an aside*) And so do I tempt the Moor to speak of his alarums and adventures. For such romantic stuff will no doubt turn the strumpet's head.

OTELLO: You wish to hear of my alarums and my adventures?

KIT MARLOWE: Well, you know, maybe another time?

OTELLO: The battles, fortunes, sieges that I have passed?

KIT MARLOWE: (*Turneth to Will*) Grab a drink, mate, this could go on all day.

OTELLO: Wherein I'll speak of most disastrous chances, of moving accidents by flood and field, of hairbreadth 'scapes in the imminent deadly breach.[*]

WILL: Grab a drink, Kit? Grab my quill! This is blooming good stuff. I need to get some of it down.[†]

KATE: (*Speaketh to Bottom in an aside. Full lusty is her manner*) Have I gone all red? Tell me if I go all red.

OTELLO: Of the cannibals that each other eat. The anthropophagi, and men whose heads do grow beneath their shoulders.

WILL: This is brilliant. How do you spell 'anthropophagi'?

OTELLO: But perhaps I speak too much?

KIT MARLOWE: Well, you know, less is more.

---

[*] These are images that would appear in *Othello*, proving again how much stuff Shakespeare pinched.

[†] And it seems he wasn't ashamed to admit it.

KATE: Oh no, General, do go on.

Otello spies Kate for the first time and full smitten is he.

OTELLO: But soft, what fair lady is this? O my fair warrior! It gives me wonder great as my content to see you here before me. My soul's joy.

KATE: You had me at 'O my'.

WILL: (*To Marlowe*) Blimey! Do you think Otello fancies our Kate?

KIT MARLOWE: It looks that way, cuz. I mean a chap's gotta be pretty smitten to lapse into blank verse.

ROBERT GREENE: (*In the manner of an aside*) Fate is kind. The old black ram be for tupping yonder white ewe as I have plotted. The trap is set.[*]

OTELLO: If after every tempest come such calms, may the winds blow till they have awakened death.

KATE: I cannot speak enough of this content. It stops me here. It is too much of joy.[†]

Bottom draws Kate aside.

BOTTOM: Calm down, Kate. You've only know the bloke for a minute and a half.

KATE: But, Bottom, didn't you hear him? He has wonderful tales of adventures, tempests and the anthropophagi. And men whose heads do grow beneath their shoulders!

BOTTOM: If I fell for anyone who span a decent yarn, I'd have to roger half the blokes in the pub! Now pull yourself together. (*To the gathered company*) Right, you lot! Tea's on table, so get fell to and get stuck in.

WILL: The phrase, Bottom, is, 'Ladies and gentlemen, dinner is served.'

---

[*] This is also an image that Shakespeare would later use in *Othello*. And yet here Greene delivers it in the manner of an aside which by strict convention Shakespeare could not overhear. The repetition must therefore be an extraordinary coincidence.
[†] Shakespeare actually appears to have pinched half his play from this encounter.

'Tis some time later. The company are at dinner. Bottom stands ready to serve. Otello boasteth most mightily.

OTELLO: First did I vanquish one, then another, until all around were vanquished.

KIT MARLOWE: Well, there's a surprise.

KATE: Oh my goodness. So exciting.

ROBERT GREENE: (*Once more in the manner of an aside*) 'Tis clear the girl doth love the Moor and he loves her. Now must I make the Moor believe the crow doth also love her. Then will he be wild with murderous jealousy. (*Doth now enact his plan, approaching Otello with some wine*) But, General, dry must be your throat after such prolonged boasting— storytelling. A little wine perhaps?

Greene pours the wine but spills some on Kate's dress.

KATE: Oh!

ROBERT GREENE: Oh! Heaven forfend, I am a dunceling clumbletrousers. Lady, I would fain lend you my kerchief, but do fear 'tis fully snotted. Sirrah, could you?

OTELLO: Gladly. The first gift I give thee. Would it were all the world.

KATE: It means the world to me, my lord.

BOTTOM: Get a flippin' chamber.

Greene doth take Shakespeare aside for the furtherance of his plotting.

ROBERT GREENE: Shakespeare, I am distraught. I just caused the great general to lose his embroidered bogey wipe. Promise me you will borrow said bogey wipe from the duchess and have another stitched in its likeness that I may gift that to the Moor?[*]

---

[*] Here we can clearly see the genesis of the whole plot of *Othello* with all its coincidences and misunderstandings. Audiences have long been exasperated with the Bard's ridiculous plots, regularly spluttering, 'But that just would never happen' into their gin and tonics at the interval. But the folios offer clear evidence that it not only could, but did. The Bard is therefore vindicated.

WILL: What? Woah woah . . .

ROBERT GREENE: And, further will I speak, you wouldst fain have your father admitted to the Company of Heralds?

WILL: Yes, absolutely. I was hoping to bring that up.

ROBERT GREENE: Then this advice will I give thee. If such a personage as General Otello were to plead your case to me, why then I could scarcely refuse such an entreaty.

WILL: Really? But why would he plead my case? He doth not know me.

ROBERT GREENE: Yes, but he does seem to be getting to know your friend the duchess rather intimately.

Otello and Kate are indeed laughing together most coquettishly.

ROBERT GREENE: Well now, General, it has been most pleasant, but I see that one more fascinating than I doth have your attention. I will take my leave. Mr Marlowe and Mr Shakespeare, perhaps you could bring the general to mine own humble home, that I might return this favour? (*Once more taketh Will aside*) The bogey wipe, Mr Shakespeare, forget not the bogey wipe. Good day.

WILL'S STRATFORD HOME – DAY

Mary and John sit before the fire. The twins do play. Susanna hath read Anne a letter.

ANNE: He wants me to stitch him a nose wipe just like this one.

SUSANNA: Yes, says it's part of some plan to get Robert Greene to agree to making Granddad posh.

ANNE: Oh dear. Two identical hankies, which will no doubt cause wrong conclusions to be drawn. Sounds just like the sort of convoluted bolingbrokes your dad would get involved with.*

JOHN: You just stitch that snot rag and send it back, for I am to become a gentleman at last.

MARY: It'll take more than a coat of arms to turn you into a gentleman, John Shakespeare. You'll have to stop eating pickled onions in bed for a start.

ANNE: You're a dirty, disgustable, grotsome old man!

JOHN: People'll be proud enough to know me when I'm posh!

MARY: He puts those pickled onions under his arms to soften them up, you know. Imagine, being bothered in the marital bed by a man with pickled onions in his armpits.

JOHN: You love it!

MARY: I do not love it, John Shakespeare. Anne's right, you are a dirty, disgustable, grotsome old man.

JOHN: Yes, but a dirty, disgustable, grotsome old man who's gonna get his own coat of arms! Which will make me a dirty, disgustable, grotsome old gentleman by law!

John doth disport himself before the fire most contentedly.

---

* Anne Shakespeare was thought to be illiterate, but yet is quite an astute drama critic.

199

KATE'S BEDROOM - NIGHT

Kate alone in her chamber. Will poketh his head round the door.

WILL: Just off to Mr Greene's dinner party, Kate. I wanted to drop Otello's hanky back.

Will enters and returneth the original hanky.

KATE: Oh, no problem, Mr Shakespeare. I've had quite a few pressies since then. A bead necklace, a hollowed-out gourd, a potpourri of scented leaves and berries contained within the dried scroting sack of a defeated foe.* (*Doth sniff the dried scroting sack with relish*) Hotty's so romantic.

WILL: Hotty?

KATE: Oh yes, 'tis my pet familiar for him. I fashioned it out of the first syllable of his name and the fact that I find him extremely and totally hot!

WILL: Yes, I think I got that.

KATE: He calls me Sweet Tits, which no doubt be a reference to adorable baby birds.

WILL: Hm ... yes, and tell me, Kate, have you yet confessed to Prince Otello that you are not in fact the Duchess of Northington but a naughty imposter?

KATE: Oh, Mr Shakespeare, Hotty won't mind that. He loves me, and *amor vincit omnia.*

WILL: Er, yes, hang on, I know this.

KATE: Virgil – love conquers all.

---

* Potpourri were very popular in Elizabethan London and used to mask the general smell of poo. Although it is difficult to imagine that a few dried herbs disguised the scent of 200,000 people crapping at close quarters on a daily basis with literally no municipal plumbing whatsoever.

WILL: Love conquers all? Could have sworn that was one of mine. Virgil? Are you sure?

KATE: Quite sure. Nearly two thousand years ago.

WILL: Right, so definitely out of copyright. (*Noteth down quote in his Occasional Book*) And tell me, Kate, how do you see this relationship developing? Do you imagine yourself as the future Mrs Otello?

KATE: Oh, I don't know, Mr Shakespeare. He's admitted to me that he's polygamous and so if we married I would in fact be one of seventeen Mrs Otellos.

WILL: Goodness, Kate, could a proud Englishwoman ever accept such a demeaning situation?

KATE: Well, you see, Mr Shakespeare, if, as a proud Englishwoman, I marry a proud Englishman, he immediately takes all my property and has the right to maketh me his slave and beat me without fear of law.

WILL: As would the Moor.

KATE: Yes, but with Otello, I would only get one-seventeenth of his attention. Whereas in England I would have to put up with some brutal bastable all on my own. For an Elizabethan woman, marriage is a percentage game.

WILL: Right, yes. I see that.

KATE: Plus, think of the adventure. To be with such a man as the Moor. A warrior who has sailed afar and seen the anthropophagi and men whose heads do grow beneath their shoulders.

WILL: Yes, well, I, I must admit that does sound like pretty exciting stuff. There was one other thing. I wanted to ask a favour. As you know, I'm hoping to petition the College of Heralds to grant the Shakespeares a coat of arms. Robert Greene has let slip that were so great a man as General Otello to plead my cause, Greene might be better disposed to consider it. So I was wondering . . .*

---

* This very same idea ended up as yet another beat in the convoluted plot of Shakespeare's *Othello*.

KATE: Of course, Mr Shakespeare. I'll have a word with Hotty and I'll lay it on really thick. I'll say you're absolutely amazing and totally wonderful. Now, you have a lovely evening with Mr Greene. I'm going to bury myself in Sir Walter Raleigh's book and dream of Hotty taking me in all those exotic places.

WILL: *To*, Kate. You mean, taking you *to* all those exotic places.

KATE: I kind of think I know what I mean.

ROBERT GREENE'S HOUSE - NIGHT

A magnificent banquet lies upon the table in the dining room. Greene is entertaining Marlowe and Prince Otello when Will arriveth.

ROBERT GREENE: Ah, Mr Shakespeare. Welcome, welcome. (*Aside to Will*) Didst thou bring the bogey wipe?

WILL: Aye, my wife did make the copy.

Greene inspecteth the bogey wipe.

ROBERT GREENE: Mm, a perfect replica. Mrs Shakespeare has talent, for a farm girl. (*Steppeth apart to deliver an aside, which by strict convention none can overhear*) And with her needle has she stitched her husband's shroud. (*Turneth back to the company*) Now come! Let us quaff and gorge as befits four gentlemen. I'm sorry, as befits three gentlemen and Mr Shakespeare.

WILL: Although I will be one when I get my coat of arms. (*Speaketh to Greene in the manner of an aside, which by strict convention none can overhear*) For soon, as you advised, one far greater than I will plead my case.

ROBERT GREENE: (*Turneth aside to deliver an aside, which by strict convention none can overhear*) Oh joy, the noose tightens.

KIT MARLOWE: Come on, Greene, this tuck won't eat itself.

ROBERT GREENE: Please.

OTELLO: Such a feast, Mr Greene. Would I were like the men with six mouths whom first I saw upon the island of Bollockapus.

KIT MARLOWE: Yeah.

The company seat themselves to dine.

OTELLO: For then would I have five more gaping gobs in which to stuff the tuck.

ROBERT GREENE: Pepper, Mr Shakespeare?

WILL: Goodness, yes, please. What a treat.

Greene doth sprinkle much spice upon Will's plate.

WILL: Such spice would cost a fortune.

ROBERT GREENE: Take as much as you please.

Now doth Greene use the pepper spoon as if it were a shovel.

OTELLO: Why, in the country of Crapatonia there be so much pepper that the natives converse only in sneezes. And their eyes do water so, the plains are often flooded with tears.*

KIT MARLOWE: Crikey, Otello mate, you have seen some stuff and then some, but to settle a bet, what is an anthropophagi?

OTELLO: Just a guy from Anthropop.

KIT MARLOWE: It makes sense.

Will sneezes several times.

ROBERT GREENE: Mr Shakespeare, you do be sneezing like a citizen of Crapatonia. Here, use this. (*He cunningly doth give the imitation bogey wipe to Shakespeare, who takes it and begins to blow. Then doth speak in the manner of an aside, which by strict convention none can overhear*) The trap shuts.

While Will is all of a sneezing, Greene doth turn to Otello.

ROBERT GREENE: Tell me but this, General. Have you not sometimes seen a handkerchief spotted with strawberries in your love's hand?

OTELLO: I gave Kate such a one. 'Twas my first gift.

ROBERT GREENE: Oh. Oh dear. I fear then she gave it to another, for see yonder Shakespeare doth wipe his beard with it.

WILL: Achoo!

Will is working the bogey wipe most revoltingly, a-snotting and a-grollying into it. Using it for one nostril, then the other,

---

* Scholars now consider that Otello's conversation here is superior to the lines Shakespeare eventually gave to his fictitious Moor. Stupid, certainly, but at least comprehensible.

*and wiping about most vigorously. General Otello doth
snarl in fury.*

OTELLO: Oh, that the slave had forty thousand lives! One is too
poor, too weak for my revenge.*

ROBERT GREENE: Oh, beware, my lord, of jealousy. 'Tis the green-
eyed monster which doth mock the meat it feeds on.†

OTELLO: Well, perhaps you're right. Don't want to jump to
conclusions.

ROBERT GREENE: No . . . But I mean, it does look really dodgy.

Will doth positively drench the bogey wipe in snottage.

OTELLO: Yes, yes!

ROBERT GREENE: One more twist will do the deed. (*To Otello*)
Perchance the knave be innocent. Question Kate and if she
speaks soft words to you of Shakespeare, then will you know that
he hath stolen her heart and so must you kill him.

OTELLO: (*Leapeth to his feet*) Arise black vengeance from thy hollow
cell! Ah blood! Blood! Blood!‡ (*Departeth in fury*)

KIT MARLOWE: Blimey. It's a bit abrupt. And so angry. Fit to murder
someone.

WILL: And he's been deep in conversation with Greene.

Will stares at the bogey wipe and then at Greene's wicked smile.

WILL: Oh my God! I had thought to use the Moor against Greene,
but he has served me likewise.§

---

* Shakespeare did pinch this line.

† And this one, which is actually pretty good. Scholars continue to argue that
Shakespeare could not have heard this line delivered in the manner of an aside.

‡ Another one that would eventually be used in the play. Since the emergence of the
Crow Folios, scholars are beginning to wonder whether Shakespeare actually wrote
any of his stuff at all.

§ Shakespeare here appears to understand the complex plot in which he is
enmeshed, something which his future audiences rarely would.

KIT MARLOWE: It's like that new line you showed me, you know, the one where the fellow totally shafted his own person.

WILL: You mean, hoist by his own petard?

KIT MARLOWE: That's the one!

WILL: You're right, Kit. Like the narcissistic contortionist, I've buggered myself.*

---

* Again, it appears Shakespeare reserved his best lines for his private life.

WILL'S LONDON LODGINGS – NIGHT

Otello in fury attempts to storm Kate's chamber. Bottom holds him back.

BOTTOM: You can't go in there! It's not proper!

Kate enters, serene and pure. A perfect chaste virgin.

OTELLO: Talk to me of Will Shakespeare!

KATE: And *bonsoir* to you too, Hotty!* (*Turneth from Otello*) It's fine, Bottom. I've been wanting to have a word with Prince Otello anyway.

OTELLO: Shakespeare, tell me now, what is he to you?

KATE: Ah well, since you ask, I think he's absolutely amazing and totally wonderful.†

Otello strikes a dramatic pose.

OTELLO: 'Tis the cause. 'Tis the cause, my soul. Let me not name it to you, you chaste stars. 'Tis the cause.

KATE: But since you're here, there was something I wanted to talk to you about.

Otello takes up a pillow and advanceth upon Kate, who is pure, chaste, gorgeous and defenceless.

OTELLO: Yet I'll not shed her blood, nor scar that whiter skin of hers than snow and smooth as monumental alabaster.

Otello seems about to suffocate Kate when Will and Marlowe burst into the room.

WILL: General, stop! She didn't give me your bogey wipe. Greene tricked me into making a copy. 'Twas that which I did snot and

---

* 'Bonsoir' was sixteenth-century French for 'good evening'. It is also twenty-first-century French for 'good evening'.

† For those who have forgotten the plot, this is what Will asked Kate to say if ever Otello enquired about him. A similar plot beat confused and irritated audiences to Shakespeare's *Othello*.

207

grolly! And if by any chance Kate's been banging on about how absolutely amazing and totally wonderful I am, it's because I asked her to, at Greene's suggestion! Kate is pure! 'Tis Greene who plots against you!*

OTELLO: Perdition catch my soul.

KIT MARLOWE: Were you really about to smother her? Because if so – not cool!

OTELLO: What? (*Still holding the pillow*) No, of course not! I'm just upset. I always hug a pillow when I'm upset. (*Casteth the pillow aside†*) But I'm upset no longer! Kate doth love me.

The maid doth now politely assert herself.

KATE: Hm, you see it was that that I wanted to talk to you about actually, Hotty. You see, I've been thinking about all those exciting stories you told me. The ones that won my heart. All that stuff about the anthropophagi and men whose heads do grow beneath their shoulders.

OTELLO: My alarums and adventures.

KATE: Mm. And it turns out it's all taken pretty much verbatim from Sir Walter Raleigh's new book.‡ I don't think you are an exotic prince, Hotty. In fact, you're probably not from anywhere very interesting at all.

KIT MARLOWE: Yes ... where do you come from?

OTELLO: Bristol.

---

* Scholars have discussed how Shakespeare's plays could be improved if someone were to burst in at the end to recap the plot.
† In *Othello*, the Moor suffocates the innocent maid with the pillow (which scholars have generally agreed makes for a better ending than this).
‡ This is true. Raleigh was an amazing sailor, navigator and adventurer. However, he was also a complete bullshitter.

WILL'S STRATFORD HOME - NIGHT

Will and his goodly wife do sit before the fire.

WILL: Turned out Otello was born in England.* He makes his living conning people that he's an African prince. Thinking Kate a duchess, he'd hoped to steal her cash. I'm as far away from getting my Shakespeare coat of arms as ever.

ANNE: Amazing story, though. You should use it in a play.

WILL: What? Dad trying to be posh? Hm, might work, I suppose.

ANNE: No! No, the noble Moor, corrupted into false jealousy by an evil snake. And suffocating his true love in her bed. You could get that Hotty to star in it. He certainly convinced you in the role.

WILL: And actually I took down a few of his lines. I . . . I mean, my lines. But a black actor in a leading role? I think that's a few centuries off. A strong supporting character perhaps. An irascible chief of the watch or a wise old judge. Possibly the villain or the hero's best mate, but the lead? Not gonna hold my breath.†

---

* Many black people were born in the port towns of England during this period. Although not quite as many as are implied in the background shots and crowd scenes in BBC costume dramas.

† Shakespeare was right. It would take many centuries before black actors played leading roles in England, and then mainly those called Idris Elba.

EPISODE 2

I KNOW THEE NOT, OLD MAN

In this manuscript exists the genesis of Shakespeare's
most celebrated comic character, the immortal
Falstaff. The general literary consensus is that
Falstaff – unlike many of Shakespeare's characters –
is actually quite funny as long as he's played by an
actor who isn't trying to be funny. Unfortunately, he
usually is.

MISS LUCY'S TAVERN - NIGHT

Will and Marlowe are present, as are the players. Miss Lucy, the tavern keeper, is being held by armed guards as the odious Robert Greene harangues her.

ROBERT GREENE: Heretic, papist! Your accounts list a hundred candles, Mistress Lucy, no doubt for use in a treasonous Catholic Mass.

LUCY: I run a pub, Mr Greene. People like to see what they are drinking.*

ROBERT GREENE: Hmm, very well, release her.

Lucy is released and is not happy.

ROBERT GREENE: But as an agent of Her Majesty, I cannot be too careful. The reformed church must be defended at all cost.

LUCY: Personally, I was born into the Odinani faith. However, I'm thinking of converting to the Maasai religion, which is very beautiful and believes that in the beginning the sky and the earth were one, but the people had no cattle so God sent them many cows down a bark rope. Then the Dorobo tribe were jealous so they cut the rope, ha, and heaven and earth were separated for ever.

ROBERT GREENE: An ignorant heathen myth. One day all the peoples of Africa will be brought to knowledge of the true faith.

LUCY: This being the faith that says God sent his son from heaven via a miraculously inseminated virgin, which is so much more logical than a string of flying cows.

KIT MARLOWE: Oh, do give it a rest, Greene. Just because you've managed to oil your way into a Walsingham spy team along with

---

* During the worst anti-Catholic excesses of Elizabeth I's reign, people were held in suspicion over the use of candles. This meant that those staying up late to finish reading a book risked being burned at the stake.

us hard guys doesn't mean there's a Catholic terrorist at every table.

Greene pointeth in fury at Will and Marlowe's table.

ROBERT GREENE: Wafers and wine, wafers and wine, Mr Marlowe! Why, you and this cohort of unrepentant heretics be celebrating Catholic communion. You will burn for it!

Greene's henchmen threaten Will and Marlowe with their spears.

WILL: Wafers and wine and cheese, Mr Greene. It's not the eucharist, it's a ploughman's lunch.[*]

KIT MARLOWE: I do hope you're not gonna be such an utter arsemongle on the Warwickshire mission, Greene, otherwise it will get very boring.

ROBERT GREENE: I shall do my duty, Mr Marlowe. The Queen's life is ever threatened and none be above suspicion. (*Threateningly*) None.

The odious Greene departeth.

WILL: Warwickshire mission, Kit? My neck of the woods?

KIT MARLOWE: Yeah. Another Jesuit snuck across the Channel from the English College at Douai, the Pope's private spy factory.[†] We've traced the swine to the Midlands. Right, better go and get the sword sharpened.

WILL: Love you loads.

Marlowe departeth.

BURBAGE: Jesuit spies, papist assassins – these are dangerous times, Will, and indeed none be above suspicion. Essex is already frozen out.

---

[*] Up until the discovery of the Crow Folios, the first record of the term 'ploughman's lunch' was in 1837 in Lockhart's *Memoirs of the Life of Sir Walter Scott*.
[†] The English College in the French town of Douai was indeed a training ground for Catholic martyrs, some of whom were infiltrated into England in plots to kill the Queen. Proving once again that one person's martyr is another's radicalized terrorist.

CONDELL: Sussex is under a dark cloud.

BURBAGE: Norfolk awaits a storm.

KEMPE: Mind you, I've heard Cornwall's lovely this time of year. Joking, maybe, riffing, rolling with it, finding, oh, the funny.

WILL: Or in this case, finding the not funny.

KEMPE: Or taking the not funny and pushing it to that special place, beyond the funny.

WILL: Thereby cunningly bypassing the actual funny altogether.

KEMPE: Yeah.

BURBAGE: Everyone's loyalty be questioned. Even we poor players are under constant scrutiny. Our productions must be faultlessly patriotic, a farrago of mendacious propaganda.

CONDELL: Like your *Richard the Third*, Will, whom you did depict as a brutal psychopath.

WILL: Well, he was a bit of a psychopath. Murdered his own nephews in the tower – definitely not cool.

BURBAGE: Yes, but in your play you had the hunchback king murder his own brother, which was a lie.

WILL: I prefer the phrase 'alternative fact'.[*]

CONDELL: You also had Richard murder his brother's wife.

BURBAGE: Yes, and his wife's former husband. And Henry the Sixth and Henry the Sixth's son Edward, neither of which he actually did.

CONDELL: And he wasn't a hunchback.

KEMPE: Just a bit of scoliosis.

---

[*] Many scholars over the years have marvelled at how Shakespeare's works speak to each new generation with equal force, that his political and philosophical vision can illuminate any age. Here, for instance, Shakespeare satirizes Trump adviser Kellyanne Conway almost four hundred years before she was born.

WILL: But the Queen loved it. Thus lies become truth. Perhaps in some future age despotic megalomaniacs will not secure power through lies, false news and the rewriting of history. But for now, the bigger the porkies you tell, the greater the power you wield. Gentlemen, I feel another Henry coming on.

All do groan most wearily at the prospect of another play from Shakespeare about a Henry.

WILL'S LONDON LODGINGS - DAY

Will be at his papers. Kate doth berate him most vexedly.

KATE: Henry the Eighth? You're going to sanitize the reputation of the meanest, cruellest monarch that ever lived?

WILL: Yes, I am. I'll play it as light romantic comedy with plenty of sauce. When Harry met Cathy. And Anne. Also Jane . . . another Anne and two more Cathys. One king, six queens, will he get his Hampton Court?

Bottom joins them.

KATE: Mr Shakespeare, Henry the Eighth was a monster. You should do Henry the Fifth – such a heroic figure.

WILL: Henry the Fifth was an utter bore and everyone knows it. A pious, humourless killjoy who attended three masses a day, forswore the company of women and marched round France killing people because apparently it was what God really, really wanted.[*]

BOTTOM: It's funny how the more religious a person is, the more murderous they seem to get.

WILL: Hmm, a brutal lesson which I learnt at school, Bottom, where the master regularly asked God for strength as he flayed the flesh from my botty buttocks. He was quite simply the most terrifying child-care professional since King Herod opened the Bethlehem crèche. His name was Simon Hunt, so you can imagine what we called him.[†]

BOTTOM: Open goal.

---

[*] This is true. Most English kings of the period thought killing Frenchmen was a sacred duty but Henry V was a true zealot. This might be the reason he has remained so popular in England over the centuries.

[†] Clear historical evidence exists that a Simon Hunt taught at Stratford Grammar School during the time of Shakespeare's boyhood, but what the pupils thought rhymed with 'hunt' will forever remain a matter of conjecture.

WILL: Yeah.

KATE: Don't you think it's deeply revealing and rather depressing that when wishing to express angry contempt men use imagery relating to the female sexual anatomy?

WILL: Kate, the man's name was Simon Hunt, what would you have had us call him? If his name had been Berty Venus, we'd have called him Spurty—

To hide her blushes Kate doth speedily interrupt.

KATE: Yes! But it wouldn't have been as potent, would it?

WILL: I don't follow.

KATE: Well, think about it. In the lexicon of male abuse, is any cod-dangle word ever as powerful an expression of hatred as a term that hails from the tufted lady grotto?

BOTTOM: I have absolutely no idea what you're on about. But I bet you'd like to tell that old bastable Hunt what you think of him now, wouldn't you, master?

WILL: Yes, I would, Bottom. I'd slaughter him with one of my brilliant insults. How about that cracker from *Richard the Third*? 'Thou elvish-mark'd, abortive, rooting hog.'

BOTTOM: You got anything stronger?

WILL: Well, there's that one from my *Titus Andronicus*: 'Villain, I have done thy mother.'

BOTTOM: Oh, that'll hurt.

KATE: And once again we see that for a really powerful insult, men must need resort to sexually degrading images of women.

BOTTOM: I still don't know what you're talking about, Kate, but maybe we should look this Hunt up if we go to Stratters, see if he's still living.

WILL: He may still be living, but not in Stratford. He refused to recant the old religion and left England in 1575. I hardly think an avowed papist is likely to turn up with Liz on the throne. Not unless he's planning to assassinate her.[*]

The company departeth for Stratford.

---

[*] Evidence exists that schoolmaster Simon Hunt did leave England that year. It is thought that he left because of his Catholic convictions, although maybe he simply got sick of the joke.

WILL'S STRATFORD HOME – DAY

John and Mary sit before the fire. The twins do gambol about. Anne is at her women's tasks and Susanna's countenance be as ever most furious.

WILL: Darling, I'm home. And if you want to know why I wasn't home yesterday, blame the Pope for turning every Catholic in Britain into a suspected terrorist. We were delayed half a day when some dung-brained arsemongle on my coach claimed another passenger looked 'a bit Italian' and he thought he'd heard him muttering Latin under his breath. Turned out the man was Welsh and that his suspected lethal weapon was a particularly knobbly leek.

ANNE: Still, lovely to have you home.

WILL: Yes, I'm returned to write my latest play. It is to be a history and Kate has come as my research assistant.

Kate doth enter, followed by Bottom, burdened with bags most cruelly.

BOTTOM: Morning, Mrs S, Mr S, Mrs S, Miss S. Where do you want the bags? I presume I'm in with the cow?

JOHN: Don't be so bloody cheeky – where would I sleep?

MARY: I do not find that funny, John Shakespeare.

JOHN: She does, she loves it.

MARY: I do not love it. I tolerate it because I feel sorry for you.

JOHN: Sorry for me? Why would you feel sorry for me? I'm a right roister doister.

MARY: You think you are but you're not. You've turned the whole town against you. Nobody will drink with him any more because of his lies and cheating and scrounging money. Oh, they used to find him amusing, with his saucy tales and drunken japes, but all be sick of it.

John pretendeth not to hear as Mary doth berate him most firmly.

MARY: They call him 'foul-stuff', John Foul-stuff. It's why he wants that coat of arms, thinks it'll make him friends again, but it won't.

ANNE: I expect you're all famished after your long journey? Well, there's a fine stew on the fire. Bottom, will you dish up?

BOTTOM: I suppose I'd better had do. Whoever it was who coined the phrase 'a change is as good as a rest' obviously wasn't a servant.

WILL: That was me, wasn't it? Yes, I think that's definitely one of mine.

BOTTOM: So when my gran used to say that to me when I was a tiny, tiny lad, she was quoting you then, was she?

ANNE: You really have got to stop taking well-known sayings and claiming you wrote them, Will. You're better than that, you know you are.[*]

Moments pass and all do now attend the table.

JOHN: So what's this new historical crap you're writing then, Will?

---

[*] History has proved that Shakespeare wasn't actually better than that.

220

WILL: I'm going for the biggie, Dad. Henry the Eighth.

ANNE: Henry the Eighth? I can't imagine anyone wanting to watch dramas about him or any of the Tudors.[*]

MARY: That devil destroyed the one true faith.

WILL: Mum, we do not call Catholicism the one true faith. It was the one true faith under the last queen. Under the current crazed harridan it is satanic heresy. Do try and keep up.

KATE: I don't think Mr Shakespeare should cover Henry the Eighth either, Mrs Shakespeare. The man's life was one long catalogue of religious hypocrisy, domestic violence and murders of convenience.[†]

JOHN: Sounds like my kind of play.

WILL: I'm sure he had a good side, some redeeming features.

SUSANNA: Dad, he cut off two of his wives' heads.

WILL: I am aware, my sweet.

SUSANNA: He didn't just say, 'Oh, you don't really get me any more, we need to give each other space.' He cut off their heads.

WILL: Well, sometimes with relationships it's better to make a clean break. Now, now, come on, everyone, we're looking for King Harry's positive points.

MARY: Well, he made Wales and England into one kingdom.

WILL: Hmm, I think I'll leave that out. Not making any friends on either side there.

KATE: Although of course the union did make sound economic sense, promoting growth by breaking down trade barriers and allowing for free movements of goods, services and labour.

---

[*] Current law dictates that at least one Tudor movie and one epic Tudor TV series must be made each year.

[†] Henry VIII had sores and ulcers on his rotting left leg. None the less he pulled six wives and countless mistresses. It might have had something to do with him being a king.

WILL: Hmm, yes, Kate, but if there's one thing we know about the British, be we Welsh, Scottish or, pardon me for living, English, it's that when it comes to a choice between sound economic sense and bloody-minded petty nationalism, then the world can get stufflington because we want our countries back, no matter how small, cold, wet or utterly impoverished they may be. Anything else?

ANNE: He wrote 'Greensleeves'.

WILL: He did not write 'Greensleeves'. That is a common misconception which no doubt will be corrected with time.*

KATE: He was a great scholar, for all his boorish, violent ways. He wrote *Assertio Septem Sacramentorum*, a staunch defence of Catholicism, for which Pope Leo the Tenth gave him the title 'Defender of the Faith'.†

WILL: Hmm, this would be the faith that a week later he started burning people for believing in.

MARY: The one true one.

WILL: No, Mum, satanic heresy! You've gotta try and get your head around that. (*To Kate*) Anything else?

KATE: Well, plenty, but none of it very nice. He passed the Succession Law, which declared his own daughters illegitimate.

WILL: Yes, not a good look. One thing *calling* your kids a couple of little bastables, we all do that, but it's another to make it an act of parliament. This is gonna be tougher than I thought.

KATE: I'm telling you, Mr Shakespeare, do Henry the Fifth, the hero of Agincourt.

WILL: I'm telling you, Kate, he was a self-righteous bore. If I wrote a play about him, I'd have to come up with some other, really memorable character to draw focus, some gross and bawdy but

---

* Except people still think Henry the Bonk wrote 'Greensleeves'.

† Henry VIII certainly wasn't thick, he just worked out early in life that writing learned religious texts in Latin just wasn't as much fun as gorging, quaffing and shagging.

ultimately pathetic figure who could lead Prince Hal astray, thus mitigating his piety and creating a good dynamic for when Hal becomes king and must renounce his gadsome ways.

KATE: Well, that sounds promising.

WILL: Yes, but what form would this character take? Who could I base it on?

JOHN: Here, Bottom, look at my parsnip. It's like a giant cod-dangle with a couple of hairy bolingbrokes – brilliant.

John doth hold up a parsnip that bears a remote resemblance to the outline of a cock and balls. All are most embarrassed at John's boorish attempt at wit.

BOTTOM: Yeah.

There be a knock at the door.

ANNE: Who can that be at this hour? (*Goes to the window and peereth out*) Oh my goodness, I don't believe it! It's the old town schoolmaster.

Will jumpeth up, all of a doodah.

WILL: Simon Hunt? Here? At our door?

ANNE: Yes.

BOTTOM: What a bit of luck! Here's your chance to call him an abortive rooting hog and say you've done his mum, like you said you would.

Will be covered in fear and jitters like a quaking palsy.

WILL: Is my collar clean? My shoes, my fingernails? Oh my God, I must scrub my fingernails!

Simon Hunt, a most stern old bastable, doth enter with angry countenance.

HUNT: Ah, Shakespeare. Is it you? Turn around and bend over.

To the astonishment of all, Will doth turn around and present his botty buttocks to the old man.

223

HUNT: Yes, that's you.

WILL: Er, yes, er, please, sir, it's me, sir, but may I ask, sir, what, what brings you here, sir?

HUNT: I have come for a visit.

WILL: Er, a visit? You, you want to stay?

Hunt, filled with angry pride, doth sit at the table all uninvited. Anne taketh Will aside.

ANNE: Will, this be Hunt. Many stories have you told me about his cruelty. Send him packing.

WILL: Yes, absolutely. I will. I'll, I'll tell him to get out of my house right now.

Will does nothing. Instead he quaketh like a quivering poltroon.

UPSTAIRS – NIGHT

Will and Anne are in John and Mary's chamber. All four are in one bed and most cramped.

ANNE: I can't believe you gave him our bed.

WILL: Oh, I know, but I'm emotionally scarred. I can't stand up to him. The wounds run too deep. I'm sure he'll leave soon, and he hasn't been any trouble so far.

The sound of Latin being chanted downstairs can be heard.

ANNE: What's that?

MARY: What's that? Why, 'tis a sound that's ne'er been heard in England since the glory days of good Queen Mary.

WILL: Oh my God.

Will doth jumpeth out of bed. All do follow.

DOWNSTAIRS – NIGHT

All the household, awoken by the sound of Latin, have gathered on the stairs.
Here they stand in shock as Simon Hunt conducts a service at the kitchen table.

WILL: He's celebrating Mass.

Mary, as if in a trance, doth approach Hunt and kneel before him.

JOHN: Oh God, she's off. Once a bleeding Catholic . . .

WILL: She's eating the wafer! They burn you for eating a wafer.*

JOHN: She'll be insisting on having marital conjugation through a
hole in the sheet again before you know it, like on our wedding
night. I was so arsemongled I couldn't find the hole. Ended up
rogering the pocket in my puffling pants.

ANNE: If we're discovered—

KATE: We will be burned alive.

JOHN: Not me. It's your house, son, he's your old teacher.

WILL: And that's your wife on her knees drinking a nice fruity red
with shades of walnut and vanilla and oh just a hint of Christ's
blood on the back of the palate.†

ANNE: You've gotta stand up to him. You have gotta get rid of him.

WILL: Obviously I have, or else live a coward in thine own esteem,
letting 'I dare not' wait upon 'I would', like the poor cat in the adage.‡

---

* Taking Catholic communion was indeed dealt with most harshly throughout
Elizabeth's reign. However, the traditional services were incredibly long and
incredibly dull and conducted in a language that only the priest spoke, so some found
being dragged off and burned a bit of a relief.
† This is the first recorded gag about wine snobbery in English literature.
‡ This is a sentence that Shakespeare would later use in *Macbeth*. Some people quote
it to this day, although evidence suggests that they tend to think 'the adage' the
cat is stuck in is some sort of room or box. In fact, an 'adage' is a proverb or saying.
Shakespeare is quoting from a now lost adage about a hesitant cat. Little wonder that
it's lost because it sounds like a very boring adage indeed.

ANNE: Will, there is no time for obscure blank verse.

WILL: How can you say that? There is always time for obscure blank verse or my whole life is a lie.

ANNE: Well, are you gonna chuck him out?

WILL: Yes, absolutely. In the morning.

DOWNSTAIRS – DAY

'Tis morning and Mary be bathing Hunt's feet before the fire in the kitchen. John, Anne and Will be also present. Will approacheth his old schoolmaster.

WILL: Um, sir, excuse me, sir, I was just wondering how long—

HUNT: Not now, Shakespeare. This poor and simple woman is washing my feet. It is a deep and symbolic communion between shepherd and flock.

MARY: I'm in a state of grace.

JOHN: You're in some sort of bloody state, that's for sure.

WILL: Sir, tiny point, sir, from, from my small store of liturgical knowledge, sir, er, I had thought it was the priest who washed the feet of the poor and simple, not, not the other way round.

HUNT: Don't cross theological swords with me, boy! I've spent the last fifteen years in study at the English College at Douai.

WILL: Of course, sir, absolutely, sir. I'm, I'm sorry. Did you say the English College at Douai?

HUNT: Concentrate, boy. I'm not accustomed to repeating myself.

WILL: Excuse me just one moment, sir. (*Approacheth Anne in great fear*) Wife, kindly prepare my reserve puffling trousers, for I fear my quakesome bowlingtons be ripe ready to barf forth a fulsome tempest of foul and steaming scaredy sludge.[*]

ANNE: What ails thee, husband?

WILL: He's the spy.

ANNE: What spy?

---

[*] Whether Shakespeare was employing poetic licence or he really was about to crap himself will for ever be a mystery.

WILL: Marlowe told me there's a Jesuit terrorist in Warwickshire. It's Simon Hunt, my old schoolteacher.*

HUNT: Yes, Shakespeare, and you have given me shelter. Your mother has taken my communion. If I burn, boy, you'll burn. I suggest you take pains to ensure my safety. I shall return this e'en.

Hunt departeth.

WILL: Lock the doors! Bar the windows! None must enter. None must ever know he's staying here.

As Anne begins to bar the windows, Marlowe entereth all cheery and merry.

KIT MARLOWE: Knock knock! Anyone home?

WILL: Kit! Oh my God!

KIT MARLOWE: What? Aren't you pleased to see me?

WILL: Yes, why wouldn't I be? What are you trying to say? It's not like we've got a terrorist staying or anything.

Greene doth also enter.

ROBERT GREENE: Ah! Shakespeare!

WILL: Ah!

ROBERT GREENE: We are come to Warwickshire as promised, ever intent upon our noble purpose – hunting Jesuits.

WILL: Well, there aren't any here. A Jesuit? In our house? Giving Mass to my mum? As if.

KIT MARLOWE: Anyway, Will, I thought you could put me up while I'm hunting the swine.

WILL: You, you want to stay?

KIT MARLOWE: Well, we get expenses but I'd rather keep them if that's all right.

---

* Shakespeare clearly forgets to talk in the manner of an aside and Hunt then overhears him.

229

ROBERT GREENE: Fear not, Mr Shakespeare. I will not be soliciting lodging in your humble cottage. I shall stay at Sir Thomas Livesey's, who will also provide constables for when we arrest the terrorist – and *all who harbour him*. Good day.

Greene departeth full of furious intent.

KIT MARLOWE: Don't mind me, Will. I know you're here for some peace and quiet to write your new play, so just show me my room, send up some ale and pie, forget I'm even here.

Marlowe sitteth on his pistol, which, much to Will's alarm, he now doth take out and inspect. Marlowe putteth his feet up in contented comfort.

WILL: Wife, those spare puffling pants, any time you're ready.*

---

* It would appear that perhaps Will did indeed foul his puffling pants.

DOWNSTAIRS - NIGHT

Will sits at his paper in the kitchen. Anne returneth.

ANNE: Well, I've got Moll next door to take Sue, Kate and the twins, so that's them safe, your mum's in Sue's room, and Marlowe's lazing upstairs and we just need to find a way to keep him there.

Marlowe descendeth the stair. He doth take Will aside for a conspiratorial aside of a ladsome nature.

KIT MARLOWE: Will, I stopped by the tavern earlier and asked them to send me round a naughty country lass for some company this evening. I hope Mrs S won't object.

WILL: Object? She'll be thrilled. Wife! Great news! Kit sent out for a prostitute.

Marlowe be a little surprised that Anne be happy to have her house used so but is content to return to his room.

WILL: Fortune favours us. With luck she'll keep him in his room till we can get rid of Hunt.

Now Hunt doth enter, hungry from his day of travels.

HUNT: Supper, if you please, Shakespeare.

WILL: Sir, an agent of the crown has lodged himself in this house. You must leave at once.

HUNT: Never. The road is dangerous and the night is wild. I shall leave early on the morrow but fear not, till then will I keep to my room and be absolutely silent and discreet.

WILL: Yes, yes, you must.

HUNT: Apart of course from celebrating midnight Mass later.

WILL: What?

HUNT: Send supper to my room.

Hunt ascendeth the stairs. There is a knock at the door. A woman stands without.

GERTRUDE: I'm Gertrude, a very sinful woman, and I'm come under cover of darkness to visit a gentleman in this house.

WILL: Good, excellent.

Will invites the woman in.

WILL: I must say the Stratter's tarting slaps have smartened up. Um, Bottom, take this young lady up to Mr Marlowe.

BOTTOM: No sooner said than done.

WILL: Now, that is one of mine, isn't it?

BOTTOM: You can't claim to be inventing the entire English language.

WILL: Can't I, Botsky? Watch this space.* Now take Miss Gertrude to Mr Marlowe. Let's hope she can keep Kit busy all night and the two of them make enough of a row to cover a midnight Mass.

Hunt returneth.

HUNT: Oh, by the way, Shakespeare, this e'en a certain member of the local gentry will be visiting to take communion.

WILL: What?

HUNT: The lady Gertrude is expected tonight.

WILL: What!!!

HUNT: Send her up when she arrives, I'll hear her confession in my room.

There is a knock and Gerty appears at the door.

GERTY: I'm Gerty, a very sinful woman, and I'm come under cover of darkness to visit a gentleman in this house.

HUNT: Ah, Lady Gertrude, I've been expecting you. Come to my chamber and we shall have a divine service.

---

* Shakespeare never claimed to have invented the English language but numerous over-excited English literature teachers have done it for him.

GERTY: Oh, that's what I'm here for, kind sir.

Will doth protest in horror.

WILL: No!

HUNT: You object, boy?

WILL: Wrong Gertrude.

To Hunt's great surprise Will doth grab Gerty and usher her up the stairs.

UPSTAIRS - NIGHT

Marlowe disports himself upon the bed in Will and Anne's chamber. Gertrude stands before him.

GERTRUDE: First I would speak with you of my deepest and most shameful thoughts.

KIT MARLOWE: Oh, loving that, yeah. Bit of dirty talk does it for me. Fire away.

GERTRUDE: And if my sins be too great for forgiveness, then must I verily be flagellated.

KIT MARLOWE: Not normally my scene, but I don't mind experimenting a bit.

GERTRUDE: And finally must I be brought to a state of ecstatic grace.

KIT MARLOWE: You and me both. Right, let's get to it.

Marlowe be full ready to embrace Gertrude when Will bursteth in.

WILL: Kit, you've got the wrong tarting slap. (*Doth usher Gerty in*) This one's yours.

KIT MARLOWE: Well then, who's this?

WILL: Um, mine, um, and Anne's. We're become swingletons. You know what goes on in boring country towns. We're all at it. We park our hay carts in quiet cul-de-sacs and watch each other.[*]

Will doth drag a surprised Gertrude from the room, leaving Marlowe with Gerty.

---

[*] The first reference in all literature to dogging, pre-dating the 1980s by many centuries.

DOWNSTAIRS – NIGHT

The evening progresses. In the kitchen, Will, Anne and Bottom listen. From above they hear creaking bedboards, but also Latin incantations.

BOTTOM: Looks like you got away with it, master. Kept 'em both busy.

WILL: Yes, but it was close. We nearly delivered a Catholic noblewoman to a government agent and a lowly tarting slap to a crazed, religious zealot.

Gertrude doth descend the stairs.

GERTRUDE: Well, I've turned some tricks in my time, but that ancient, doddering old arsemongle was the weirdest. He just wanted to serve me wafers and wine and talk Latin to me. Still, whatever turns them on. The price is still the same, a copper penny.

Will be most surprised. Gertrude holds out her hand for money. Will, stunned, takes a penny from the box and gives it to her. Gertrude departeth.

ANNE: Oh my goodly godlingtons. Gertrude was the tartling slap.

WILL: Which means Gerty was the noblewoman and we sent her to Marlowe.

Gerty descendeth the stairs, looking happy but most tousled.

GERTY: Well, I must say, that was the most divine service I've ever had. I feel I've been to heaven and back. The eucharist has certainly changed since I last had it ministered. In the old days you kept your clothes on and the priest only put a biscuit in your mouth. Now, money.

WILL: Money?

GERTY: For the offertorium. A good Catholic never forgets alms for the poor. Here is a copper penny.

Gerty drops a penny into the money box that Shakespeare is holding.

235

GERTY: Believe me, it was worth it. Priests were never like that before the Reformation.

Gerty departeth.*

BOTTOM: Just goes to show you shouldn't judge a book by its cover. Still, all's well that ends well.

WILL: Now those two are definitely mine.

BOTTOM: Stop it, master, really. It's embarrassing.

ANNE: And it hasn't ended well, Will.

WILL: I don't know, wife. We got our penny back.

ANNE: But we're still harbouring a heretic who'll be turning our kitchen table into an altar at midnight, and with Marlowe still upstairs.

WILL: We've gotta get Kit out of the house. But how? It's impossible.

BOTTOM: Just get your old man to take him down the pub.

WILL: As I was about to suggest. Dad! Get your coat!

JOHN: What's that, son?

WILL: Astonishingly, we need you. I mean, what were the odds?

---

* Since the discovery of the Crow Folios, scholars have speculated that had Will used this curious episode from his private life as inspiration for a play, he would have invented the bedroom farce.

DOWNSTAIRS - NIGHT

'Tis past midnight. In the kitchen Simon Hunt performs a Mass to Mary, whilst Will and Anne look nervously on.

WILL: How long does this thing go on? It's been three hours.

ANNE: Oh, your dad can't keep Marlowe drinking for ever. If he comes home and sees this, we'll burn. You've got to act now.

WILL: You're right, wife, this is really it, time to man up. For there is special providence in the fall of a sparrow. If it be now, 'tis not to come. If it be not to come, it will be now. If it be not now, yet it will come – the readiness is all.*

ANNE: When I said do something, I did not mean recite a soliloquy.

WILL: Right, yes. Fair point.

HUNT: God bless this woman.

MARY: I am a wicked sinner.

Finally Will doth find his courage.

WILL: No, Mum! He is the wicked sinner, er, and a disgrace to his God.

Mary gaspeth in horror. Hunt turneth in full fury.

HUNT: How dare you, boy! Show me some respect and call me sir!

WILL: I will not call you sir, sir, because you are a disgusting sadist, sir, who used his position of power and authority to abuse defenceless schoolboys, sir.

HUNT: Well, it didn't do you any harm, did it?

---

* Shakespeare uses this line later in his immortal *Hamlet*. Sadly it didn't make any more sense then. Sparrows? What's all that about?

WILL: No, apart from the deep emotional and physical scars, I'm absolutely fine!* Now get upstairs, keep quiet and at first light futtock off!

All stand amazed that Will hath finally grown a pair of bolingbrokes.

---

* Here, Shakespeare defines the concept of post-traumatic stress, for which psychologists of the 1970s often take credit.

DOWNSTAIRS – NIGHT

Marlowe and John return from the tavern full pisslingtoned. They do stagger about the kitchen and 'shh' each other.

KIT MARLOWE: Shh shh.

JOHN: I love you, Kit. You're my mate.

KIT MARLOWE: Oh, I love you.

JOHN: I wish you were my son, not Will. You've got bolingbrokes. He won't even stand up to his old schoolteacher.

KIT MARLOWE: Schoolteacher?

JOHN: Simon Hunt.

KIT MARLOWE: Oh.

JOHN: Priests, I 'ate 'em.

KIT MARLOWE: I have no idea what you are talking about.

DOWNSTAIRS - MORNING

Hunt standeth in the kitchen with his bag. Will doth urge him to the door.

WILL: Go now and don't come back. You'd have been caught last night if Walsingham's agent hadn't got himself drunk.

Marlowe appears on the stair.

KIT MARLOWE: Drunk, Will? It takes more than four or five gallons of sack to get this bad boy squiffy. I only stayed drinking with your boring, vain, nasty old dad because I guessed a sad-act town foul-stuff like him would have information, and he did.

Marlowe points his pistol at Hunt.

KIT MARLOWE: Simon Hunt, Jesuit, traitor, follower of the heretic Campion, I arrest you for treason.[*]

WILL: But, Kit, he's, he's found in my house. You condemn not just Hunt but me. I shall surely burn for harbouring a traitor.

Greene bursteth into the house, followed by guards.

ROBERT GREENE: Oh, how sweet it is. To capture a heretic is one thing, but to snare the crow is a thing sublime. You'll burn for certain, sirrah.

KIT MARLOWE: Now hang on just one minute, Greene. Will? Burn? He's a hero. 'Twas he that entrapped the traitorous Hunt, luring him here under the excuse of their days together at Stratford School and summoning me and keeping him close till I arrived.

ROBERT GREENE: You mentioned none of this before.

KIT MARLOWE: What? Trust deep intel to a Johnny-come-lately like you? You've only been a spy a week and the best you've done is harass Miss Lucy for serving cheese and biscuits.

---

[*] Campion was a saintly Catholic martyr, or a heretic terrorist, or an absolute nutter, depending on your point of view. He was eventually hung, cut down while still alive, his dick and balls were then cut off and his entrails removed and burned before his still conscious eyes. His head was then cut off and his body quartered. They did not futtock around in those days.

HUNT: Shakespeare boy, did you betray me?

WILL: Well, er—

ANNE: Yes, yes, he did betray you.

HUNT: Then am I grateful.

WILL: Grateful?

HUNT: For now I can embrace the martyr's death. As a Christian, I can think of nothing more glorious than to be tortured and killed by other Christians over minor details in the church service.

ROBERT GREENE: Take him away!

The guards take Hunt away. John doth descend the stairs.

JOHN: What's all this noise? Have I missed something? You're not off, are you, Kit? I thought we could have another night out roistering.

Marlowe's attitude be no longer laddish and matey. His countenance be stern and noble.

KIT MARLOWE: Roistering? With you? You bothered the barmaids, you never bought a round, you tried to filch some poor fella's purse, and you told the same dreadful joke about a poultry farmer's disappointing cock fifteen times.

John be most downcast.

KIT MARLOWE: Never, ever again.

JOHN: I thought we were mates.

KIT MARLOWE: I know thee not, old man. Fall to thy prayers. How ill white hairs become a fool and jester.[*]

Marlowe retreateth, leaving John a saddened man.

MARY: I told you, John. People find you out. At first they think you're good company but in the end they realize you're just a greedy, revolting old man.

---

[*] Shakespeare uses these words in *Henry IV Part 2*. Ironically, it seems he actually stole them from Marlowe.

Will be struck by inspiration.

WILL: Oh my goodly godlingtons. That's it.

ANNE: What's it, duck?

WILL: The comic character for my Henry. It's Dad. It's been Dad all along. The amusing yet ultimately pathetic figure who forms a counterpoint to Prince Hal's heroic destiny. It's you, Dad. It's John Foul-stuff.*

---

* Here, finally revealed, is the inspiration for John Falstaff, Shakespeare's most famous comic character and a huge favourite of Queen Elizabeth, who even demanded he be resurrected for a spin-off (*The Merry Wives of Windsor*). It was Shakespeare's deeply dodgy dad.

DOWNSTAIRS – NIGHT

Anne and Will sit before the fire with their pipes.

WILL: Well, I won't write Henry the Fifth just yet, or Henry the Eighth for that matter. I'm not in the mood to celebrate religious zealotry just now, since it be but an excuse for intolerance and murder.

ANNE: I know, it's so weird, and for the same God too.

WILL: Why can't we be like the Muslims? They have their Shiites and their Sunnis as we have our Protestants and Catholics but unlike us they don't seem to feel the need to start a holy war over it.[*]

ANNE: You wait, someone will stir them up in the end. Anyway, the trip's not been a total failure. You've come up with a brilliant new comic character and I think one of these days John Foul-stuff will be a very big hit.[†]

John Shakespeare sitteth nearby upon the privy pot.

JOHN: That's right. I'm a bleeding inspiration and don't you forget it.

John Shakespeare doth grimace most gurningly, summoning up the effort to eject a stool.

---

[*] The propensity for wanting to murder people who believe in the same God as you do but with minor differences in worship seems, in fact, to be common to all religions.

[†] As previously noted, Shakespeare's boastful, boozy charlatan John Falstaff was indeed a huge hit in both parts of *Henry IV* and, unlike pretty much all of Shakespeare's other comic characters, remains quite funny to this day.

I DID ADORE A TWINKLING STAR

Scholars have discussed whether Shakespeare ever
travelled abroad. There is no evidence that he did,
and the fact that he makes two geographical errors
in thirty-seven plays has been used as evidence
that he didn't. Which is, of course, just potty.
How many people boarding the next EasyJet to
Megashag know where they're actually going, let
alone anything about the world in general? Anyway,
that aside, this episode establishes beyond doubt
that he did travel at least to Italy and, like many
travellers since, his bags were lost.

WILL'S LONDON LODGINGS – DAY

Kate darns and Bottom polishes. Marlowe practises fencing. Will enters, his face aglow with happiness.

WILL: Bring ale, bring pie. Let all be merry for at last our theatre has acquired a patron.

BOTTOM: What's that mean then, master?

WILL: Well, Bottom, it means that this is England and therefore no matter how creative, industrious or successful a workforce may be, they will still require a talentless, over-entitled, freeloading posh boy to give them social and legal status. Fortunately for us, the Lord Chamberlain doth love the drama and so we have become his men.[*]

KIT MARLOWE: Ah, a powerful friend indeed, Will.

WILL: One who must be flattered and indulged. His secretary, the odious Robert Greene, who doth hate my gutlings, tells me his lordship demands a bloody and vengeful history. Luckily, I am very good at those.[†]

KIT MARLOWE: Ah, well then, it's top news all around, mate. Got a pretty nifty new gig myself. Walsingham is sending me to Verona on a spy mission. Yeah. Fine wine, fabulous food, top Italian totty.

KATE: I presume you'll also be expected to do a bit of actual work.

KIT MARLOWE: No, not really. Job's a doddling skive. Just got to contact some contessa who's a Protestant and wants to spy for us.

---

[*] The term 'patronizing' derives from 'patron'. There can be no doubt that in sixteenth-century England the rich and powerful exploited the talents and industry of others while purporting to be on their side. Thank goodness that doesn't happen any more.

[†] While Shakespeare was uncannily astute when it came to the inner workings of other people's minds, he had little understanding of himself. Will was, in fact, not always as good at histories as he claims. As anyone who has slumbered through *King John* or *Henry VIII* will attest.

Seems she has a list of the Pope's assassins she wants to give us. Only bother is I'm supposed to learn some Italian.

KATE: (*Demeanour most surly and grumpish*) Goodness, having to make some small effort. How awful for you.

KIT MARLOWE: Beshrew me, Will. Methinks me bolingbrokes be being busted.

WILL: Forgive her, Kit. Kate doth ever chafe at the lack of opportunities afforded to women. Suffering as she does with the curious illusion that talent and brains in some way mitigate the absence of a cod-dangle.* Learning Italian, you say?

KIT MARLOWE: Hmm. Walsingham's orders. Do you know, I think he's worked out that I don't take being a spy as seriously as he'd like.

KATE: You can see how he got to be head of the intelligence service.

KIT MARLOWE: I'm sorry, is there a problem?

WILL: Yes, Kate. You are being a teeny bit of a pain in that which though it be sat on, be not a chair. Though it doth trumpet loud, be not a military fanfare. And though it be divided in two with a crack in the middle, be not a frozen lake on which stands a nervous skater who has overestimated the strength of the ice.

BOTTOM: He means arsingmongle.

KATE: Yes, Bottom. Got that. And, like most men, he seems to be talking out of it.

KIT MARLOWE: What is your problem, Kate?

KATE: You, for a start. You live only for pleasure. You gorge, you quaff, you treat women as playthings.

KIT MARLOWE: Yes. And what is your problem?

---

* Before the twentieth century, men of almost all societies, cultures, religions and ethnicities believed that whatever qualities a woman might have, possessing a cod-dangle made every man on earth her superior. A brief browse of the internet shows that this belief is dying only very slowly.

WILL: Come along now, you two. Let's not fight. Look, here's an idea, Kit. I'm off to Stratters to write my new play. While I'm away, why doesn't Kate teach you Italian? For then, you will have your lessons and she some occupation for her very large but frustratingly female brain.

KIT MARLOWE: Do you speak Italian, Kate?

KATE: *Naturalmente che parlo italiano, grande idiota.*

KIT MARLOWE: Oh right, that was Italian, was it?

WILL'S STRATFORD HOME – DAY

All the family are present. Will doth enter, muddied from his journey.

WILL: Father is returned.

JUDITH: Did you get us sugar sticks?

WILL: Yes, I got you sugar sticks. The way children eat sugar these days, by the time they are twenty, you'll scarcely be able to count their ribs.

ANNE: Bad journey was it, love?

WILL: Just a touch, my sweet. There be a dispute twixt coaching management and staff. One side claimeth that a single worker is all that is required to shout 'Giddy up' and poke the horse's arseington with a stick whilst also ensuring that there be sufficient turding straw laid about the carriage, while t'other side insists that two men must needs do the job for the comfort and safety of all. A situation which produces in mine little heart a tortuous duality of emotion. Naturally, of course, I support those who withdraw their labour in order to protect their jobs and maintain standards. And yet I canst not help sort of wishing they burn in hell till the end of time.*

SUSANNA: That's right. Because it's all about you, isn't it? None of us ever have any problems. I hate you. Shut up!

WILL: Zounds, daughter, that's an impressive explosion of random intolerance even by your volcanic standards.

ANNE: Don't mind her, love. She's a bit sensitive. It's a boy.

SUSANNA: Mum!

ANNE: The springtime woodland gadabout approaches. Sue would like to go with this boy, but he's shy and he won't ask her.

---

* This observation uncannily predicts the nature of the Southern Railways dispute of 2016 and most commuters' reactions to it.

SUSANNA: And of course I'm not allowed to ask him.

MARY: Well, I should say not. A maid ask a youth to gamble in the greenwood? All order would end. Chaos would be come again.

SUSANNA: Except actually, Gran, it wouldn't.

WILL: Well, I'm not sure, Sue. Methinks perhaps there is a certain social covenant that prevents a kind of chaos. If girls started to act as boys then would there come a time in Albion where gangs of maids were seen of a Friday night staggering from tavern to tavern? Collapsing in the gutter and passing out in their own vomit?*

JOHN: Man must ever be the master of woman, because man is made in God's image and he sits at the pinnacle of creation.

John Shakespeare doth make this statement while he sitteth upon the privy pot.

SUSANNA: I hate him!

ANNE: Never mind all that. So what are we going to do about Sue and the shy and timorous youth Darren?

WILL: Why, the answer's obvious. We must invent some stratagem whereby he be persuaded to approach our Sue.

ANNE: Any bright ideas?

WILL: Anne, please, it's me you're talking to. Bright ideas are what I do. Susanna must woo this foolish boy by proxy. Dressing as her own cousin Shane, come a-visiting from Solihull. I can't see how it can possibly go wrong.

JOHN: Funny how many of your ideas involve girls dressing up as boys. I think it's a pattern.

WILL: It's not a pattern.

JOHN: It looks like a pattern.

---

* Shakespeare's prescience is extraordinary. 'Ladette' culture would not emerge until the 1990s.

WILL: It is not a pattern. Now, if you excuse me, I've got a bloody and vengeful history to write. I'm planning a cheeky little Roman number called *Titus Andronicus* in which fourteen characters are brutally murdered and a mother forced to eat her own children baked in a pie. Our patron will love it.[*]

---

[*] Amazingly, this is actually what happens in *Titus Andronicus*. The play makes *Reservoir Dogs* look like a Disney picture.

ROBERT GREENE'S OFFICE – DAY

Will doth sit before stern Robert Greene, petitioning for his play.

ROBERT GREENE: This will not do!

WILL: What do you mean, it won't do? You, you told me to write a blood-soaked history.

ROBERT GREENE: Did I? Goodness, so I did. Sorry. My badlington. What I meant to say was *don't* write a blood-soaked history. The Lord Chamberlain hates them. Rather, His Grace demands a light romantic comedy set in an exotic location.

WILL: But I've never written a play like that in my life. I wouldn't know where to start.

ROBERT GREENE: Which is why I suggested the idea. You will fail in your commission, lose your new patron and be disgraced. A laughing stock.

WILL'S LONDON LODGINGS – DAY

Kate and Marlowe do practise their Italian. Bottom busies himself with his household work.

KIT MARLOWE: *Vorrei comprare del pane, per favore.*

KATE: *Bene, Signor Marlowe. Bene.*

KIT MARLOWE: Well, it's all credit to you, Kate. Couldn't have had a better teacher.

KATE: *Si prega di parlare italiano, Signor Marlowe.* You know my rules. We must *parlare solo italiano.* This house is not in London but Verona. I am not Kate, the landlady's daughter, but La Contessa Silvia. And Bottom be named in the Latin style, as is the Italian fashion, and thus he is an A-nus.

BOTTOM: That's been said before.

KATE: What is more, Mr Marlowe, you must be ever proficient in fine phrases. Flirty flourishes, gentle sighs. For Italian society would expect a noble gentleman to be well versed in the sweet words of . . .

There is a tremble in Kate's voice as her eyes meet Marlowe's. He doth sigh likewise.

KIT MARLOWE: *Amore?*

Marlowe speaketh in the manner of an aside, which by strict convention none can overhear.

KIT MARLOWE: Oh God, I think I'm falling for her, which is just raving tonto. But when she doth speak italiano, so damn saucy it makes me call for a more copious codpiece.

KATE: Aye, sirrah, *amore.*

Kate speaketh in the manner of an aside, which by strict convention none can overhear.

KATE: How can this be? I feel my pulse quicken and my boobingtons do palpitate most mightily. 'Tis very madness. And yet when he practises the sweet words of romance, I do totally find myself going diddly doodah.

Bottom speaketh in the manner of an aside, which by strict convention none can overhear.

BOTTOM: They're doing a lot of talking to themselves. Which in my experience means things are going to start going very wrong.

KIT MARLOWE: Kate. Babes. *Bambina.*

KATE: *Sì.*

KIT MARLOWE: I love you. Like the wild pig I long to snuffle your truffle. Can I hope that you love me?

KATE: Yes! Yes! I love thee too!

KIT MARLOWE: Result! And yet late tonight I must to Verona. My ship awaits.

KATE: Aye, sirrah. 'Tis against such a day that we have studied here in our little Verona. I, your contessa, with A-nus always at your service.

KIT MARLOWE: Pardon?

BOTTOM: She means me.

KIT MARLOWE: Right, yes. Absolutely. A bit of a leap. Anyway, right now, I must to the tavern, there to meet my sidekick, Valentine. But I shall return tonight for one final farewell.

KATE: Until tonight, gentle Christopher.

KIT MARLOWE: Please call me Kit. I am your Kit. Oh, such irony. I, your Kit, must get off, when all I desire is for you to get your kit off.*

---

* Once more the Crow Folio provides evidence of the nature of Marlowe's sexuality. While historical evidence leaves little doubt that he was extremely attracted to men, clearly he also harboured romantic and erotic feelings for some women. Particularly classy, brainy ones like Kate and Emilia Lanier, the Dark Lady of the sonnets.

Kate doth sigh with love. Marlowe departeth.

KATE: Such a poetic soul.

BOTTOM: Kate, weren't you listening? He said he wants to get your kit off.

KATE: Yes, but in a nice romantic way.

Will, the master of the house, returneth.

WILL: Clear the decks. Cancel all appointments. Greene has tricked me into writing the wrong play for our new patron. He wants a light romantic comedy set in an exotic location.

BOTTOM: What you gonna do? You're absolute crap at comedy.

WILL: I am not crap at comedy.

KATE: You are a teeny bit crap at comedy, Mr Shakespeare.

WILL: How can you say that? It's just mad. Every single history I've ever writ has contained at least one hilarious scene in which poor people of low social status with amusing names like Doll Tearpants and Ned Snatchbutt acted stupidly. So funny. But I've only ever done comedy *scenes*. Never a whole comic play.[*]

KATE: Well, at least all will be peaceful here, Mr Shakespeare. My Italian lessons are done. Brave Kit must away on his country's service.

WILL: Yes, I passed him on the stair. He seemed different, as if some strange and luminous light shone from within. Possibly he bit on a bad oyster and was struggling to keep his buttocks clenched till he didst make the shitting ditch. Child, there is a blush to your cheek and your boobingtons do palpitate most mightily. Have you been eating maggoty cheese?

KATE: 'Tis not maggoty cheese which doth palpitate my boobingtons.

---

[*] Mercifully neither of these characters can be found in any of Shakespeare's known works (although there is a Doll Tearsheet in *Henry IV Part 2*).

BOTTOM: No, it's a cheesy maggot.

KATE: Bottom! 'Tis not so.

BOTTOM: She's only going diddly doodah over Mr Marlowe.

WILL: Kate, can this be true? Be you diddly doodah over Mr Marlowe?

KATE: Yes! And he is not a cheesy maggot. He's just a bad boy who needs a good girl. And what's more, he's diddly doodah over me.

WILL: Kate, I'm sure he thinks he is but that's Kit. He's a gadabout. Like the newly discovered American hummingbird that doth flit from bud to bud, spreading wide the soft damp petals, plunging deep its beak and lapping full fervent at the nectar within using its curiously long and agile tongue.[*]

Kate doth sigh most ardently.

KATE: Gosh, Mr Shakespeare.

BOTTOM: You're not helping, master!

---

[*] The curious nature of the hummingbird's tongue was scarcely understood at this time. Shakespeare's knowledge of it suggests a private and erotic interest in agile tongues.

MISS LUCY'S TAVERN -NIGHT

Marlowe attends Miss Lucy's tavern in the company of Valentine, a handsome spy.

LUCY: So, you boys be off to Verona.

KIT MARLOWE: Aye, Mistress Lucy, but Valentine here travels separately so the papal spies may ne'er know he's my sidekick.

VALENTINE: Yeah, except that wouldn't happen, would it? Because in fact you're *my* sidekick.

Valentine doth cuff Marlowe in a manner designed to irritate.

KIT MARLOWE: He's my sidekick.

Marlowe doth cuff Valentine.

VALENTINE: So, sidey-balls. Got any cool new gear from the boffins at the tower?

KIT MARLOWE: Ooh, just a bit, side-dangle. An innocent ostrich feather? No no no. A lethal throw-dart. Witness buzzy bee on yonder flower.

A bee buzzeth about a flower. Marlowe doth pluck a feather from his cap and with it doth spear insect mid-flight.

VALENTINE: That's fine. If you're attacked by a bee. An innocent coddling pouch? No. A dangle-mounted blunder-banger.*

Valentine doth point his coddling pouch at the pot in which the plant doth flower and fire a shot which doth cause it to explode.

KIT MARLOWE: Yeah, well, they offered me that, but no room. My coddling pouch is already fully loaded.

LUCY: Boys, boys. Don't have a dangle-off in my pub. Because, believe me, I will win. And I haven't even got one.

---

* The practice within the British Secret Service of maintaining a clandestine science division to come up with improbable weapons that can only be used in very specific circumstances clearly pre-dates James Bond.

Will enters all of a hurry.

WILL: Kit, thought I'd find you here. I was just rushing to the theatre but I wanted a quick word.

KIT MARLOWE: Not a problem. Valentine's just leaving. He's my sidekick.

VALENTINE: In your dreams, sidekick boy.

Valentine doth flick Marlowe's nose and depart.

KIT MARLOWE: Such a sidekick. Anyway, Will, what's up? Make it snappy, I leave for Verona tonight and I would first bid farewell to my true love.

WILL: Yes, that's what I hurried over to talk to you about. This true love. That would be Kate, right? Our Kate.

KIT MARLOWE: Damn, she's hot. Do you know, I always thought she was a proper Penny Pure-pants.

WILL: She is a proper Penny Pure-pants.

KIT MARLOWE: But you haven't heard her speak Italian. Oh! The passion.

LUCY: Pah! If you think Italian be sexy-talk, you should hear a bit of Igbo. Ha! (*Speaketh in an African tongue*) Which means your chest is broad and your testicles large and hairy.

WILL: Phew. Thoroughly invigorating stuff, I must say. But look here, Kit. This crush on Kate. You know what you're like. You fancy anything in a farthingale. What happens if while you're away, you fall for some Italian tottling gobble and come home covered in garlic-flavoured love bites? If you break Kate's heart, I'll—*

In fury doth Marlowe take a knife to Will's throat.

KIT MARLOWE: You'll what?

---

* The farthingale was the weird birdcage-like arrangement of hoops that women wore beneath their skirts in order to prevent them from getting through doors.

WILL: I'll write a pretty stern sonnet about it. You see if I don't.

KIT MARLOWE: Fear not, Will. No, my roistering days are done. Never more will Marlowe the bonking rodent be. Let all know that he be Kate's true kissy love gerbil.

LUCY: Ah, why not take her these roses from my garden, eh? All girls love flowers.

Now doth Marlowe sneeze most mightily.

KIT MARLOWE: Sorry, Lucy. No can do. See, I do suffer from the summer snottage. Roses in particular make my eyes water. Wouldn't want my bird to see me blub now, would I? Thanks anyway. Settle the drinks, will you, mate? Love you loads.

THE RED LION THEATRE - NIGHT

Mr Burbage, Mr Condell and Mr Kempe do confront Will most impatiently.

BURBAGE: Where is your play, Will? Our new patron is impatient for our first production.

CONDELL: How about we bring back *Richard* for another run? I know the crowds miss my Margaret. I get so many letters.*

BURBAGE: I can't imagine there'd be much public interest in digging up *Richard the Third*.†

WILL: Of course there would, but the Lord Chamberlain wants a comedy.

KEMPE: So play it for laughs. Job done.

---

* The announcement of improbable and unquantifiable public support is something many actors claim, particularly after receiving a bad review.

† Burbage was wrong. There was enormous public interest in digging up Richard III, particularly from BBC 1's Time Team who, having spent years failing to find so much as a significant teacup, had to face the fact that some navvies found a dead king in a car park.

BURBAGE: Play *Richard the Third* for laughs? What comedy is to be found in such an evil and grotesque villain?

KEMPE: Dark comedy, yeah? Edgy comedy, eh? You've done the groundwork making Richard a hunchback. Now you got to ramp it up.

CONDELL: Ramp it up, Kempe? How so?

KEMPE: Well, for instance, do a scene where everyone's trying really hard not to mention his stoop, but they can't stop themselves.

CONDELL: That would be funny, would it?

KEMPE: Er, yeah. Like, Richard's with his knights, and Norfolk goes, 'Oh, fancy a spot of hunch? Oh . . . sorry, I meant *lunch*.' Brave, edgy, challenging taboos.*

WILL: You're not changing a line of my *Richard*. It's perfect. All four hours of it.

BURBAGE: Yes. But the Lord Chamberlain demands a new play now, Will.

WILL: I'm trying. He wants a light romantic comedy set in an exotic location and I've only ever done histories. Maybe Kempe's right. Maybe I should do a comical history. Go with what I know. *Henry the Sixth Part Four*. Henry meets Joan of Arc at her trial and instead of burning her, takes her for a naughty weekend at Lyme Regis. Might work.

---

* Comedians performing offensive material under the guise of irony was previously believed to be a post-modern phenomenon.

261

WILL'S LONDON LODGINGS – NIGHT

Kate and Kit do canoodle most soppily.

KATE: O, how this spring of love resembleth the uncertain glory of an April day, which now shows all the beauty of the sun, and by and by a cloud takes all away.

KIT MARLOWE: You see? You see? Got to dig all that poetry stuff. I mean, so sexy.

KATE: It's a bit of Mr Shakespeare's, actually. Isn't it perfect? Our love is like the bright sun and your leaving be a cloud upon it.*

KIT MARLOWE: Is that what that meant? I could never tell. Oh, you're such a classy bird, Kate. Can't believe I've wasted my life a-roistering and a-rogering when I should have been a-worshipping you. Let us exchange tokens so that, while we are parted, we may always know to whom our hearts belong.

KATE: Oh, Kit. Let's.

Kate doth present a ring with a maidenly sigh of love.

KATE: My grandmother's communion ring. She wore it on her finger. Then my mother on hers. And now I on mine. I gladly give it thee.

Now Marlowe reaches into his shirt and also produces a ring.

KIT MARLOWE: My grandfather's nipple ring. He wore it through his nipple. My father through his, and now I through mine. I give it to thee.

KATE: Hmm. Thanks. I'll just put it on a chain around my neck, if that's all right.

KIT MARLOWE: Well, suit yourself. But you are missing something pretty cool. So erotic when you play with it.

KATE: Really I'm fine.

---

* Kate was quoting from *The Two Gentlemen of Verona*, which suggests that while Shakespeare had not yet had the inspiration for his Verona play, he was already toying with some of the verse. It should be noted that this is one of the clearer passages of the play.

WILL'S STRATFORD HOME – DAY

John and Mary sit beside the fire. The twins play. Anne doth help Susanna with the raiment of a boy.

SUSANNA: I feel stupid.

ANNE: Well, it's your dad's idea and he's a genius so you're going to have to give it a go. I can't take another week of you moping and mooning about.

MARY: It is not proper for a young lady to go about in britches.

JOHN: I think he looks very fetching.

SUSANNA: Don't be creepy, Granddad.

ANNE: Do you want this lad to invite you to the gadabout or don't you? Now let's go through it again.

Susanna doth attempt the deep soulless monotone of a gormless youth.

SUSANNA: 'Hello, Darren. I'm Sue's cousin Shane and Sue really likes you and I think you should ask her to the woodland gadabout.' Mum, this is never going to work.

ANNE: It will, love, honestly. You look really convincing.

SUSANNA: So you think I look like a boy.

JOHN: A very attractive boy.

SUSANNA: Shut up, Granddad!

WILL'S LONDON LODGINGS – DAY

Will attempts to work while Kate standeth at the window cloaked in melancholy.

KATE: I just miss my Kit so much. I fear he will forget me. Ah me. Ah me. Oh woe! Ah me!

WILL: Seriously, Kate. You have got to stop pining. It's very frustrating. Here am I trying to conjure up a brilliant plot involving parted lovers in an exotic foreign location and there you are making it impossible for me to think because you're parted from your lover who's gone off to an exotic foreign location. Hang on. Hang the futtock on.

A CONTESSA'S PALAZZO IN VERONA – DAY

Marlowe sits in an antechamber with quill and pen, writing a letter.

KIT MARLOWE: My dearest snugglebunny, I write from a contessa's antechamber where I await her presence. I wish she'd get a move on, as I long to return only to you.

Enters a servant.

SERVANT: La Contessa di Verona.

The Contessa Silvia enters. She is very beautiful. Instantly Marlowe forgets his letter, screws up the parchment and tosses it away.

SILVIA: Welcome, Signor Marlowe. I hope you will allow me to practise my English on you.

KIT MARLOWE: You can do anything to me you like, you captivating little pomodoro.

SILVIA: My secretary is preparing a list of the Pope's assassins, which I think will be of interest to Signor Walsingham. You will deliver it to him.

KIT MARLOWE: Never mind the secret list. Will you have dinner with me tonight?

SILVIA: Oh, Signor Marlowe. Well, that would be so nice, except I have already agreed to have dinner with another English visitor, Signor Valentine.

Valentine enters. Marlowe's visage be most furious.

A CONTESSA'S PALAZZO IN VERONA – DAY

Will and Bottom arrive in the garden of the contessa's home.

WILL: Unbelievable. When you buy a boat ticket to Verona, you expect to be taken to Verona. Not a tiny fishing village on the channel coast which, outrageously, the shipping line have renamed 'Verona north', with coaches laid on to cover the 750-mile transfer to 'Verona actual'.

BOTTOM: That's what you get if you sail budget.

WILL: Which actually turned out to be not very budget at all once you factor in the extras, like the outrageous indulgence of actually wanting to travel with a bag.*

BOTTOM: Which they lost.

WILL: I mean, how? Just how? They load the bag on, they take the bag off. Where is the window of opportunity to futtock that up?

BOTTOM: Put on the wrong boat.

WILL: Exactly. Even as we speak, my brand-new holiday puffling pants, which I was really looking forward to wearing on the piazza, are off to North Virginia where they will no doubt end up adorning the bottom of a scabby-arsed beaver trapper.

Kate hurries into the garden dressed as a handsome youth in the finest raiment.

KATE: Sorry, got distracted. So many amazing shops. Is this the contessa's garden?

WILL: Yes, Kate, it is. And here you are, as I instructed, in guise of gadsome youth. Good effort, by the way.

KATE: Thanks. Knocked it up out of two curtains and a carpet.

---

* Startling evidence that the cabin-luggage-only model pre-dates the age of EasyJet.

WILL: And now let us hide ourselves behind this small tree, which by strict convention will render us invisible. No doubt shortly Kit will come a-strolling and, when he does, you must approach him and become his servant. Thus not only will you be close to your love, but also should his gladsome eyes start to stray, you'll be in the position to plead your own cause. Ever reminding him of his devoted Kate.

KATE: Oh my God, it's brilliant.

WILL: It's double brilliant because I'm going to take it all down and use it for my play.

BOTTOM: But, master, Mr Marlowe's known Kate for years. He's going to recognize her the second he sees her.

WILL: Of course he won't, Bottom. She's wearing puffling pants and a boy's hat. He's not clairvoyant. Shh, come on, quick.[*]

Will, Kate and Bottom hide behind the small tree and are thus rendered invisible. Marlowe emerges into the garden, sighing most sadly,

KIT MARLOWE: Oh, my lady love. Canst thou e'er be mine? Oh bugger, roses. That's all I need.

Now doth Marlowe begin to sneeze for he doth suffer most vexingly from the summer snottage.

KATE: He weeps, he pines. He longs to get my kit off.

WILL: Now's your chance to get near him and pledge your own troth. Off you go.[†]

Kate, all in boy's garb, doth approach Marlowe.

---

[*] Countless generations of actors and audiences alike have put Shakespeare's reliance on absurd disguises in his comedies down to lazy plotting. However, the folios suggest he actually believed that putting on a hat made a person completely unrecognizable, even to their lover.

[†] 'To pledge or plight one's troth' means to ask someone to marry you. Most people don't know this and presume it means to try and cop off with someone. Clearly Shakespeare didn't know either.

KATE: Ho, sirrah!

KIT MARLOWE: Who comes? Sorry, bit blurry. These damn roses have made my eyes water. I do suffer from the summer snottage.

KATE: (*In the manner of an aside*) Sweet. He doth seek to hide his love from me with the old summer snottage excuse.

WILL: See? He didst not recognize her.

BOTTOM: His eyes are watering. He's got the summer snottage.

WILL: It is not the bloody summer snottage. It's because she's wearing puffling pants and a boy's hat.*

KIT MARLOWE: Tell me, what is your business here?

KATE: Why, only to serve you, my lord. I am but a poor English boy, far from home.

KIT MARLOWE: (*In the manner of an aside*) Gadzooks, here's a happy chance. A servant will be useful in my pursuit of the divine contessa. (*To Kate*) Very well, boy, you may enter my service and know straight away that I do love.

KATE: Joy. (*In the manner of an aside*) He thinks only of me.

KIT MARLOWE: See, my love comes.

The contessa comes now a-strolling, looking hotter than fresh baked pie.

KATE: What?

KIT MARLOWE: Now hide we must, behind this small tree, which by strict convention will render us invisible.

Marlowe doth hurry Kate behind a second tree while Shakespeare and Bottom still hide behind the first.

WILL: I thought this might happen. Kit's eye has lit upon another. Brilliant. That's the Act Two opener right there.

---

* It seems strange that Shakespeare couldn't see the obvious point that Bottom is making. On the other hand, if he had accepted Bottom's logic, he'd have needed to rework the plots of most of his comedies.

BOTTOM: Poor Kate. Her heart will be broken.

WILL: Not for long. Soon will she reveal herself as a girl and Marlowe's love will be rekindled.

BOTTOM: Or not.

Marlowe and Kate observe the contessa from behind their own small tree.

KIT MARLOWE: 'Tis mine own Silvia. Be she not radiant?

KATE: Aye, sirrah. Radiant indeed. And yet, be there no sweet English girl at home whom you hold in your heart?

KIT MARLOWE: Well, there was one. A bookish Polly Pure-pants whom I thought I did love but I am so over her. La bella Silvia be my love now. So far have I plighted my troth in vain. Therefore I will send you in my stead. You are a charming, pleasant-voiced youth and 'tis certain Silvia will lend you her ear. Here. Give her this token of my love.

Marlowe doth take out the very ring that Kate gave him and bids her take it to the contessa. Kate's eyes do fill with tears.

KATE: Oh, this ring, sir. But surely 'tis most precious to you.

KIT MARLOWE: No, not really. Got it off a landlady's daughter. Can't really see her having anything valuable to give away.

Kate be devastated.

KATE: (*In the manner of an aside*) Save perhaps her heart.

Will and Bottom do still observe the scene from their hiding place.

WILL: Kit sends Kate to plead on his behalf with the very love token she gave him. Boom. Act Three just wrote itself.

BOTTOM: What a total bastable.

WILL: Don't worry. When she reveals herself, all will be well and I'll have my finale.

BOTTOM: Or not.

269

Sad Kate do as Marlowe has bidden and approacheth the contessa.

KATE: Madame, forgive my intrusion but I bring word from my master, Christopher Marlowe.

SILVIA: Signor Marlowe? What says he, girl?

KATE: Boy. I am a boy.

SILVIA: I see you are confused with your gender. Or perhaps just curious. It's more common than people think. Well then, boy trapped in a girl's body, what message have you for me?*

KATE: Only that my master does love you, full well. And as a token of his love does offer you . . . this nipple ring, which didst pierce the nipples of his forebears.

Now doth Kate offer the contessa not her grandmother's ring but the ring Marlowe had given her. Marlowe doth observe this from behind the tree.

KIT MARLOWE: Zounds. This lad doth have the very gift I gave Kate . . . It is Kate! Come in disguise, the better to be near me. And I've just sent her to declare my love for Silvia. Awkward.

SILVIA: You will tell your master that both of my nipples be already pierced with finer jewels than this. Besides, I do love another. My Valentine.

Valentine entereth the garden.

VALENTINE: And I love thee.

Will, still observing from behind his tree, doth almost dance for joy.

WILL: A second lover! Brilliant. I'll certainly use that. And now will Kate reveal herself.

KATE: You were right to spurn Marlowe, Contessa. For once he did love me.

---

* It is interesting to note that the Italians had an awareness of transgender issues and, as now, the Brits were probably a bit uptight about that sort of stuff.

Kate removeth her hat and her hair doth fall about her shoulders most prettily.

WILL: See how she doth shake out her hair most ravishingly. Now will Marlowe love her once again.

KIT MARLOWE: Kate! I've been a fool. Forgive me.

WILL: Boom, textbook stuff. I predict a double marriage.

BOTTOM: Or not.

VALENTINE: Silvia, will you give me your hand?

SILVIA: Yes!

KIT MARLOWE: Kate, will you give me your hand?

KATE: Yes.

WILL: What did I tell you?

Kate puncheth Marlowe full in the face.

SILVIA: Ah, the English foreplay. I've heard of this. Summon the priest. Bring the candles. Burn the incense. Let the twin wedding begin.

Marlowe appears about to speak. Kate doth punch him again.

WILL'S LONDON LODGINGS – DAY

Will, Marlowe, Bottom and Kate are gathered in London once more.

WILL: Back in Blighty at last with my play as good as writ. I shall use it all. The only tiny change is that in my play I'll have both couples marry at the end, instead of only one while the other lover gets punched unconscious.

KIT MARLOWE: To be honest, I think I kind of dodged a bit of a musketball. I mean, you're a cracking-looking bird, Kate, but a little bit scary.

KATE: I think I dodged a musketball too, Mr Marlowe. You're a handsome chap but a shallow, cheating bastable.

KIT MARLOWE: Guilty as charged. I want to thank you, Kate, for making me one of Walsingham's favourites.

WILL: Yes, it was clever of you, Kate, to notice that the contessa called for a priest and all the trappings of a Catholic wedding despite claiming to be a Protestant.

KIT MARLOWE: Turned out she was a papist double-agent and a secret assassinist – a total plant.

KATE: I still think you should have told your sidekick Valentine that he was marrying a mortal enemy of the crown.

KIT MARLOWE: Yeah, right, got to do that.

KATE: But really, Mr Shakespeare, are you seriously going to write a story where the heroine, having been completely cheated on and actually sent by her false boyfriend to woo another girl with the very ring she gave him, just takes the bastable back and marries him?

WILL: Absolutely. That is how *The Two Gentlemen of Verona* will end.

KATE: Honestly, it is not going to be one of your best.*

---

* Kate was right, it absolutely wasn't.

WILL'S STRATFORD HOME - NIGHT

Will and Anne do sit before the fire with their pipes.

ANNE: Well done, Kate. I wouldn't have taken Marlowe back either.

WILL: Can't put that in the play, though, wife. The Lord
 Chamberlain wants escapist romance, not gritty realism. What's
 more, so do the punters. I've writ my first comedy. Now I plan to
 write a shed-load more.

ANNE: Really, love? Do you think that's a good idea?*

WILL: Absolutely. Anyway, enough of my doings. How did Sue get on
 with the shy youth? Did my stratagem work?

ANNE: Well, it sort of worked.

Susanna doth enter, still in the attire of a youth.

SUSANNA: Darren fell in love with me . . . as Shane.

---

* Tantalizing to speculate what a deal of arse-numbingly boring productions could
have been avoided if Anne had been more forceful in her efforts to dissuade Will
from taking up comedy.

FOOD OF LOVE

Of all the revelations contained within the Crow Folios, this episode of the Bard's life is perhaps the most stunning. Will Shakespeare invented the jukebox musical. It seems that had there been no Bard there would have been no *Mamma Mia*, no *We Will Rock You*, and no *Jersey Boys*. Who'd have thought? The producers of outrageously overpriced 'souvenir' programmes and merchandised mugs and t-shirts have much to thank Shakespeare for.

WILL'S STRATFORD HOME – DAY

Will and his family are at their ease.

JOHN: I want to be a gentleman. I want to be posh. You promised.

WILL: All right, Dad. I'll petition the College of Heralds again.

MARY: He's been on about that coat of arms for years. As if they'd give one to him. He's been before the courts and shamed us all.

JOHN: It was only a bit of fiddling. They should go after the real criminals. The dodgy financial dealers.

WILL: Dad, it is a matter of public record that you manipulated wool prices, fixed interest rates and reneged on personal debt. Exactly what part of dodgy financial dealer is it that you are not?

MARY: He's a common thief.

WILL: Which I admit is not normally considered an impediment to ennoblement in England.* But in this case, it is, because Robert Greene, who doth hate my gutlings, has made Master Herald. And Robert Greene would rather be personal hairdresser to a snake-headed gorgon than do me a good turn.

JOHN: I want a coat of arms.

WILL: And I'll do my best, Dad. But I am quite busy, you know? The public's demand for new plays is insatiable. And I have not a single solitary second to spare. I be like the springtime lark, who must needs build her nest, feed her young, tend her delicate plumage, whilst all the while singing merry songs that the fairies may dance in the greenwood glades.

ANNE: Is that you making the point that you haven't got a second to spare?

---

* In this respect, it is clear that nothing has changed in Britain since. Being a selfish greedy immoral bastard is still a common cause of ennoblement.

WILL: Yes, absolutely. Underlining, so to speak. I'm so pushed that I barely have a moment to illustrate my observations with extended metaphor and fantastical whimsy. Theatre is booming and its demands are insatiable. My *Two Gentlemen of Verona* filled a gap but already Burbage needs another, and out is it stressing me most vexingly.

ANNE: Well, I know you're busy, love, but you absolutely cannot miss Hamnet's school Latin recitation.

WILL: Latin? Still? At eleven? In my day, we were on to Greek by then. The whole curriculum's been completely dumbled down.[*]

ANNE: The other dads come. 'Where's your Bill?' the other mums say, and I have to make excuses.

WILL: What . . . like, I have a life? That I exist independently of my children? How weird. How selfish. What is it with modern youth that they canst not kick an inflated pig's bladder the wrong way up a sporting field but that both parents must be standing on the sidelines shouting, 'Goodling job, poppet. Goodling job'?

ANNE: A father should take an interest in his children.

WILL: Why? Mine never did. That wicked old bastable didn't so much as glance at me till I was fourteen and he could put me to work.

JOHN: I wasn't bloody interested.

MARY: He wasn't interested. Look to your son, I'd say. And he'd say, 'Who?'

JOHN: 'Who?' I'd say. Wasn't interested.

ANNE: All I'm asking is for you to get involved sometimes. It's healthy for their emotional development.

WILL: I don't think it is. I think it's corrupting. A whole generation is growing up who on reaching adult estate will scarce be able to let

---

[*] Boys of Shakespeare's time were expected to be familiar with both Latin and Greek, but then they had more time than boys today as they didn't study media.

loose a fartle-barfle without their parents shouting encouragement and promising to bottle it for Grandma.*

Susanna enters singing merrily.

SUSANNA: 'April is in my mistress' face, and July in her eyes hath place.'

WILL: Susanna, will you please stop singing 'April Is in My Mistress' Face'. Sing something else.

SUSANNA: 'Now is the month of Maying, when merry lads are playing.'

WILL: But not 'Now Is the Month of Maying' or any other madrigal by Thomas bloody Morley.

SUSANNA: Thomas Morley is the best madrigal writer of the English Renaissance. He is God. I would die for him. I'm a Thomatic.†

WILL: He is not God, daughter. He is a sugar-coated ditty guffer, whose every song be two-thirds fa-lala-la-la, and the other third some arsing porridge about merry maids in May, naughty nymphs in November or juicy jugs in July.

JOHN: Never mind Thomas blooming Morley. What about my coat of arms?

WILL: I'm working on it. Establishing a noble lineage is a process. You can't fake four hundred years of family history overnight.

---

* Shakespeare was identifying a trend in parental behaviour which has continued to our own day where kids whose parents refuse to watch them being crap at football and netball are offered counselling.
† Thomas Morley was indeed the foremost madrigal writer of the English Renaissance but, then again, there wasn't a lot of competition.

ROBERT GREENE'S OFFICE – DAY

Shakespeare doth sit before Robert Greene.

ROBERT GREENE: Mr Shakespeare, heraldry is a complex discipline. You can't fake four hundred years of family history overnight.

WILL: Well, how long might it take, do you think?

ROBERT GREENE: How long? Well now, let me see. In your case, hmm, well, give or take a week or two, I'd say eternity. The Shakespeares will never be gentlemen.

WILL: But we could be tomorrow, if you'd just grant us that family coat of arms.

ROBERT GREENE: Yes, *if* – such a tiny mewling word and ever the lament of the turnip-chewing country bumshank. If only I were higher born. If only I'd been to Cambridge University instead of leaving the town duncing school at fourteen to work in my dad's glove shop.

WILL: There is no terror in your threats, Greene, for I am armed so strong in honesty that they pass by me like the idle wind of a small . . . somewhat constipated squirrel.

ROBERT GREENE: Hmm. Tails off a bit at the end, don't you think?

WILL: It will get there. Probably just needs a couple hundred more syllables.[*]

---

[*] When Shakespeare did eventually use this phrase (in *Julius Caesar*) he merely concluded the 'idle wind' phrase with 'Which I respect not'. Which is clearly not even as good as 'small constipated squirrel'. He should have stuck with his instincts.

279

WILL'S LONDON LODGINGS – DAY

Kate doth read a book, Marlowe quaffs, Bottom sweeps. Will doth enter.

WILL: Bottom, bring ale and pie. Ah, I see it is laid. Hello, Kit. You're here.

KIT MARLOWE: Yeah, I heard you were back. Thought I'd drop in for a quaff and a gorge.

KATE: 'Tis apple season, Mr Shakespeare. Have a little fruit.

Kate doth juggle apples most amusingly.

KATE: Ale-up, ale-hazzah! Ale-diddly-doo. Juggling and such tricks are, as I'm sure you are aware, key skills for any theatre professional.

WILL: Kate, please, I know you want to be an actor but I'm not in the mood to watch juggling. In fact, I'm never in the mood to watch juggling, an activity which I consider to be second only to mime in its somnambulistic tedium.[*]

KATE: I love mime.

WILL: You do not love it, Kate. You merely tell yourself you love it, because you are kind and have a natural sympathy for the terminally deluded and the pathologically talentless. I, however, am made of sterner stuff and would lock every mime in Christendom up in his imaginary glass box and throw away the notional key.

BOTTOM: Good journey, was it, master?

WILL: Well, Botsky, it was dirty, overcrowded and late. On the other hand, it wasn't diverted via Aberystwyth or cancelled due to unusually wet leaves. So I suppose within the very limited context of my minimal expectations, you could say that in a purely comparative sense, yes, I had a good journey.

KATE: And I expect your family were pleased to see you.

---

[*] It's almost as if Shakespeare had actually visited the modern piazza at Covent Garden on a sunny day in the school holidays.

WILL: Not really, Kate. 'Twas all too brief and they complain
I neglect them. I'm just so overworked. I need more time. I wrote
a history on the coach. The tragical history of Edward the Second.
It's a quite brilliant first draft but it needs a lot more work.

KIT MARLOWE: Hang on, hang on. Here's a thought. I know how
you can save yourself all that work.

WILL: Really, Kit? That would be great.

KIT MARLOWE: Give the play to me. I'll just chuck it on as is. I'm
not proud. And be fair, you've had loads of hits.

WILL: Through talent and hard work. What I have, I have by merit.

KIT MARLOWE: You say that as if it's a good thing.

WILL: Isn't it?

KIT MARLOWE: Well of course not. I mean, if all men advanced by
merit, what becomes of us stupid posh boys? Or do we not count?
Never had you down as an elitist, Will. Stop being such a snob.
Give us a play.*

WILL: No, Kit. I am resolved and even an insanely convoluted
argument such as that cannot sway me. I've sent my *Titus Andronicus*
round to Burbage but I'm really not sure about it. What do you think,
Kate? You read it. Too gory? Be absolutely honest. I can take it.

KATE: Since you ask, yes, it was.

WILL: Well, thank you very much. That's very helpful. Nice to have
your support. I don't think.

KATE: I'm sorry. But *Titus Andronicus* is a degrading orgy of abusive
sex and unspeakable violence.

BOTTOM: Sounds brilliant. I'd go.

KIT MARLOWE: Me too. Love all that.

KATE: People's lives are filled with abuse and violence, Mr
Shakespeare. Surely as an artist you should be offering them

---

* History shows that Marlowe needn't have worried. Five hundred years after he
voiced this fear, posh boys continue to advance in Britain without merit.

something inspiring. Uplifting. Which brings joy and lightness to their existence.

WILL: But what about that Comedy of Mistakes, Misunderstandings and Coincidences I was working on.

KATE: I thought it was contrived.

WILL: Contrived? How can you say that? Two identical twins separated at birth who happen to have been given the same name, with servants who are also identical twins, also separated at birth and also happen to have been given the same name, end up in the same town and mistakenly hook up with each other's girlfriends. That could easily happen.

KATE: I just don't think it's a play, Mr Shakespeare. But it's not entirely irredeemable.

WILL: Irredeemable? It's the most deemable thing I've written all week.

KATE: Deemable is not a word.

WILL: It is if I bloody say it is because in case you've forgotten, that's what I do.*

KATE: It's got some nice madness about it, but the drama exposes its limitations. You need to come up with a new art form which allows for such exuberant absurdity. Some extra element which takes us to a heightened world where we can accept such joyful nonsense. A new style which defies dramatic logic and appeals directly to the senses, the emotions, the soul.

WILL: Gosh, Kate, if I could do that, then all my problems would be solved. I could get away with really stupid plots while still delighting the crowds and running for years.

KATE: Yes!

WILL: But no such extra element exists. Theatres put on plays. There is no new form, and meanwhile I have bills to pay and a family to feed. I need a show.

---

* Shakespeare never put 'deemable' in a play; it never actually became a word.

BOTTOM: Well, when I'm really stuck on something, I find it helps to sing a happy song.

WILL: Yes, thank you, Bottom. I'm trying to concentrate.

Bottom doth sing most lustily.

BOTTOM: 'Now is the month of Maying, when merry lads are playing.'

Kate and Marlowe joineth in.

KATE/KIT MARLOWE/BOTTOM: Fa-lala-la-la-la-lala.

WILL: Trying to think!

KATE/KIT MARLOWE/BOTTOM: Fa-lala-la-la-lala.

KATE: I love Thomas Morley. He is a God.

BOTTOM: Oh, how does he do it? I mean, they're just so catchy. So many hits. 'April Is in My Mistress' Face.'

KATE: 'My Bonny Lass She Smileth.'

KIT MARLOWE: 'Flora, Wilt Thou Torment Me?'* I mean hit after hit after hit. Appealing directly to the senses.

KATE: Oh, the emotions.

BOTTOM: The soul!

WILL: Hang on. Hang the futtock on. That's it. By Neptune's salty nipples, that's it!

KATE: What's it, Mr Shakespeare?

WILL: The new form! The key to getting away with really silly stories while providing joyful, uplifting popular entertainment. I must to the theatre. A cultural revolution begins!

---

* These were indeed the titles of enormously popular sixteenth-century English madrigals. As is still the case today, many pop songs were about men's attraction to women (although Thomas Morley did not refer to April as his bitch or comment on Flora's fine ass and pussy).

THE RED LION THEATRE – DAY

Burbage, Condell and Kempe discuss their scripts.

BURBAGE: What is to be done? This *Titus Andronicus* be little better than pornography. Titus kills Tamora's oldest sons. Tamora has Titus's sons beheaded. Tamora's sons gang-rape Titus's daughter and Titus cooks Tamora's sons in a pie and makes her eat it!*

CONDELL: I certainly shan't be recommending it to Mother.

KEMPE: I'm telling you, make it a comedy, like we should have done with his *Richard*. Problem solved.

BURBAGE: Suppose it might work as a kind of dark pantomime.

KEMPE: Except, no laughter.

CONDELL: I thought you said play it for laughs.

KEMPE: I said comedy, mate. Not laughs. Laughing is anti-comedy. I don't want to be told when to laugh.

CONDELL: Other people's laughter isn't telling you anything. It's just an innocent expression of collective jollity.

KEMPE: Collective jollity? What's collective jollity got to do with comedy? Comedy should be exclusive and elitist. If everybody gets it, then what's to get?

BURBAGE: The joke?

KEMPE: And there's your problem right there, Burbage. In comedy, jokes are worse than laughter.†

Will doth enter.

WILL: Mr Burbage, halt rehearsals, I've had the most brilliant idea. A way to uplift and inspire. To fill our theatre with joy. To move

---

* Early Shakespeare proves he was the Tarantino of his day.
† It would take another five hundred years, but eventually Will Kempe's vision of comedies without either jokes or laughter would come to pass.

people so much that they tell their friends, and perhaps even return a second time themselves.

BURBAGE: Oh, do not jest, Will. Word of mouth and repeat business are the Holy Grail of the theatre owner. For such things, we would sell our souls.

WILL: Then pop your soul in a bag, mate, and I'll take it with me, cos I've got the answer. Music.

BURBAGE: Music? Oh dear, Will, you really have lost your touch. We already use music. Had you not noticed?

CONDELL: We strum our lutes at the beginning and we blow our pipes at the end.*

KEMPE: And from what I've heard, Condell, you blow a few pipes at the interval too. Whoopsiphobic or brave and edgy? You decide. Ha ha ha!

CONDELL: God, he's doing his laugh again.

BURBAGE: I thought you said you didn't like laughter, Kempe.

KEMPE: Group laughter, mate. Everyone laughing together. That's never right. But solo laughter. Me laughing, very loudly and intrusively at something that nobody else finds funny? That's the mark of a comic genius.

WILL: Excuse me, I'm trying to tell you my brilliant idea. I didn't just mean music at the start and the finish, Burbage. I meant throughout. For add music to theatre and what do you have?

BURBAGE: Theatrical music.

WILL: Yes! No! Musical theatre.

CONDELL: Oh my God. I love it.

BURBAGE: Love what, Condell? Mr Shakespeare's scarcely begun to explain himself.

---

* Extremely boring musical interludes were indeed a feature of Elizabethan theatre. Scholars have speculated that these moments were very much seen as wee breaks.

CONDELL: I don't care. I love it anyway. Just those two words. Musical theatre. They speak to my soul.

WILL: Of course they do. I'm talking about a play with songs. What's not to love?

KEMPE: Um, everything?

BURBAGE: Let me think this through, Will. Are you suggesting that we find somebody to write songs to fit your plays?

WILL: Well, I thought that at first. You know, work with a composer on an original score. But then I thought, no, we need guaranteed hits. Lots of them. And how do we get those?

BURBAGE: By using songs that are hits already!

WILL: Yes! By St Bernard's buttered barn-cakes, yes! I'm on fire today. First I invent the original stage musical and then instantly make it obsolete by inventing the greatest hits musical.*

BURBAGE: Talk me through the detail.

WILL: Well, how does my *Henry the Sixth Part One* open, for example?

BURBAGE: At the funeral of Henry the Fifth, Bedford, Gloucester, Exeter, Warwick, Winchester, Somerset are gathered to mourn the king.

CONDELL: Each speaks at length. A soldier brings news that France is lost. Further extended monologues ensue. It's a very long scene.

BURBAGE: Very long.

KEMPE: Like mad long.

WILL: It is not long at all. Twenty-five minutes at most and it flies by.† But I admit that you don't exactly go home humming it. But imagine if instead of opening with fifteen pages of blank verse, we opened with 'Now Is the Month of Maying'.

---

* The debt which Abba, Queen and The Four Seasons owe Shakespeare has never been properly noted.
† Shakespeare protests too much. It is in fact a very, very long scene.

BURBAGE: My God. 'Tis a thought.

CONDELL: A brilliant magical thought. I love, love, love it. I can see it now. Act one, scene one. London, 1422. The street is filled with lovable cockney characters. Cheeky street urchins. Costermongers. Pretty flower girls. A perambulating top or two.

BURBAGE: Enter the new king!

CONDELL: Strike up the players!

BURBAGE: And the whole company sing 'Now Is the Month of Maying'!

WILL: Two minutes later, the entire audience will be on their feet with their arms swaying in the air. Fala la la la la la la!

All raise their arms and sway from side to side singing 'Fala la la la la la la' together most lustily.

THOMAS MORLEY'S HOUSE – NIGHT

Burbage and Will come a-calling upon the great composer Thomas Morley, a fellow of somewhat debauched and decadent appearance.

BURBAGE: I must say how very kind it was of you to invite us to your beautiful home, Mr Morley.

THOMAS MORLEY: Technical point: not actually my home. Belongs to a subsidiary branch of an offshore holding company incorporated in Lichtenstein. Which is, I must stress, an entirely legal tax arrangement, entered into on the advice of my accountants.[*]

BURBAGE: Yes, of course. No doubt.

THOMAS MORLEY: I just want to make music, man.

BURBAGE: Absolutely. And if you allow us to use your songs, then you might also make a great deal of money.

THOMAS MORLEY: Yeah, technical point: not actually my songs. The copyrights are owned by a subsidiary branch of an offshore holding company incorporated in Baden Eisenbach. An entirely legal tax arrangement, entered into on the advice of my accountants. I just want to make music, man. And I'm loving this new direction. Morley, the musical. Very cool.

BURBAGE: Yes, it does have a certain ring.

WILL: Sorry, Morley the musical?

THOMAS MORLEY: Well, Tom, Tommo. Tomster. Tomster the musical?

WILL: You think the show should be called after you?

THOMAS MORLEY: Too on the nose? Could be. What about 'Norwich Boy', the story of a one-man hit factory?

BURBAGE: Yes. Yes, I can see the groundlings flooding to see that.

WILL: I was just wondering if the show should be about you at all?

---

[*] Then, as now, some popular musical personages devoted much of their creative talent to avoiding tax.

THOMAS MORLEY: Why not? It's my musical.

WILL: Our musical. I provide the script.

THOMAS MORLEY: Yeah, you or some other geezer.

WILL: What other geezer?

THOMAS MORLEY: I don't know. Anyone. I got people.

WILL: People?

THOMAS MORLEY: Yeah, people who sort stuff.

WILL: What, like creating original stories and sparkling dialogue?

THOMAS MORLEY: Could be. They're my people. They sort what I tell them. Organize a few parties. Drum up a few grouping slaps. Write an original story with some sparkling dialogue. That's why you have people. To get stuff sorted. You want the gig or not?

Burbage doth speak to Will in the manner of an aside, which by strict convention none can overhear.

BURBAGE: Have a care, Will. Mr Morley's created the most valuable back catalogue in Christendom.

WILL: And I've written three hits called *Henry the Seventh* and a fourth called *Richard the Third*. I admit that my Verona piece wasn't as big but it's that difficult fifth play that isn't named after a numbered monarch, isn't it? The point is, I'm not going to write some tawdry hagiography designed to massage the ego of Thomas bloody Morley.

BURBAGE: Then with deepest sadness, I must needs commission some other geezer and you will have no play, no income and be ever further from buying the coat of arms on which you've set your heart.

WILL: Right. So, 'Norwich Boy' it is.

THOMAS MORLEY: I just want to make music, man.*

Morley doth sit by Will, throw a leg over his knee and kiss him.

---

* This may be the first recorded moment of what has come to be known as the 'U2 feint'.

ROBERT GREENE'S OFFICE – NIGHT

Robert Greene hath invited three cock-snobbled folderols to conference.

ROBERT GREENE: Fellow poets, brother scholars, we meet today in the face of perhaps the most heinous attack on high culture since the first clown showed his bottom to the mob. I speak of Mr Shakespeare's plan to produce in London a greatest hits musical based on the smasheroo madrigals of that loathsome ditty guffer Thomas Morley.

A COCK-SNOBBLED FOLDEROL: We must stop this aberration.

ANOTHER COCK-SNOBBLED FOLDEROL: Madrigals are popular music.

A THIRD COCK-SNOBBLED FOLDEROL: The theatre is no place for popular entertainment.

ROBERT GREENE: Quite so. Mine own sublime *Friar Bacon and Friar Bungay* is well known as the most impenetrably obscure drama in all of literature.

A COCK-SNOBBLED FOLDEROL: We must destroy this heinous assault on our pre-eminence.

ANOTHER COCK-SNOBBLED FOLDEROL: But how?

ROBERT GREENE: How, sir? Why, in the manner by which an English pamperloin always gets what he wants. Abuse of privilege, gentlemen. Abuse of privilege.

They do laugh most evilly.

WILL'S LONDON LODGINGS – DAY

Bottom tendeth the fire. Will and Kate converse over his papers.

WILL: So, 'Norwich Boy: the Tommy Morley Story' told through his greatest hits.

BOTTOM: Sounds brilliant. I'd go.

KATE: You're going to make it a biography? Sounds a bit cheesy.

WILL: Well, strangely, Kate, I have a feeling that in musical theatre, being cheesy might turn out to be a bit of a plus.*

KATE: But the whole idea was that music would provide the extra element for your Comedy of Mistakes, Misunderstandings and Coincidences.

WILL: But Morley insists that it be about him. Thus must I chronicle the inspiring life struggle of the Norwich boy. A mixed-up, wild-eyed loner with a crazy dream, a cute smile and a lute. His thrill-packed journey from humble Norfolk chorister to chief organist at St Paul's.

KATE: Ooh, it's not very thrill-packed.

WILL: During which Tommy and his identical twin Tommy, plus their identical twin servants, turn up in the same city and mistakenly hook up with each other's girlfriends.

KATE: Oh my goodness, Mr Shakespeare. That's incredible.

WILL: Well, I think it will fit.

KATE: Fit? It's uncanny. You said such a thing could happen, and it turns out, it has, and not only that, it's happened to the very person you're supposed to write a musical about. I mean, it's just spooky.

WILL: Tommy didn't actually have an identical twin. I'm just going to say that he did.

KATE: That's dishonest.

---

* Once more Shakespeare's uncanny prescience makes him truly a man for all ages.

WILL: Kate, I'm writing a celebrity biography. What has honesty got to do with it?

KATE: A dishonest and self-serving celebrity biog? I hope you're not setting some kind of precedent.*

BOTTOM: Isn't Mr Morley going to mind you giving him an identical twin?

WILL: Of course not. He gets double Tommy. He'll love it. Now, where to start?

KATE: Well, since Tommy's a composer, why don't you give him that line you showed me? The one about music and love.

WILL: If music be the food of love, play on.

KATE: Wonderful. That's perfect.

BOTTOM: Yeah, that is quite good.

WILL: Give me excess of it, that, surfeiting, the appetite may sicken, and so die. That strain again! It had a dying fall. O, it came o'er my ear like the sweet south, that breathes upon a bank of violets, stealing and giving odour.

KATE: Oh. Maybe just use the first bit.

BOTTOM: See, you always do that.

WILL: What?

BOTTOM: Well, you come up with a brilliant one-liner and then ruin it by going on and on and on. Speeches should be two lines, tops. Make it a rule.†

KATE: Anyway, let's get on. In your comedy, you have Adriana, wife of Antipholus of Ephesus—

---

* Kate's fears were to prove accurate. Our modern-age reality celebrities regularly release titles chronicling their long struggles with being self-indulgent arseholes before publishing another one the following Christmas.

† Shakespeare did not take Bottom's advice and stuck with the entire passage, although all anybody ever remembers is the first line.

WILL: Now Tommy of Norwich.

KATE: . . . mistake his identical twin, Antipholus of Syracuse—

WILL: Now Tommy of Lowestoft.

KATE: . . . for her husband, Tommy of Norwich—

WILL: Cue for a song. Tommy of Lowestoft sings 'Good Morrow, Fair Ladies of the May'.

BOTTOM: That's brilliant. Fits perfectly.

KATE: Is it May?

WILL: It is now.

KATE: Very well. Next in your comedy, you have the Syracuse—

WILL: Lowestoft.

KATE: . . . twin falling for the Ephesus—

WILL: Norwich.

KATE: . . . twin's wife's sister, which shocks the wife because she thinks he's her husband.

WILL: Exactly. She punches out the wrong Tommy and, on realizing her mistake, tries to revive him by singing 'Arise Get Up My Dear'.

BOTTOM: Brilliant! That's one of me favourites. I couldn't think how you were going to get it into the plot.

WILL: Well, that's the job, Bottom. Grab the hits and crowbar them in with a wafer-thin pretence of relevance. Then reprise the lot at the end in a great big sing-along.

BOTTOM: Can't wait to see how you fit in 'Flora, Wilt Thou Torment Me?'

WILL: Well, I thought about having a character called Flora whose love torments him. Or I could just make it a song about hay fever.

THE RED LION THEATRE – DAY

Morley sits at his clavichord. The players rehearse. Will attends.

BURBAGE: 'Alone! Cut off! No friends, no shelter!' Do you think I have your voice, Mr Morley?

THOMAS MORLEY: Brilliant, geezer. It's all so true. I was down, I was out. I mean, my parents were supporting me, obviously. But I had to take a summer job to buy my first lute.[*]

WILL: Perhaps we could get to the end of the scene.

THOMAS MORLEY: Sorry, geezer. Just loving it.

WILL: Enter Mr Condell as Flora, Tommy's childhood sweetheart.

THOMAS MORLEY: My first bird was called Gladys.

WILL: In which case you might have thought to write a madrigal called 'Gladys, Wilt Thou Torment Me?' But since you didn't, we'll just stick to the script, eh?

THOMAS MORLEY: All right, geezer. Just loving your work.

WILL: And music . . .

THOMAS MORLEY: Two, three, four . . .

Mr Condell doth dance and sing most prettily.

CONDELL: Arise, get up, my dear, arise. / My dear, make haste to be gone thee, / Lo where the bride, lo where the bride, faire Daphne, bright, / Where the bride faire Daphne bright tarries on thee.[†]

THOMAS MORLEY: I am loving this.

---

[*] Morley seems to have been the first popular musical star to claim an early struggle on the thinnest of evidence. He certainly wasn't the last.

[†] This was a massive hit in the late sixteenth century, although the lyrics then, as in pop music now, were a bit crap and meaningless.

THE RED LION THEATRE – NIGHT

'Tis the first night of Will's musical. A packed crowd are cheering the finale.

BURBAGE: Come on, London. One more time!

The cast lead the audience swaying their hands in the air.

ALL SING: Fa-lala-la-la-lala-la-la. Fa-lala-la-la. Fa-lala-la-la-la. Fa-lala-la-la-laaaaa!

The audience cheer and shout. It is verily a hit. But Robert Greene doth spy at the window most wickedly. 'Tis clear he has a plan.

MISS LUCY'S TAVERN - NIGHT

All do celebrate the night's success.

BURBAGE: More ale, Miss Lucy! The first preview was a smash. They loved it.

LUCY: They certainly did, Mr Burbage. Everyone says they are going to go again and again.

All raise their glasses and cheer.

LUCY: A-a, eh-eh. You should do an African musical next. Eh? My people have wonderful music using polyphonic ostinato. Also call-and-response choral rhythms. Oh, you could do a story about a lion cub who can't wait to be king.*

WILL: I can't really see people wanting to watch a story like that, Lucy.

BURBAGE: And besides which, the theatre is full. *Norwich Boy* will run for ever!

ALL: Hurray!

Robert Greene doth enter, all wicked malevolence.

ROBERT GREENE: Its run is already over, Mr Burbage. Today's preview was the first and last performance.

BURBAGE: Just how do you intend to stop us, Master Greene?

ROBERT GREENE: Why, by abusing my power and my position, of course. All men crave social status, particularly lowly artists.

WILL: Oh, I get it. I'll handle this, Burbage. So, Master Greene, you see that I have a hit and in your jealousy are come as Master of Heralds to offer noble rank in exchange for pulling the show.

ROBERT GREENE: Well, 'tis certain a gentleman could ne'er be associated with such an endeavour as this.

---

* Scholars speculate that Disney may have seen stolen excerpts of the Crow Folios and pinched the idea for *The Lion King* from Miss Lucy.

WILL: Sorry, Greene, but it won't work. I would love for my father to gain his family coat of arms, which is his dearest wish of all. But sod him. I will not cancel my greatest hits musical.

ALL: Hurrah!

ROBERT GREENE: Mr Shakespeare, you misunderstand me. This is not about you.

Thomas Morley enters the scene.

THOMAS MORLEY: Sorry, geezer, I'm pulling the gig. You can't use my songs.

BURBAGE: But, Tomster, we have a hit. Surely there's nothing that a-rocking and a-roistering popular music star wants more than a hit.

ROBERT GREENE: Well, there is one thing, Mr Burbage. Unfortunately I was able to recommend to the Queen that he gets it. Was I not, Sir Tommy?*

THOMAS MORLEY: Very nice. Very tasteful. Loving that.

WILL: Knighted? Him? But the bloke's a shameless tax avoider.

THOMAS MORLEY: I've done a lot of work for charity.

ROBERT GREENE: Yes, the knighthood is principally for Sir Tommy's charity work.

THOMAS MORLEY: Which I've done a lot of.

WILL: What? What bloody charity work? We never get told, do we?

THOMAS MORLEY: Couple of posh galas for the orphans. The occasional sumptuous dinner for the starving.

WILL: So you're being knighted for avoiding tax and showing off.

ROBERT GREENE: Yes, I think that is generally considered to be the proper heraldic process.

---

* Shakespeare reflects so many of our modern sensibilities. The one thing pop stars want more than anything else is to be knighted.

WILL: God, I hate this sceptred bloody isle.

ROBERT GREENE: Sir Tommy understands the ways of the world, Mr Shakespeare. Because, you see, he is a gentleman. Something nor you, nor your father, will ever be. Good day.

THOMAS MORLEY: I just want to make music, man.

Robert Greene and the Tomster exit.

BURBAGE: Will, we cannot let the theatre go dark. We'll be ruined.

WILL: Well, we could just do the play straight with lengthy monologues instead of songs.

BURBAGE: I suppose we have no choice. But what would you call it?

WILL: 'A Comedy of Mistakes, Misunderstandings and Coincidences.'

BURBAGE: Basically, it's just a comedy of errors.

WILL: Errors. Oh, I like that. That's good. I'll use that. 'A Comedy of Mistakes, Misunderstandings, Coincidences and Errors.' Brilliant.*

---

* Shakespeare eventually shortened the title. Sadly he didn't shorten the play.

WILL'S STRATFORD HOME – DAY

The family do sit about. Will enters.

WILL: God, it's good to be home. Home to the gentle, welcoming bosom of my family.

ANNE: You missed Hamnet's Latin.

JOHN: You didn't get my coat of arms.

WILL: Guilty as charged, but I did get something for Susanna. It's an undershirt signed by Tommy Morley.

SUSANNA: Don't like him any more. He sold out.

WILL: How so, my love?

SUSANNA: He did a musical.*

---

* This curious snobbery existed even in Shakespeare's day. Pinter can be endlessly revived and ancient Gershwin musicals can be presented at the National and Disney can recreate their cartoons word for word on the physical stage all to great critical acclaim, but if some rock band has the gall to think that their much-loved melodies might be appreciated and enjoyed in a new and theatrical context, then apparently they're sell-out bastards.

WILL'S STRATFORD HOME - NIGHT

Will and Anne sit with their pipes before the fire.

WILL: Well, we put on *A Comedy of Errors* without songs and despite everyone's doubts, it's actually a big hit.

ANNE: Well, that's nice. Maybe you were just a bit ahead of your time, trying to invent the musical.

WILL: You're probably right, wife. Still, it was fun for a night. People gathered together, singing, laughing, waving their arms in the air. Just having a joyful night out.

ANNE: What's wrong with that?

WILL: What indeed? I hope that one day in some future age, London will be full of theatres, and they'll all have musicals in them. 'Tis a joyful dream.

ANNE: Or a living nightmare.

WILL: Yes, I suppose opinion will always be divided on that one.

EPISODE 5

BEWARE MY STING!

The following episode tells the story of
Shakespeare writing *The Taming of the Shrew*. In the
modern age, when the issue of male entitlement
and sexual harassment is finally and properly at
the forefront of the national conversation, it seems
unlikely that Shakespeare's appalling 'comedy' of
sexism and sexual abuse will ever be staged again.
Unless, of course, someone chooses to play the
'irony' card.

WILL'S LONDON LODGINGS – DAY

Will doth sit at table before a large pie.

WILL: Bottom, bring me a hammer and a cold chisel. This pie crust be so too tough, pixie cobblers could use the crumbs to fashion the fairies' dancing shoes.

Bottom respondeth most grumpishly.

BOTTOM: You could always try cooking a pie yourself, of course.

WILL: Yes, Bottom, or a third way would be for me to employ a servant whose skill set comes slightly closer to matching their job description.

KATE: Let me bring you a sharper knife, Mr Shakespeare. Hold, sirrah! Parry! Advance! Hold! (*Advanceth upon Will holding a table knife in fencing mode*) Stage fighting is a key skill in the actor's armoury.

WILL: Hmmm, yes, for 'skill' read two mincing preeners slowly circling each other while occasionally hitting their swords together with a big clang.*

KATE: So exciting.

WILL: I know you long to play the ingénue in my still unfinished teen romance, but girls be banned from acting.

KATE: But it's so obvious that real girls would be better at playing girls.

BOTTOM: Yeah, cos that's just really logical, isn't it?

KATE: Um, yes!

BOTTOM: Maybe you think we should get real kings to play the kings? Or real ancient Romans to play the ancient Romans.

---

* Shakespeare does actors a disservice here. There is more to stage fighting than he describes. Besides circling and clanging, they also periodically come close together, pushing their swords against each other before both leaping backwards with a fierce cry as if the other has forced them back.

KATE: Um, that's not quite the same . . .

BOTTOM: Or real witches to play the witches.

KATE: I get what you are trying to—

BOTTOM: Or a real St George for St George and the dragon, and a real dragon. Real armies for the battles, real fairies for the enchanted woods. *Theseus and the Minotaur?* Where are we going to find a minotaur?

KATE: Yes, all right, Bottom! I get it.

BOTTOM: Yeah, and you know I am right too. Besides which, a girl onstage would be nothing but a proslington and a whoreslap.

KATE: Oh, another brilliant argument, Bottom, because delivering blank verse in the character of a dead queen is obviously just code for 'Hello, ducks, I'll fondle your fandangles for a farthing'.

BOTTOM: Dirty talk won't win your argument.

KATE: Finish your great teen romance, Mr Shakespeare. Let me be your Juliet.

WILL: No, Kate. Quite apart from anything else, I just don't think the public wants to see a love story.

KATE: Certainly not one like your *Two Gentlemen of Verona*, where the hero brazenly cheats on the heroine and you yet have her marrying the hornsome bastable anyway.

WILL: I needed a happy ending.

KATE: Well, it might have been nice if it had developed out of plot and character instead of simply being nailed on at the end.

WILL: I'faith the maid is right; I did just nail it on at the end.*
(*Doth turn away, speaking in the manner of an aside*) I canst only

---

* It is useful to have evidence that Shakespeare was aware of the glaringly illogical and inconsistent nature of the ending of the *Two Gentlemen of Verona*. This may finally relieve scholars and schoolteachers alike of the onerous duty of pretending it's somehow clever.

hope the verse with which I nailed it be so obscure that future generations trusting in my genius will just think they are being stupid and have missed something.[*] (*Turneth to Kate once more*) Look I'm . . . I'm sorry, Kate, I know you want to play Julian.

KATE: Juliet.

WILL: As I said, Juliet, and I would love to see the play performed but as you know it's a work in progress. I've got my double-death ending but much else remains unwrit.[†] For instance, I need a lot more lines for the amusing nurse.

BOTTOM: No, don't do it, master. Less lines. Trust me. Kate read me a bit. The nurse really gets on me nerves.

KATE: She could be getting a teeny bit irritating with her endless clucky duckyness, Mr Shakespeare.

WILL: Which is why she needs more lines. You know my rule: if you are in a comedy hole, keep digging.[‡] I'm not going to do it now, it's a romance and I can't risk a kissy-wissy, gropy-pokey load of soppy old mushington right now. My next play must be a smasheroo. You know my dream.

KATE: To be recognized now and for all time as indisputably the greatest writer that ever lived and to buy the second biggest house in Stratford.

WILL: Exactly. That's it in a nutshell.

BOTTOM: In a nutshell? What does that mean?

WILL: Oh, 'tis just one of the numerous inspired phrases which I'm wont to coin and which I am confident will enter the common idiom.

---

[*] Shakespeare was right to hope.

[†] The double-death ending was of course inspired by the youth Florian in the first episode of the First Crow Folio.

[‡] Bottom and Kate are right. The nurse is extremely irritating, requiring an inspired comic actress to breathe life into the clucky duckyness.

BOTTOM: Well, good luck with 'in a nutshell' cos I think it's stupid. I mean, you couldn't really get anything at all inside a nutshell cos they are very, very small and also full of nuts. Clue's in the name.

WILL: Your observations, Bottom, are neither here nor there.

KATE: Is that another one?

WILL: Yes, just invented it. When it comes to language, the world's mine oyster. In fact, I'm so clever I could end up with too much of a good thing.

KATE: Maybe you should stop now.

WILL: Can't. They just pop up all of a sudden but, give the devil his due, there's method in my madness.

KATE: Really, stop it.

WILL: Why 'tis a foregone conclusion that they'll leave you bedazzled and in stitches and before long you will be demanding more with bated breath.

BOTTOM: The world's your oyster? Why would that be a good thing?

WILL: Tad obscure, er . . . what the dickens! I'll spoil my spotless reputation. Must be tired; I didn't sleep one wink. If I'm not careful, you'll send me packing on a wild goose chase and I'll vanish into thin air or be dead as a doornail.

KATE: Stop it. I really mean it. You are very clever, Mr Shakespeare, but you can be an awful show-off.

WILL: But with a heart of gold.

KATE: No! Just a show-off.

WILL: Ay, there's the rub.

KATE: Stop it. And actually I happen to know you didn't originate the phrase 'dead as a doornail'.

WILL: I bloomin' did.

KATE: You bloomin' didn't. William Langland did in his Middle English allegorical narrative poem *Piers Plowman*.

305

WILL: (*To self*) In faith, the bothersome girl is right. Filched have I some of my finest phrases from prior sources and common usage. I can only hope that as the years go by the original derivation will fade from memory and I'll get all the credit.

KATE: But never mind Langland, we were talking about you writing a new play.

WILL: Yes, but I am sorry but it's not going to be my teen romance. I need to design a hit. Women love theatre so of course I must write a heroine that will appeal to them. Gutsy.

KATE: I like that.

WILL: Tough and independent.

KATE: I love that.

WILL: Witty and headstrong.

KATE: Feisty.

WILL: Feisty, Kate? I know not what you mean. Be it a foreign term?

KATE: No, I am doing what you do, creating a new word. 'Feisty', to refer to a gutsy, independent, headstrong woman.

WILL: Hmm, not sure.

KATE: It's brilliant. In fact, I am a bit worried it will end up getting overused to the point of banality, eventually being appropriated by any loud-mouthed harridan who seeks to lend an empowering gloss to being a gobby bitchslap.*

WILL: Hmm, perhaps best leave new words to me, Kate, because 'feisty' just ain't gonna fly.

KATE: Well, however she's referred to, you are going to create a strong woman who is both strong and a woman. Bravo.

WILL: Yes, and then I am going to crush, abuse and humiliate her.

---

* Before the Crow Folios, scholars believed that the word 'feisty' originated in the late nineteenth century.

KATE: Crush, abuse? But why?

WILL: Because while women may love the theatre, 'tis men who pay for entry. Thus have I in mind a sort of battle of the sexes where a strong woman is tamed by a man.

KATE: I have no words.

WILL: Yes, well, luckily, Kate, that's my job.

MISS LUCY'S TAVERN – DAY

Kate and Lucy sit at a table in the tavern.

KATE: I have come to see you, Mistress Lucy, because you are a strong woman. You have independence, your own business. How did you do it?

LUCY: I cut off the penis of the cur who enslaved me, stole his gold, jumped ship at Tilbury and bought a pub.

KATE: I am not sure any of that will help me get on to the stage.

LUCY: Pah! Lady acting is against the law, Kate, because the law hates women. Your only hope is to do as I did: use a man to get what you need. Oh ho! Will Shakespeare is your friend.

KATE: You think I should cut off Mr Shakespeare's penis?

LUCY: No, no, no, just get him to help you. Persuade him to write a sublime female lead and convince him that only you can play it.

KATE: Oh yes, but how?

LUCY: Ah, ah, eh, eh. Kate, you are a woman. A woman has special skills to move a man.

KATE: Wait, you think I should embroider him a cushion cover? I suppose it might work.

WILL'S STRATFORD HOME – DAY

The family be present. Will doth enter.

WILL: Home am I, wife, let joy be unbounded. Father has returned.

ANNE: Good journey, love?

WILL: Well, it's funny you should say that, Anne, because you know how up until now I've never, ever had a good journey?

ANNE: Yes.

WILL: Well, amazingly, I still haven't. I had to stand the whole way. Two days with my face in the armpit of a man who appeared to be actually sweating urine. I am knackmungled. Susanna, bring ale and pie.

SUSANNA: Get it yourself. Leave me alone, I want to die. Shut up.

ANNE: Don't mind her, Will. (*Whispering*) She's a bit more sensitive than usual. She hath taken up that burden which every woman must carry at the journey of each moon.

WILL: Oh I see. (*Loudly*) Mum says you started your periods, Sue.

SUSANNA: Shut up!

WILL: What? What did I say?

ANNE: God's bouncing boobingtons, husband! For a bloke who reckons himself to be the world's greatest poet you've got about as much tact and sensitivity as Mrs Moomoo's flatumongous arseington.

MARY: She's not talking about Susanna's women's business anyway. It's her character. The girl is totally out of control.

ANNE: She's so gutsy and headstrong.

WILL: Feisty.

ANNE: Ooo, that's a really good word for it. A new one of yours?

WILL: (*Shiftily*) Yes. Just trying it out.

MARY: Well, she's feisty all right, and 'tis not a goodling look for a maid.

John Shakespeare be ever sat upon the privy pot.

JOHN: You should never have taught her to read. Women aren't supposed to be all sophisticated like us men.

ANNE: And the thing is, our Judith is so sweet and kind that all do love her, and it would be awful if Judith were married and Sue left an old maid. Life is dangerous for a single woman, particularly a clever one.

MARY: They be suspected of being witches.

JOHN: Because most of them are witches.

ANNE: Sue will need a husband.

MARY: But who will have the feisty little bitchington?

SUSANNA: I am still here, you know!

WILL: Well, what about this for an idea? If Judith be so pretty and popular and Sue such a feisty little bitchington, then why do not I, a stern father, announce that any young knave who doth tip his cap to our Judy must first find another who will take our Sue?

ANNE: Will, all the world is not a stage, and all the men and women aren't merely players.

WILL: Bit of a tortured image, my love.*

ANNE: Setting Sue up through Judy might work in one of your comedies but it won't work in the real world.

WILL: You're right, you're absolutely right, and it's brilliant.

ANNE: Brilliant? I've just said your stupid plan won't stop Sue ending up isolated, pitied, despised and endangered for life.

WILL: Yes, but you also said that it would work in a comedy, and it absolutely would.

---

* Clearly Will was to remember this phrase and use it in *As You Like It*. In fact, it's generally considered to be the most memorable line in the entire play.

THE RED LION THEATRE - DAY

The players are visited by the odious Robert Greene.

BURBAGE: I am sorry, Mr Greene, I know you are anxious to see staged a revival of your *Bungling Bacon*.

ROBERT GREENE: *Bacon and Bungay.*

BURBAGE: But we await a new play by Mr Shakespeare.

Now doth Greene speak in the manner of an aside, which by strict convention none can overhear.

ROBERT GREENE: Shakespeare, Shakespeare – ever doth the upstart crow peck at my botty buttocks. Curse him for his feverish fertility, but I will finish him yet. (*To the players*) Remember, sirrah, that I am Master of Revels. Perchance when the oafish bumsnot delivers his play I will find excuse to deny it licence.

BURBAGE: You overstep yourself, Mr Greene. I'm London's leading actor-manager and not without friends. Unless Will's new play be actual treason, I will see you hanged before it is denied licence.

ROBERT GREENE: Oh, you actors think you are so special, do you not, Mr Burbage? You likewise, Mr Condell.

KEMPE: And me, I'm mad special.

ROBERT GREENE: You flatter yourselves that you have social and political influence. Well, *ha!* You would be better to remember that you are naught but preening lovey kisses, puffed-up, strutty, shouty boys who people actually find quite irritating.* Do not make an enemy of me, sirrah. Good day!

Greene doth take his leave.

BURBAGE: 'Puffed-up, strutty, shouty boys'?

CONDELL: 'Preening lovey kisses'? Outrageous slur!

---

* It is interesting to note that the status of actors in society has changed very little over the years, even though these days they get knighthoods.

KEMPE: Well, you two are a bit.

BURBAGE: Shut up, Kempe! Of course actors are special and influential.

CONDELL: Hugely special and influential.

KEMPE: Mad special and influential.

BURBAGE: It's a great burden of deep responsibility.

CONDELL: I feel it very deeply.

BURBAGE: We have a great duty to use our influence for good.

CONDELL: To point out, for instance, that poverty is horrid and that cruelty is cruel.

BURBAGE: Oh, absolutely. Actors have an enormous responsibility to point out that poverty is horrid and cruelty is cruel.[*]

KEMPE: Cos otherwise who'd know?

BURBAGE: I doubt it would occur to people.

CONDELL: Course it wouldn't.

---

[*] Many modern-day actors also feel this great responsibility.

312

WILL'S LONDON LODGINGS – DAY

Marlowe, Bottom and Kate are all present as Will describes his play.

WILL: So, we're in Padua, right?

BOTTOM: Where's that?

WILL: Dunno. Italy I think, but I may have made it up. I left school at fourteen. I don't do geographical detail.

KIT MARLOWE: You should watch that, Will. Centuries after you are gone people may use it to claim you were too thick to have written your own plays.*

WILL: Don't be absurd, Kit. The idea that I never wrote my own plays could only appeal to the sort of naive fact-averse fantasists who claim that the monks sacked their own monasteries to make Henry the Eighth look bad and that man never walked on the New World.

BOTTOM: I don't believe he did. I think Raleigh faked the potato in a garden shed in Catford by crossing – by crossing a turnip with a radish.

WILL: Then you're an insane, conspiracy-mad coach-spotter, and I can only thank benign providence that ignoramuses like you will never wield political influence.† So, we are in Padua, and Lucentio wants to marry Bianca. Beautiful, sweet, obedient, and of course as hot and steaming as a fresh cowpat in a frosty meadow.

KIT MARLOWE: I must say I like her.

BOTTOM: My kinda girl.

---

* As mentioned previously, the fact that Shakespeare got two geographical details wrong in thirty-seven plays has led many pompous snobs to claim one so ill-educated could not have written such masterpieces.

† Many people have credited Shakespeare with almost second sight in his understanding of humanity but he certainly didn't predict the Trump and Brexit campaigns.

KATE: You don't think it might be nice to give her a few tiny extra elements?

WILL: What elements did you have in mind, Kate?

KATE: Well, I don't know. A character maybe? A personality?

WILL: Kate, you weren't listening. I told you: she is mild, sweet, obedient and hot. How much character and personality do you want?

KIT MARLOWE: Must say, you're on to a winner here, mate. Cool Lucentio fools the hot Bianca and marries her. Perfect plot, job done. Let's go to the pub.

WILL: Oh, but I am not finished. That's not all of it.

KIT MARLOWE: You've got enough, mate. Quit while you are ahead.

BOTTOM: That's what I keep saying.

KIT MARLOWE: You do this all the time.

BOTTOM: Over-complicate things.

KIT MARLOWE: Come up with a perfectly nice plot of boy meets girl, boy gets girl, and then you ruin it with all your usual rubbish of mistaken identities, absurd coincidences, supernatural interventions.*

BOTTOM: People not recognizing their own lovers cos they are wearing tiny, tiny masks? It's just daft.

KATE: Actually, I think Mr Shakespeare's plot be already too complex.

WILL: Really, Kate, how so? I have scarce begun it.

KATE: Well, boy meets girl, boy gets girl. Why not say 'boy owns girl' and leave it at that, perhaps displaying your leading lady alluringly clad and in a cage.

---

* Christopher Marlowe may not have been much of a playwright but he would have made an astute literary critic.

KIT MARLOWE: Actually, that's not a bad idea.

WILL: Look, I don't need a new idea or a new plot, complex or otherwise. I've got a plot and it's brilliant. Lucentio loves Bianca but Bianca has a sister, Katherine, who be all that Bianca is not. She be bold, assertive, opinionated and feisty.

KATE: Can I play her?

WILL: No, Kate. So of course no one would dream of marrying her.

KIT MARLOWE: Well, *obviously*. You'd have to be insane!

WILL: Thus Bianca and Katherine's dad declare that none may marry sweet Bianca until he has offloaded bolingbroke-busting Katherine.

KIT MARLOWE: Now this is good.

WILL: Enter Lucentio's pal Petruchio, a charming but feckless fella.

KIT MARLOWE: Loving him already.

WILL: He needs a fortune and he doesn't care who he marries to get it.

KIT MARLOWE: What a rogue! My kind of guy.

WILL: He offers to take Katherine and commences to break her spirit by starving her, refusing her clothing and depriving her of sleep for days on end.

Bottom and Marlowe both laugh most merrily at what Will describes.

KIT MARLOWE: That's perfect!

KATE: And does Katherine cut this pervert's throat in the night with a rusty knife?

WILL: No, she allows herself to be happily broken and is soon hilariously agreeing with everything her husband says. I have a lot of fun with that.

Whilst the men laugh, the maid Kate is stunned.

315

WILL: Driven to a compliance bordering on dementia, Katherine accepts that the sun is the moon and an old man is a beautiful young maiden.

Bottom and Marlowe do weep with laughter.

KIT MARLOWE: That's gonna get a big laugh. Bossy bird goes raving tonto. Love it!

BOTTOM: I am chuckling already.

WILL: Anyway, Lucentio marries Bianca and Katherine marries Petruchio and at the wedding the reformed harridan delivers a lengthy monologue about women being obedient to men.

KIT MARLOWE: What, there is even a moral? Ohhh, I don't know how you do it, Will!

BOTTOM: Yeah, I'm going to say it's a winner. It'll be your most popular comedy yet.*

KATE: Mr Shakespeare, please do not write this appalling story.

WILL: Too late. I did it on the coach from Stratters. Burbage has it now. It's called *The Taming of the Shrew*.

KIT MARLOWE: Best title ever! End of!

KATE: I have invented a new phrase, Mr Shakespeare, especially for you.

WILL: Really, Kate? That's very flattering.

Kate doth seethe with righteous fury for the wrongs done to her sex.

KATE: Yes, it is, for you are strong as if made from chain, exciting like a pageant. You have risen up from nowhere as if a city on water. You are a guiding light and the very heart of a man.

---

* Bottom was right. Once again, this simple serving man proves himself remarkably astute in his analysis of his master's works. Perhaps Shakespeare's career would have been even more spectacular had he paid more attention to Bottom's comments and advice.

WILL: Your words move me, sweet Kate, but I would fain know their meaning.

KATE: Why mail is made from chain, a pageant is a show, the city on water be naught but Venice, the light that guides is a star, and the heart of a man is his soul. Put them all together and you get . . .

WILL: Mail, show, Venice, star, soul.

KATE: I'll leave it with you.[*]

---

[*] Astonishingly, the word 'chauvinism' was not coined until the late nineteenth century and is derived from the name Nicolas Chauvin, who was a particularly patriotic Napoleonic officer. Kate is therefore showing prescience even more incredible than Shakespeare's own.

THE RED LION THEATRE – DAY

Burbage and Condell do rehearse a scene from The Taming of the Shrew. *Kempe doth watch most dubiously.*

BURBAGE: 'Come, come, you wasp; i' faith, you are too angry.'

CONDELL: 'If I be waspish, best beware my sting.'

BURBAGE: 'Who knows not where a wasp does wear his sting? In his tail.'

CONDELL: 'In his tongue!' Oh, I do think this is good.

BURBAGE: Yes, it's his funniest scene yet.

The odious Greene doth enter.

ROBERT GREENE: Which is an insult to the person of Her Majesty.

BURBAGE: An insult to the Queen? How be it insulting, sirrah?

ROBERT GREENE: Why, by speaking ill of her sex, 'tis very treason. I shall not even offer it up for her consideration.

BURBAGE: This be not fair, Mr Greene. The piece is a harmless comedy and you know it. You overstep your authority, sirrah.

Greene sneers with most ugly visage.

ROBERT GREENE: Um, dur. I think you know what to do. (*Sotto voce*) *Bacon Bungay.* Good day.

WILL'S LONDON LODGINGS – DAY

Kate doth tidy most prettily. Marlowe enters.

KIT MARLOWE: Good morrow, Kate. Will home?

KATE: He's gone back to Stratford, Mr Marlowe.

KIT MARLOWE: Ah, shame. Now his *Shrew* is in rehearsal, I was gonna have another stab at persuading him to give me his Edward the Second.

KATE: He may need it himself. Mr Greene refuses to show his awful, abusive play to Her Majesty for fear of offending her with its dreadful attitude to women.

KIT MARLOWE: Ha! That bastable would use any excuse.

KATE: It seems to me that Mr Greene has done Mr Shakespeare a favour. For Gloriana is a proud member of her sex and her wrath to see women so offended might have been terrible.

KIT MARLOWE: Do you think? I'm not sure.

KATE: Hmm. Perchance you don't know much about women, Mr Marlowe.

KIT MARLOWE: Er, kinda do, particularly Queens, especially Ginger Liz.

WILL'S STRATFORD HOME – NIGHT

In their chamber, Will and Anne do lie a-bed.

WILL: Well, my love, all is not lost. It occurred to me that I could at least use the work I have done on my play to help our Sue.

ANNE: How so, husband?

WILL: Why, to tame her, wife, as Petruchio does tame the shrew. I can't see how it can fail. Tomorrow we begin the taming of the Sue. Did you see what I did there?

ROBERT GREENE'S HOUSE - NIGHT

Marlowe has come a-visiting the odious Robert Greene.

KIT MARLOWE: I just came round to thank you for saving Will's life. I mean, I know you hate his gutlings so it was big of you.

ROBERT GREENE: Saving Shakespeare's life, Mr Marlowe? I know not what you mean.

KIT MARLOWE: Why, by refusing to show the Queen his traitorous, seditious new play.

ROBERT GREENE: Traitorous, seditious? It be but a foolish sex comedy.

KIT MARLOWE: Yeah, but about a strong, clever, determined woman who refuses to marry whilst all around would see her wed. Remind you of anyone?*

ROBERT GREENE: God's boobikins! I catch your thought.

Marlowe doth take his leave. Greene doth muse.

ROBERT GREENE: How did I not spot this? I thought only to set aside his play for mine but now I see the crow is truly in my clutches. I will be done with him for ever.

---

* Marlowe here refers to Queen Elizabeth, whose failure to take a husband led to the presumption that she died a virgin. Yeah. Right.

WILL'S STRATFORD HOME - DAY

The Shakespeare family be at breakfast.

SUSANNA: Can I have another bit of bacon?

Will doth whisper to Anne.

WILL: Mark me, wife. Let the taming begin. (*Doth leap up and shout at his startled daughter*) Bacon! Never! I will see thee starve.

SUSANNA: What? You are so weird. Shut up. Give me bacon.

Will's manner changeth to a sweet and loving tone.

WILL: Why, sweet Susanna, this bacon be not good enough for one so charming.

JOHN: Is he pisslingtoned?

SUSANNA: You are such an arsemongle.

Will doth feign delight at this insult.

WILL: Arsemongle, am I? Kind Sue doth dub me arsemongle. Oh, that all the world would call me arsemongle.

JOHN: You're an arsemongle.

Will doth whisper to Anne.

WILL: It's going brilliantly. The girl be all confused by my hilariously contrary manner.[*]

SUSANNA: Why has Dad gone all weird? Tell him to stop.

WILL: Why, daughter, look through the window – is not the most beautiful moon you ever saw?

SUSANNA: Er, it's the sun, Dad. It's morning. Are you all right?

Will doth feign the most shouty fury.

---

[*] Just as audiences ever after would be confused by the blinding insanity of *The Taming of the Shrew*.

WILL: It's the moon, daughter, because I am your lord and father and I say it is the moon!

SUSANNA: All right, it's the moon. Who cares? Whatever. Why are you being weird?

WILL: (*Doth whisper to Anne*) See, wife, it's working! She doth own the sun to be the moon. Was ever a girl so tamed? Now to trick her once again with my sparkling wit. (*Turneth to his daughter*) Susanna, spy you that pretty maid sat next to Granny. Be she not a fragrant beauty?

MARY: You're right, husband. Our son be pisslingtoned.

SUSANNA: You mean Granddad?

WILL: Not Granddad, child, for Granddad is a wrinkly old man with a face like a slapped scroting sack. 'Tis a fresh-faced maid.*

SUSANNA: All right, it's a maid. Have it your way. I don't care. Stop being weird.

WILL: Aha! And so the shrew be tamed.

SUSANNA: Shrew?

WILL: You no doubt all thought it passing strange that I be so contrary with Susanna.

SUSANNA: Shrew!

WILL: But now must own that by such tricks have I cured her of her feistiness and made of her a sweet, compliant maid.

SUSANNA: Shrew!

WILL: A girl who will agree with everything her father says and thus also the husband who will one day replace me as her master. Job done. God I am good.

Susanna leapeth up in fury.

---

* These are exactly the tricks that Petruchio plays on Kate in his *Taming of the Shrew* and which audiences have pretended to understand and find funny. It seems Shakespeare's own daughter wasn't so easily pleased.

SUSANNA: You are the worst person in the whole world! I know everyone else thinks I am a gobby bitchington but I thought at least you respected me and now you are calling me a shrew? I hate you. I hate you! Don't ever talk to me ever again!

Susanna doth storm from the house in fury.

ANNE: Well, that went well.

WILL: Yes, well, it, it, it may be that the taming will require one or two more witty contradictions before it takes full effect.

Marlowe enters.

KIT MARLOWE: Morning, Mrs S, Mr and Mrs S senior. Any ale and pie? I've ridden overnight from London.

ANNE: Course, Mr Marlowe.

WILL: Kit! Well, what in the name of Titania's tiny toenails brings you here?*

KIT MARLOWE: I'm telling you to get your sweet country arseington back to the theatre. I tricked Greene into showing the Queen your *Shrew*.

WILL: Really? How? He swore it would offend her.

KIT MARLOWE: Aye, cuz, but I told him it would do worse than that. I pointed out that it could even be a construed as a call for Gloriana *herself* to be tamed and forced to marry.

WILL: Oh my God! That never even occurred to me. You've condemned me.

KIT MARLOWE: Oh, don't get your puffling pants in such a twist. She loved the play, as I knew she would.

WILL: But how could you be so sure?

---

* Titania would feature in Shakespeare's later play *A Midsummer Night's Dream*. Clearly he was already toying with the cloying whimsy which was to make the actual play such hard work.

324

KIT MARLOWE: Will, Liz has been on the throne for thirty-three years, daily making laws on everything from what language can be used in prayer books to what colour clothing people of different classes should wear, and in all that time has she done one single thing to improve the lot of women?*

WILL: Well, can't think of anything offhand.

ANNE: Bit disappointing, when you put it like that.

KIT MARLOWE: Far from feeling solidarity with other birds, Gloriana clearly loves being quite literally the only woman in the country that matters. She likes keeping the rest of her sex in her place. I knew she would adore *The Taming of the Shrew*, and she did.†

WILL: She adored it? Really?

KIT MARLOWE: Oh yes, and in fact I confidently expect history to record it was one of her favourite comedies. Can we get this pie to go, Mrs S? Wouldn't want to miss opening night.

---

* Queen Elizabeth was an able and prolific law-maker, involving herself in every type of social change with the single exception of helping out her sisters. This is a side of her character that those who seek to hold her up as a female hero conveniently ignore.
† *The Taming of the Shrew* was said to be Elizabeth's favourite comedy. It seems Marlowe was right. Elizabeth had absolutely zero interest in empowering other women. In fact, the opposite: she wanted to be the single woman that counted in a world of men. Like Mrs Thatch.

THE RED LION THEATRE – NIGHT

Burbage, Condell and Kempe do present The Taming of the Shrew.

CONDELL: 'Thy husband is thy lord, thy life, thy keeper, thy head, thy sovereign. Such duty as the subject owes the prince, even such a woman oweth to her husband.'

In the audience the men cheer while the women grimace.

KIT MARLOWE: Hear, hear! It's brilliant!

KATE: I think I'm gonna be sick.

CONDELL: 'And when she is forward, peevish, sullen, sour, and not obedient to his honest will, what is she but a foul contending rebel and graceless traitor to her loving lord?'

The men do applaud. The women look glum.

WILL'S LONDON LODGINGS – NIGHT

Will sitteth at table. Kate brings him beer.

WILL: Well, my *Shrew* was a huge hit but I take little pleasure in it for it has cost me the good opinion of two women whose respect I value. Yours, for one.

KATE: I still respect you, Mr Shakespeare, for although I think your play doth sorely insult women, you are a creature of your times, and in truth even now your misogyny be less offensive than most. At least you take trouble to write your women some fine verse.*

WILL: And you do realize that the last big speech in the play, the one where Katherine calls on women to worship and obey their husbands, it's supposed to be ironic. I ... I mean ... I ... I mean that's clear, isn't it?

KATE: Mr Shakespeare, please. Did you really write it ironically or are you hoping that in later, more enlightened ages scholars will try to get you off the hook by pretending that's what you intended?

WILL: Well, you know – either way.

KATE: But, intrigued am I, who is the other woman whose respect you fear you've lost?

WILL: Why, my lovely Sue. She knows 'twas her who inspired my Shrew and is hurt most mortally. I would fain make amends but I know not how.

KATE: Well, just because a girl is feisty and full of spirit like your Sue, doesn't mean she values not romance. You should write another play. One featuring a sensitive, articulate, headstrong, tragic, beautiful, captivating, feisty maid of Susanna's age.

WILL: All right, Kate, you win. I'll finish *Romeo and Julian*.

KATE: *Juliet?*

WILL: *Juliet*, yes.

---

* The crap other Elizabethan playwrights wrote for their female characters (if they had female characters at all) simply beggars belief.

WILL'S STRATFORD HOME – NIGHT

Will and Anne do sit before the fire with their pipes.

ANNE: I didn't find your *Shrew* play too offensive when I saw it. I thought it was quite funny, actually, if you just see it as a load of illogical, stupid, potty old bolingbrokes.[*]

WILL: Thank you, wife. That's a lovely thing to say.

ANNE: And it's nice to have a stonking great hit raking in the cash.

Susanna doth enter. She holds a script.

SUSANNA: Dad, Juliet's beautiful.

WILL: Really, daughter? I ... I ... remember you once saying nobody talked like that.

SUSANNA: I was thirteen, you know. I'm fourteen now. I'm mature. And I just love it.

WILL: The end not too sad?

SUSANNA: Er, of course it's too sad. It's endlessly sad, heart-breaking, eternally sad. I love it. And you really based Juliet on me?

WILL: Well, yes, absolutely. You know, you're a girl and Juliet's a girl so ... direct lift really.

---

[*] Which is absolutely the only way that this play can be enjoyed.

EPISODE 6

SWEET SORROW

In this last episode of the Second Crow Folio we see Shakespeare finally completing and staging his immortal teen snog fest *Romeo and Juliet.* That he only completed it as a result of the machinations of his landlady's daughter is a new and fascinating revelation, as is the sex of the first ever Romeo.

MISS LUCY'S TAVERN – NIGHT

The players, Marlowe and Will do quaff ale served by Miss Lucy.

BURBAGE: Our new theatre be scarcely built, yet already the God-prodding Pure-titties on the city council petitioned Our Majesty for its closure. They say it be nothing but a den of debauchery. Ha!*

LUCY: Hmm. I have seen more debauchery at the Eokoto e-kule.

WILL: The Eokoto e-kule, Lucy?

LUCY: Mm. The Maasai milk-drinking ceremony, in which a strong and virile young warrior is allowed to drink milk by himself for the first time since his circumcision. Oh oh, it is a very boring ceremony. Bah! But not as boring as *Henry the Sixth Part Three.*†

WILL: Ha ha! You jest, of course. Hard to see how a five-act, forty-seven-character play written entirely in blank verse about a third of the life of a lesser-known Henry could be described as boring. Still, I do agree. It is a puzzle how the city council justify their charge that putting on my plays will result in the use of prostitutes.

KIT MARLOWE: Sometimes it's just the only way to stay awake during the last act.

BURBAGE: Point is, that is their charge. Once more, we're in desperate need of a titled patron.

LUCY: Eh eh. I thought you were the Lord Chamberlain's men?

---

* Theatres in Shakespeare's time and indeed for long after were thought to be places where the pursuit of every vice was more important than the actual plays being presented. Anyone who's sat through a Pinter play might well have wished that the tradition had not died out.

† Extensive literary research has led some scholars to conclude that there is nothing as boring as *Henry VI Part 3*. Clearly they hadn't read *The Merry Wives of Windsor*.

BURBAGE: Sadly no longer, Lucy. He is fearful of the Pure-titties and has withdrawn his favour.

KIT MARLOWE: What about that young Henry Southampton? I mean, he hates the Pure-titties and would love to snook their cocks. You know him well. That posh boy you used to fancy.

WILL: I did not fancy him. I merely happened to mention in passing that he was lovelier than a summer's day and that his eternal beauty would live as long as men still breathed and had eyes to see. Entirely ambiguous lines, I think you'll agree, and not remotely suggestive of a deeply personal and agonizing private passion. I really had hoped that this whole silly idea that I be part hugger-tugger might have done its dash by now.[*]

KIT MARLOWE: Yes, I kind of think that one's going to hang around, mate. Look, I see young Southie on the dilly from time to time. I can ask him if you like.

WILL: Won't do any good. He hates the theatre. Can't stand histories.

BURBAGE: What about one of your romantic comedies?

WILL: Hates them more. He's an incorrigible romantic and resents the way the theatre only ever uses love as a source of fun.

KIT MARLOWE: Well, why not write a romantic tragedy? Might lure him in.

BURBAGE: Romantic tragedy? No, it's never been done.

WILL: That's right, Burbage. But doing what's never been done is exactly what I do. For instance, this morning, I came up with three entirely original words: multitudinous, newfangled and scuffle.[†]

KIT MARLOWE: I don't know what the world'd do without you, mate.

---

[*] Shakespeare would be surprised to know that the theory is still going strong four centuries later. Although those who knew him probably wouldn't be.
[†] Shakespeare is indeed credited with inventing these words and many others. Sometimes he actually could be pretty clever.

WILL'S LONDON LODGINGS - DAY

Will doth converse with Kate and Bottom.

WILL: And so you see, Kate, 'tis finally time to present my teen romance.

KATE: So exciting. English theatre's first proper romantic tragedy, and is all complete?

WILL: Pretty much. Although I'm still not entirely happy with the balcony scene. Something tells me it's going to be a biggie. What do you think? 'Goodnight, goodnight. Parting is just so boring that I could say goodnight till it be morning.'

KATE: I like the intention. She's sad because her love must leave, but she's only sad because she loves. It's a sort of sweet sorrow.

Will doth jot down this phrase most surreptitiously.

WILL: You literally read my thoughts.

KATE: Such an honour.

WILL: 'Goodnight, goodnight. Parting is such sweet sorrow. Mustn't grumble. Mustn't wallow.' Nailed it.

KATE: I'm not really sure about the second bit.

WILL: You're right, of course. It's missing two iambic beats. How about, 'Mustn't flipping wallow'?*

KATE: It's not really the scansion. I just preferred your idea about looking forward to the glad morning. Uplifting, hopeful. Like a young girl's love.

WILL: Yes, but morning doesn't rhyme with sorrow.

BOTTOM: Morrow does.

WILL: As I was about to say, Bottom.

---

* This iambic pentameter obsession was a bit like a mental illness. Scholars have rightly asked the question: why? Just why?

BOTTOM: Don't think you were.

WILL: I most definitely was. 'Goodnight, goodnight, parting is such sweet sorrow that I could say goodnight till it be morrow.'

KATE: Brilliant.

BOTTOM: The last word is the best bit.

WILL: I'm loving this conflicted-emotion sweet-sorrow stuff I came up with. I think I should use it for Juliet's actual dismissal of Romeo from the balcony. She needs to tell him to leave, but also that she wishes he could stay.

KATE: Oh, she would make him her captive.

WILL: But bound only by bonds of love.

BOTTOM: Well, when I were a boy, and my life were very harsh and brutal—

WILL: Please, Bottom. I'm working.

BOTTOM: Sometimes, in me pain and loneliness, I'd trap a lark or a sparrow and hold it fast with a thread of silk.

WILL: Bottom, I'm trying to concentrate.

BOTTOM: It were, like ... so beautiful and delicate and sweet of song, and I knew I should release it but the only freedom I could bear to grant it were the length of the thread.

Both Will and Kate pause most thoughtfully.

KATE: Actually, that is quite an effective and appropriate image.

WILL: Well, yes, I suppose it might work at a pinch. I'll just bung it in for now, until I can think of anything better. What do you think?

Will has scribbled some words and now Kate doth read them.

KATE: 'Tis almost morning. I would have thee gone, and yet no farther than a wanton's bird, that lets it hop a little from his hand, like a poor prisoner in his twisted gyves, and with a silk thread plucks it back again, so loving jealous of his liberty.' Loving jealous! Like sweet sorrow. Another heart-breaking confliction. It's beautiful.

BOTTOM: That's my line, that is!

WILL: Bottom, it is not your line. I admit that your shameful history of cruelty to animals may have given me a vague hint, but it is definitely my line.*

---

* This line was to appear verbatim in the finished script and any modern copyright lawyer would claim at least partial credit for Bottom.

WILL'S STRATFORD HOME – DAY

The family be gathered. Will doth enter.

WILL: Home am I.

The twins rush excitedly to greet him in the hope of treats.

WILL: Last trip before *Romeo and Juliet* rehearsals begin.

SUSANNA: Is my play really finished then?

WILL: Pretty much, my darling. I've just been reworking the balcony scene with Kate. Tell me what you think.

Will doth give his daughter the manuscript.

SUSANNA: I can't believe you wrote this for me. I know I used to think it was all crappage, but if you really read it and give it a chance, and come back to it, quite a few times, and slowly familiarize yourself with the language and the imagery, weirdly, you can start to sort of enjoy it.

WILL: Yes, I rather think that's the way it's going to be with my stuff.[*]

JOHN: I still think it's all crappage.

MARY: But you don't mind spending the money he makes.

JOHN: Of course not. If people want to sit for hours, busting for a wee and wishing they were dead so's I can have plenty of ale and pie, good luck to 'em.

ANNE: Anyway, did you have a good journey, love?

WILL: Astonishingly, no. Didn't get to sit down till Leamington Spa.

JOHN: You got to get there early if you want a good seat.

WILL: I know that, Dad, and I did. Three hours early. And I got a lovely seat, at the back, by a window. And mark this, there sat none beside me. I put my cloak and pork pasty upon the

---

[*] This is indeed the only way to vaguely enjoy Shakespeare.

adjoining place, avoided all eye contact as others boarded, and my ruse worked. Despite the coach being passing full, I myself had room to spare.

MARY: A double seat.

WILL: Aye, Mum, a double seat is indeed such stuff as dreams are made of. But soon did it become a very nightmare as the hour of our departure comes and yet we do not move. We sit and we sit. Now come travellers who would have missed this coach had it left upon its hour. 'Coachman, bar the door,' I shouted. 'These travellers have missed this coach. The fact that it is still here is a technicality.'

MARY: Quite right. You have to make a fuss in this world.

WILL: But I fussed in vain, Mum. The shabby grottling just grinned at me through toothless, rotting gums as first one, then another tardy traveller crowded in upon us. My coat and pasty was soon challenged, of course. 'Is anybody sitting there?' Why do people ask that? Yes, actually, there is. But he's invisible. Of course nobody's sitting there. That's the whole futtocking point.

MARY: And so you had to shift your pasty.

WILL: Yes, while a girthsome yeoman, who appeared to have eaten a turd omelette for breakfast, crushed himself against me and began to scratch inside his codpiece. And still, the coach doth not depart. Now, we are jammed together like two boobies in a bodice. The stinksome bumshank of an unwashed peasant be in my face. My pasty knocked to the floor, which the dangle-scratcher picks up for me, using his dangle-scratching hand, so that now I cannot eat it but must still thank itchy dangle for his kindness through clenched teeth.

MARY: And I don't suppose any explanation was given.

WILL: Why would there be when imposing arbitrary inconvenience on the travelling public is the sworn duty of all who administer Albion's transport infrastructure?

JOHN: But it moved in the end, son. I mean, you're here, aren't you?

WILL: No, Dad. It did not move, for finally there comes a voice. This coach has developed a fault and we must needs abandon it. Another awaits behind. So now you see the satanic conclusion to my tale. Suddenly, having been first on—

ANNE: Oh my God, you're last off!

WILL: Yes. A perfect storm of transport horror. I waited three hours to get a good seat and now the mooching hooligans who should have missed it are first in the new queue.

MARY: Well, you should have said something!

WILL: I did say something! 'Coachman, ho!' I shouted. 'Those who boarded last must do so again. Lock the new coach until I who was first can enter!'

ANNE: And did he?

WILL: Yes, yes, he did. Except no, he didn't! He just laughed and all made merry at my expense as I struggled on last and the door was forced closed behind me with my arsing cheeks caught in the gap. God, I hate this sceptred bloody isle.

Susanna be crying.

WILL: Sue, what's wrong? Don't cry. Honestly, it wasn't that bad a journey.

SUSANNA: No, Dad, it isn't that. It's my play. It's so beautiful and so sad. It's like Jules says, it's sweet sorrow.

WILL: Sue, I think that might be the nicest thing anyone's ever said about my plays.

JOHN: I don't imagine there's a lot of competition.[*]

---

[*] John Shakespeare was wrong. People had and would continue to say more nice things about his son's plays than any other writer who ever lived. Even if secretly they didn't mean it.

UPSTAIRS – NIGHT

Anne be already a-bed. Will doth enter the chamber.

ANNE: Do you know, I think this *Romeo and Juliet* could be as big as *Richard the Third* was. Bigger, even.

WILL: Finally. Another proper hit. And I owe it to two wonderful women.

ANNE: Susanna.

WILL: Aye, sweet Sue. And also—

ANNE: Me.

WILL: Kate.

ANNE: Kate? I thought you were going to say me. Because of the sweet sorrow and loving jealousy of our own courting days.

WILL: Well, yes. Obviously, absolutely. That's a given. Although, our courting days weren't exactly days, were they? I mean, more like hours really. Minutes, to be fair. I came round to buy a chicken, knocked you up in the barn, and the next thing we knew, we were walking up the aisle with your dad's pitchfork prodding me in the arseington.*

ANNE: We found love, didn't we?

WILL: Of course we did. And of course you are the inspiration for my Juliet – in a very abstract sense. I only mention young Kate because her sensitive readings of the text have inspired me.

ANNE: You're not going all diddly doodah on her, are you?

WILL: Anne, please. 'Tis simply that I appreciate her faultless oral work. She has a fine chest and I particularly admire her assonance.

Anne is not happy but Will is oblivious.

---

* Scholars have long known that Shakespeare married Anne when she was pregnant but it is useful to have it confirmed.

WILL'S LONDON LODGINGS - DAY

Will, Bottom and Kate, who be most excited.

KATE: Juliet! Me? Oh my goodly godlingtons. Thank you! Thank you! Thank you! This be so unexpected. (*Speaks in the manner of an aside, which by strict convention none can overhear*) And yet by my troth, it be not unexpected at all. For first, did I revive his interest in the play by invoking the image of his sweet Susanna. Then did I ensure that every word he writ, I spoke until he could hear his Juliet in no other voice but mine.

WILL: Well, let's face it, Kate. 'Twas you that revived my interest in the play by invoking the image of my sweet Susanna, and then every word I writ, you have spoke till I could hear my Juliet in no other voice but thine.

Again, Kate doth turn away to speak in an aside.

KATE: God, I'm good.

BOTTOM: You better not futtock up my line about the captured bird.

WILL: It is not your line, Bottom.

BOTTOM: You can tell yourself what you want, master, but you know the truth.

KATE: But the main thing is, how are we going to sneak me into Burbage's company? Girly acting being illegal.

WILL: And we must also deal with Mr Condell, who as you know is as anxious to play Juliet as you are.

BOTTOM: He's even had his nostrils waxed.

KATE: But methought that last year, when you first considered the casting of the role, you deemed Mr Condell too old to play the ingénue.*

---

* See the First Folio.

WILL: Ah, but that was before he became an investor in our new theatre. As a stockholder, he has a casting veto. Or in this case, a casting ego. He'll insist on playing the female lead.[*]

KATE: But he'll be a dreadful Juliet.

WILL: Exactly. And likewise Mr Burbage as Romeo. For of course he will expect the title role and, much though I do admire him, he be very old and fully twenty-seven stone.

KATE: So you're saying that while Mr Condell and Mr Burbage be wrong for the teenage lovers, being middle-aged and most hairy, they'll still want the roles?

WILL: Yes. I'm beginning to think that actors might be a tiny bit vain and self-obsessed.[†]

KATE: Oh no. I simply can't agree. Actors are very, very special people.

WILL: So they will tell you at exhausting length. Vanity, thy name is actor. And 'tis their vanity that will undo them.[‡]

---

[*] The modern practice of company shareholders ruthlessly acting in their own interests and not that of their clients (in this case the audience) appears to be a long-established one.

[†] Much has changed in British theatre since Shakespeare's day but this at least remains the same.

[‡] To the casual scholar, this appears to be Shakespeare working on the line 'Vanity, thy name is woman'. In fact, he never wrote this line. He wrote 'Frailty, thy name is woman' in *Hamlet*, which might be considered as offensive.

THE RED LION THEATRE – DAY

Condell and Burbage rehearse in costume as Romeo and Juliet.

CONDELL: 'Oh Romeo, Romeo, wherefore art thou Romeo?'

Will enters.

WILL: Ah, Mr Burbage. Mr Condell. I see that you're already in rehearsal.

BURBAGE: Indeed, Mr Shakespeare, and I have good news. Kit Marlowe sends word that the Earl of Southampton, for who you have writ and dedicated many poems—

WILL: Platonically, yes. I certainly never fancied him.

BURBAGE: Will attend thy opening night, and if he approves of your play, will be our new patron.

WILL: How can he not approve with you and Mr Condell in the title roles? For above all, Condell and Burbage must play the title roles.

BURBAGE: Well, obviously.

CONDELL: Obviously.

WILL: Which is why I wonder that you be all bedecked as the minor juvenile love interest. Be you working at the blocking for the two unknown beginners who'll play the kids?

BURBAGE: Kids, Will? Romeo and Juliet be the title roles.

WILL: What? Oh, I see, you're working off that draft. Oh, that's all changed.

CONDELL: What's changed?

WILL: The title. It's not called 'Romeo and Juliet' any more. It's called 'Prince Escalus and the Nurse'.

BURBAGE: Prince Escalus, is he in it?

WILL: Is he in it? Is he in it? He's only the voice of stability and authority who restores the natural hierarchical order at the end of the play after the chaos caused by forbidden love.*

BURBAGE: Oh. Oh. Well, I must say, that does sound rather important. And it is the title role.

WILL: Oh, absolutely. For sure. Probably.

CONDELL: The nurse does have some fine lines. The title role, you say?

WILL: Totally. Good as. Now, we need to audition for the juveniles.

BURBAGE: Well, I know who you'll want for the girl. There's a new lad, wowing them across the river at the Curtain. Augustine Snootyloin gave a superb Isabella in Tommy Kyd's *Spanish Tragedy*.†

CONDELL: Superb? I thought *he* was the tragedy. Too showy. No depth.

WILL: We'll see him, of course, but I think we need to keep an open mind. And of course, also, for Romeo.

BURBAGE: There I must draw the line. He may no longer be the title role, but Romeo remains pivotal. We'll need an established company member. A genuine draw-card.

The actor Will Kempe doth enter.

KEMPE: Oh, someone who's big in Italy, maybe? Oh, who said that? I did. So, mmm.

---

* Shakespeare often used this trick in his plays, having failed to come up with a convincing ending based on character and motivation. He would simply truck on some previously unmentioned nobleman to give the impression of drawing a proper conclusion. The only discernible upside of this outrageous feint is that it has given generations of tired old luvvie-kissies the chance of a speaking role.

† *The Spanish Tragedy* is a useful addition to the canon of Elizabethan tragedy because if ever students tire of having to wade through Shakespeare they only have to take a quick glance at this play to realize how much worse things could be.

ROBERT GREENE'S OFFICE – DAY

Robert Greene doth interview Augustine 'Gussie' Snootyloin, a preening young luvvie-kissie.

ROBERT GREENE: The upstart crow flies ever higher. Lord Southampton himself will attend the curiously titled 'Prince Escalus and the Nurse', and 'tis whispered that if he approves, he will stand patron to the company. Mmm, with so powerful a protector, the crow will be beyond my clutches. I must sabotage the show. You are Augustine Snootyloin, currently the most fashionable young actor in London?

GUSSIE: Whatever, the fame thing is such a joke. I'm a jobbing actor, a craftsman applying his trade. My body is my tool. Basically, I'm a tool.

ROBERT GREENE: I think that much is clear.*

GUSSIE: And can we please get over the fact that I'm posh and I went to Eton?

ROBERT GREENE: Yes. Now 'tis said you are hotly tipped to be cast as the ingénue in Mr Shakespeare's new romantic tragedy.

GUSSIE: I've met the director. We've talked.

ROBERT GREENE: You will make sure that you are cast, sirrah. And on opening night, if somebody sets fire to the theatre during the balcony scene, for a generous fee . . .

GUSSIE: Shouldn't be a problem. I'll be on fire anyway.

---

* It seems that the actorish habit of humble-bragging their great art by constantly referring to it as a trade and a craft is much older than previously thought. Interestingly, these same actors do not claim to be but simple players when being shown to the best tables in restaurants.

THE RED LION THEATRE – DAY

The players and Will do conduct auditions. Gussie is onstage performing Juliet.

GUSSIE: 'What's in a name? That which we call rose by any other name would smell as sweet.'

BURBAGE: Thank you. Most impressive. He has exactly what it takes to be a star these days. There's no doubting that.

WILL: Are you mad? He's just a weird-looking Eton boy with a rather pretentious name.

BURBAGE: As I said, he has exactly what it takes to be a star these days.

CONDELL: I disagree, Burbage. Like all these young boys, he has no substance, no depth.

KEMPE: No pubic hair in his eyebrows.

BURBAGE: I am decided. Gussie Snootyloin be our Juliet.

WILL: Stay your hand, Burbage. There be one audition remaining.

Kate doth come onstage all dressed as Juliet.

CONDELL: Not as pretty as the other boy.

WILL: Let's at least listen to him.

KATE: 'Come, gentle night. Come, loving, black-browed night. Give me my Romeo, and when he shall die, take him and cut him out in little stars, and he will make the face of heaven so fine that all the world will be in love with night.'

All are stunned by Kate's virtuosity.

BURBAGE: My heavens, 'twas brilliant. The young boy maketh a very window into the heart of a young woman, and through its prism to inspire the very essence of the female soul. How came he by such talent? What is the secret of his acting craft? He didn't go to Eton. Hasn't got a pretentious name. Doesn't even look all that weird.

CONDELL: She's a girl, Burbage. I swear the lying, cheating little bitchington is a girl.

Kate doth verily adopt the coarse voice and manners of the common roister knave.

KATE: Oh yeah? I'll show you who's a girl, you pocksed-up old hugger-tugger. Cop a load of this bad boy when he's at home.

Kate doth lift her skirts. None but Will and the players can see what lies beneath but by their expressions 'tis certain something impressive. Kate doth turn to the wings where Bottom is holding a string of raw sausages. They wink at each other. Now all is clear. Kate has been wearing a false cod-dangle. The jealous Gussie has witnessed this exchange and discovered her secret.

ROBERT GREENE'S OFFICE – DAY

Gussie sits before Greene.

ROBERT GREENE: So, you failed. I have no more use for you. Be gone from my sight.

GUSSIE: I didn't fail, Mr Greene. There was reason I didn't get the role, and I think it's worth as much to you as me sabotaging the production.

ROBERT GREENE: Really? Well, if you have information that I can use against Mr Shakespeare, I will pay handsomely for it.

GUSSIE: They've cast a real girl.

ROBERT GREENE: How can you be sure?

GUSSIE: Because I saw her sausage and it was a sausage.

ROBERT GREENE: Oh, happy day. The crow is in my clutches. If they disport a girl upon the stage, all those involved will be arrested. Lord Southampton will flee in fear of association, and, without a patron, Burbage and the crow will be at the mercy of the Pure-titties.

GUSSIE: Exactly. My monies please, Mr Greene.

ROBERT GREENE: My dear Gussie. The thing about making a transaction is always to demand payment before delivering the goods. You, I'm afraid, gave your valuable information gratis. And now have naught to sell.

GUSSIE: You're giving me nothing?

ROBERT GREENE: On the contrary. I'm giving you a valuable lesson. Good day.

THE RED LION THEATRE – DAY

The company doth rehearse the play with Kate as Juliet and Kempe as Romeo.

BURBAGE: So, the Capulet ball. Tybalt has departed in disgust. Romeo, fearless in his enemy's house, spies the exquisite Juliet across the room. Instantly is smitten. The gadsome youth has found true love. Their eyes meet. He approaches her. He takes her hand. The world stands still. He speaks.

KEMPE: Congratulations. You've been pulled.

WILL: The line, Kempe, is: 'If I profane with my unworthiest hand this holy shrine, the gentle sin is this: my lips, two blushing pilgrims, ready stand to smooth that rough touch with a tender kiss.'

KEMPE: Yeah, and my line's better.[*]

BURBAGE: Kempe's line was rather more succinct. Yours is a tad obscure.

CONDELL: Oh, very obscure.

KEMPE: Like, mad obscure.

WILL: It's not obscure at all. It's as clear as fairy snot. Romeo sees Juliet's hand as sacred, like a shrine. He says if she's offended by his touch, she should imagine his lips are two visiting pilgrims and let him kiss it better.

KEMPE: You're joking. That's what it means?

BURBAGE: That's amazing. I had no idea.

CONDELL: Nor me.[†]

---

[*] Some scholars on first discovering this passage in the folio were forced to concede that Kempe had a point.

[†] The actors Burbage, Condell and Kempe were the first people in history to fail to understand the weird shit that Romeo and Juliet gabble when they first meet at the masked ball. Countless audiences that followed would sympathize.

WILL: Juliet coquettishly replies:

KATE: 'Good pilgrim. You do wrong your hand too much. For saints have hands that pilgrims' hands do touch. And palm to palm is holy palmers' kiss.'

BURBAGE: Oh, their hands kiss. Palm to palm. Oh, I like that. That's sweet.

WILL: And of course there's also the highly amusing internal pun.

BURBAGE: There's a pun? Oh God.

WILL: Obviously there's a pun. People love my puns. They love how obscure they are. Palmer is archaic slang for pilgrim. So Romeo, having called himself a pilgrim, is now offering a palmers' palm. So funny. It will stop the show.*

KATE: Maybe you could afford to lose that one, Mr Shakespeare. Bit weak.

WILL: It is not weak. It's a bolted-on pant-wetter. And in my view, it will get even funnier as the meaning of the pun fades ever further into history. Now, proceed. Romeo asks – Kempe:

KEMPE: 'Have not saints lips?'

WILL: And Juliet teases back:

KATE: 'Ay, pilgrim. Lips that they must use in prayer.'

WILL: She's flirting. Saying, naughty boy, you should use your lips for prayer, not kissing.

BURBAGE: Yes, I think I got that one.

WILL: Then Romeo says, 'Oh then, dear saint, let lips do what hands do. They pray, grant thou, lest faith turn to despair.'

BURBAGE: Now you've lost me again now.

CONDELL: I must confess, I did start to glaze over.

---

* Nobody has ever, ever got this in the entire history of theatre, which is probably a good thing as it's even less funny if you understand it.

WILL: Oh, for God's sake. Romeo is praying for a kiss, and if Juliet doesn't grant it, he'll lose his faith.

KATE: So Juliet teases, 'Saints do not move, thou grant for prayers' sake.'

WILL: A holy saint isn't going to be giving out kisses, even to answer a prayer. Then naughty Romeo, who by this time be as hornsome as the newly discovered African rhinosaurus, which has, as you know, a very large horn, says, 'Then move not, while my prayer's effect I take.'

KATE: Pucker up, babes.

WILL: And Romeo kisses Juliet.

Kate and Kempe kiss.

KATE: Oh, now that is a cracking good scene.

BURBAGE: Yes, it's pretty good, Will, I must say. Congratulations.

CONDELL: Now I understand it, I consider it destined to become one of the most celebrated lovey kissy moments in all English theatre.

WILL: One of? One of? Oh, thanks very much, Condell. Talk about damning with faint praise.

KEMPE: It's a good start. Yeah. Two teens hook up at a party. Like it. But to make it brilliant, and edgy, they should get totally lathered. Go get tattoos. And Juliet passes out in the kitchen. Oh. Romeo cops off with her best mate. Aha. Then Juliet wakes up stuck with his name tattooed on her bum.[*]

WILL: Mr Kempe, let us hope that the day never dawns in Albion when tales of young love will be reduced to mere celebrations of drunkenness and copulation.[†]

KEMPE: Keep wishing, mate. History's on my side.

---

[*] One can only speculate at how brilliant *Romeo and Juliet* would have been if Shakespeare had listened to Kempe.

[†] Fortunate for Shakespeare that he never lived to be commissioned by Channel Four.

THE RED LION THEATRE – NIGHT

The first night of Romeo and Juliet. *Lord Southampton doth attend the crowd in the company of Marlowe.*

LORD SOUTHAMPTON: I want a drink and some sweets, and make sure nobody with big hair sits in front of me.

KIT MARLOWE: Of course, my lord.

LORD SOUTHAMPTON: Oh, and make sure you have an extra hanky or two because I'm a terrible old sobbling pup and bound to cry in the sad bits.

Lurking in the shadows be Greene who doth speak in the manner of an aside, which by strict convention none can overhear.

ROBERT GREENE: Oh, you will cry, my lord – when the crow is arrested and you disgraced for attending such a show with an actor with a tufting muffle where a cod-dangle should be.

RED LION THEATRE BACKSTAGE – NIGHT

All is a-hustle and a-bustle as the players prepare. Burbage doth spy the poster which full clearly declareth 'Romeo and Juliet'.

BURBAGE: You said the title had changed!

WILL: A genuine oversight, Burbage. I really meant to tell the printer.

BURBAGE: Well, it's too late now. We'll just have to go with 'Romeo and Juliet'.

Gussie doth appear all full of spite.

GUSSIE: Just 'Romeo', I think, Mr Burbage. Because this little bitchington has no right to be an actor. He's a girl!

BURBAGE: Juliet, a girl? Ha! Impossible!

Condell doth inspect the maid must sneeringly.

CONDELL: Oh, she is a girl. She's using real boobingtons instead of coconuts. Which is just cheating.

BURBAGE: We're ruined.

WILL: Kate, I'm so sorry.

KATE: Don't worry, Mr Shakespeare. You tried and I love you for that.

WILL: I tried because you deserved it. If anyone had a right to play a star-crossed lover, it was you. If only there was a way.

THE RED LION THEATRE ONSTAGE – NIGHT

The play be going brilliantly. Lord Southampton, who indeed is an old soppington, is in raptures.

LORD SOUTHAMPTON: Oh my God, he's going to try to pull her. I love it!

ROBERT GREENE: Stop the performance! A heinous offence is being committed. The disgusting personage playing Juliet is a girl!

Juliet is revealed to be Gussie, who turns on Greene.

GUSSIE: How dare you, sir? I shall sue.

Clearly Greene's accusation is false. He is disgraced.

GUSSIE: Valuable lesson in life, ducky. Eton boys always win.[*]

LORD SOUTHAMPTON: Shame on you for interrupting this beautiful play with such foul slander. Guards, arrest him!

ROBERT GREENE: My lord! My Lord Southampton!

Greene be dragged from the theatre in disgrace.

LORD SOUTHAMPTON: Now, can we please get to the kissy bit?

Romeo doth speak, and it is Kate.

KATE: 'If I profane with my unworthiest hand this holy shrine, the gentle sin is this: my lips, two blushing pilgrims, ready stand to smooth that rough touch with a tender kiss.'[†]

Kempe approaches Will backstage.

KEMPE: Still can't see how I locked myself in the privy.

---

[*] This was true then and four centuries later (except when the tax authorities occasionally catch up with them).

[†] It is perhaps some small comfort to all actresses who have had to put up with worse roles and lower pay than the men that Shakespeare's most famous lover was first played by a girl.

WILL: Yes, funny that. Lucky Kate knew the lines.

BURBAGE: She is rather excellent.

CONDELL: It's a very good thing there's a law against her.

Romeo and Juliet kiss. The crowd be enraptured with delight.

LORD SOUTHAMPTON: Oh! Beautiful!

MISS LUCY'S TAVERN – NIGHT

All are gathered for the aftershow.

KIT MARLOWE: Well, you got yourself a new patron. Southampton absolutely loved it.

WILL: Did he? Did he really? What, what was his favourite bit?

KIT MARLOWE: Oh, without question it was that amazingly moving image of the captive bird on a silken thread.

BOTTOM: Yeah, that was my—

WILL: Some more ale please, Bottom.

BOTTOM: You're showing a very unpleasant side, if you don't mind me saying, master.

Bottom doth depart to get the ale.

WILL: So, Kate, you didn't get to play Juliet but you got the next best thing.

KATE: The best thing, if I'm honest, Mr Shakespeare. Because, not surprisingly, Romeo, being the male protagonist, is informed by a complex set of personal and social issues, whereas Juliet, being the girl, is informed exclusively by her attitude to the male protagonist.*

WILL: Ah, you spotted that, did you?

KATE: And Romeo has seventy-four more lines.

---

* This is undoubtedly true. Juliet was one of the first great heroines of drama to be identified entirely in terms of her attitude to the leading man. But she wouldn't be the last.

WILL'S STRATFORD HOME - NIGHT

Will and Anne do sit before the fire with their pipes.

WILL: I, for one, hope that one day lady-acting will be made legal.

ANNE: Except that, if it ever were, I expect most of the girls' parts would be hackneyed clichés, and like as not they'd be expected to show their boobingtons.*

WILL: I fear you may be right. And also 'tis certain they'd earn less too.

ANNE: For doing the same job as a man? Surely not. Well, that would be just ridiculous.

WILL: Perhaps you're right, my love. Only time will tell.

---

* Shakespeare wasn't the only one with remarkable powers of foresight.

GLOSSARY

Arseington – slang for anus.

Arsemongle – person who acts like an anus.

Bastable – person of dubious parentage or someone who just isn't very nice.

Bolingbrokes – slang for testicles.

Boobingtons – polite term for bosoms, from which is derived the modern 'boobs'.

Bumshank/le – both an anus and a person who acts like an anus.

Cock-snobbled folderols – slang for entitled posh boys.

Cod-dangle – slang for penis.

Country bumshank/le or bumsnot – any person who lives outside London.

Doodle – early English version of the modern 'dude'.

Dunceling clumbletrousers – clumsy person.

Fartle-barfle – flatulence.

Futtock/futtocking – archaic, profane.

God-prodding Pure-titty – Puritan.

Going all diddly doodah – previously unknown Elizabethan phrase meaning to fall in love.

Hugger-tugger – slang for a person of homosexual orientation.

Kissy love gerbil – term of affection with erotic overtones.

Knackmungled – extremely tired, as in 'my knackers are totally mungled'.

Lickspittle nincombunion – a low fool.

Pamperloin – person of wealth and power.

Penny Pure-pants – chaste and virginal maid.

Puffling pants – stupid, nappy-type underpants worn on the outside of tights.

Saucy prancings – weird courtly dances often depicted on TV, which it is impossible to imagine anyone actually enjoying.

Stranger with the purple helm – slang for penis.

Summer snottage – hay fever.

Tarting slap – woman of presumed easy virtue.

Tufting muffle or tufted lady grotto – slang for vagina.

Up the duffington – with child.

Wankington – A foolish fellow or one who is in the habit of personally pleasuring his cod-dangle.

Whoreslap – woman of presumed easy virtue.

ABOUT THE AUTHOR

Ben Elton is one of Britain's most provocative and entertaining writers. From celebrity to climate change, from the First World War to the end of the world, his books give his unique perspective on some of the most controversial topics of our time.

He has written fourteen major bestsellers, including *Stark*, *Popcorn*, *Inconceivable*, *Dead Famous*, *High Society*, *The First Casualty* and *Two Brothers*.

He has also written some of television's most popular and incisive comedy, including *The Young Ones* and *Blackadder*.

He is married with three children and lives in Western Australia.